The Role of Annuity Markets in Financing Retirement

The Role of Annuity Markets in Financing Retirement

Jeffrey R. Brown
Olivia S. Mitchell
James M. Poterba
Mark J. Warshawsky

The MIT Press
Cambridge, Massachusetts
London, England

This book was set in Palatino by Best-set Typesetter Ltd., Hong Kong, and was printed and bound in the United States of America.

Library of Congress Cataloging-in-Publication Data

The role of annuity markets in financing retirement / Jeffrey R. Brown ... [et al.].
    p.   cm.
  Includes bibliographical references and index.
  ISBN 0-262-02509-4 (hc. : alk. paper)
  1. Annuities. 2. Retirement income. 3. Annuities—United States. 4. Retirement income—United States. I. Brown, Jeffrey R. (Jeffrey Robert), 1968–
HG8790 .R65 2001
332.024′01—dc21

2001030653

Contents

1   Introduction and Overview

As the baby boom cohort nears and moves into retirement, analysts, policymakers, and advisors in many nations are devoting increased attention to issues of old-age income security. Dramatic advances in life expectancy in the United States over the last century mean that today's typical 65-year-old man and woman can expect to live to age 81 and 85, respectively. Perhaps even more striking is the fact that almost a third of 65-year-old women and almost a fifth of 65-year-old men are likely to live to age 90 or beyond. Similar trends have been experienced in developed and developing nations around the world. Longer life expectancy is widely viewed as a positive outcome. Without appropriate adaptation in saving behavior and financial planning during retirement, however, increased longevity also means that individuals face a greater risk of outliving their resources and may be forced to substantially reduce their living standards at an advanced age. This volume examines the role that life annuities can play in helping people protect against this important source of old-age risk.

A life annuity is an insurance product that pays out a periodic (e.g., monthly) amount for as long as the annuitant is alive, in exchange for an initial premium. The primary appeal of a life annuity is that it offers retirees the opportunity to insure against the risk of outliving their assets by exchanging these assets for a lifelong stream of guaranteed income. Insurers pool individuals and couples with similar longevity expectations but varying longevity outcomes as a means to help protect them against longevity risk.

In the United States as well as in many other Western nations, retirees have typically had access to three main sources of annuities: universal publicly provided Social Security payouts, payouts from employer-sponsored defined benefit pension plans, and payouts from privately purchased annuities offered by insurance companies. Social Security has traditionally been the most important of these three.

Whether Social Security will remain the dominant source of annuity payouts in the future is not clear. In most developed countries, the government-run system faces substantial actuarial imbalances requiring near-term reform. Some of the reform options that have been suggested in the U.S. context supplement or partially replace the existing pay-as-you-go public defined benefit system with an individual-accounts defined contribution program. Related plans have recently been implemented in the United Kingdom, Argentina, Chile, Mexico, Hong Kong, and elsewhere.

While Social Security reform is under discussion in many nations, employer-sponsored pensions are also undergoing massive change. The growth of defined benefit pension plans in the first few decades after World War II has slowed and in some cases reversed, and it has been replaced with explosive growth among defined contribution plans. Because defined contribution plans typically offer retirees a lump sum payout rather than an annuity, the growth of defined contribution plans raises new challenges for retirees seeking to protect themselves against the risk of outliving their resources.

Private annuity markets, the third source of annuity income, are likely to attract growing attention as the cohort of workers with substantial defined contribution plan balances reaches retirement age. The private annuity market offers one way for retirees with substantial wealth accumulation to structure their withdrawals from this wealth stock over an uncertain retirement period.

In this book, we bring together several studies that explore how private annuity markets operate, why annuities are important to retirees, and how the availability of annuity products affects the design of public and private retirement systems. This work is the product of a number of collaborative research projects investigating various aspects of the annuity markets in the United States and other nations. The roots of this research can be traced to Warshawsky (1984), which represented the first systematic attempt by economic researchers to compare expected annuitant payouts with the premium costs that buyers face when purchasing an annuity policy. It also evaluated, in expected utility terms, the benefits of annuitization. Two of the chapters in this volume build directly on that early work.

Other components of this book reflect growing national and international public policy interest in annuity markets. These studies consider a range of topics including the availability of annuity products that offer some inflation protection rather than fixed nominal payouts, the tax treatment of annuity products, and whether private annuity markets provide a cost-effective method for drawing down accumulated balances in retirement saving accounts.

This introductory chapter, which sets the stage for the six chapters that follow, is divided into six sections. It begins with a description of the structure of annuity contracts. There are many different types of annuity products on the market, and insurance companies could potentially offer many more. All offer some insurance against longevity risk. The second section describes the role of annuity products in providing retirement income. It explores the value of annuities in enhancing the expected utility of retirees, as well as the size of the current annuity market.

The third section considers the role that individual annuity markets might play in a modified version of the current Social Security system. It focuses in particular on "mandatory annuitization" options that would compel Social Security participants to annuitize their resources at retirement.

Section four of this introduction provides brief summaries of the subsequent six chapters. Section five explains some of the methodological issues that link the chapters and alerts readers to some of the subtle differences across chapters. Finally, the last section draws several general lessons that emerge from our studies of private annuity markets.

1 What Is an Annuity?

Annuities are generally defined as contracts that provide periodic payments for an agreed-upon span of time. They include *annuities certain*, which provide periodic payouts for a fixed number of years, and *life annuities*, which provide payouts for the duration of one or more persons' lives. This book is primarily concerned with life annuities, which protect individuals against outliving their resources.

The simplest annuity contract is a "fixed immediate single-life annuity." It involves a one-time premium payment by the annuitant, in return for which the insurance company immediately (within a month or quarter) begins making periodic payments to the annuitant. These payments continue until the death of the annuitant. Actual annuity contracts come in many additional varieties. They can be written to commence payouts at a later date, to cover multiple lives, to have payment rates that vary with some underlying portfolio, or to have various "bequest" options that make payments to the insured's beneficiaries after death. While the more complicated products differ along these and other dimensions, as life annuities they must all provide payments that continue for as long as the insured individual is alive.

To classify different types of annuity products, it is useful to consider separately their accumulation and payout phases. The accumulation phase is that period during which assets are set aside for future conversion to an income stream. The payout phase is that period during which the individual receives the payout. During the accumulation phase, it is possible to distinguish annuities along two dimensions:

• *Immediate versus deferred annuities*: Immediate annuities begin making payments immediately after the payment of the premium. In contrast, deferred annuities do not begin making payments until some date in the future. Deferred annuities receive favorable tax treatment during the accumulation phase, and in many cases it is possible to withdraw assets from these annuities without conversion to a life-long income stream.

• *Rates of return on deferred annuities*: With deferred annuities, payments commence at some future date. Before that, the premium dollars can be invested at a fixed rate or in a portfolio of risky assets. In the latter case, the annuity is known as a variable annuity.

During the annuity payout phase, annuity policies also differ on several dimensions. One pertains to the *number of lives covered*. Single life annuities pay until the insured individual dies. Joint-and-survivor annuities continue to make (generally reduced) payments as long as at least one of the covered individuals is alive. Another attribute that distinguishes annuities in the payout phase is their *bequest option*. Many private market annuities offer *period certain* guarantees or refund options that provide some additional payments to a beneficiary in the event that the insured individual dies shortly after annuitization. Ten-year and twenty-year certain periods are common. Yet a third distinction among different types of annuities concerns the *type of payout*. Fixed nominal annuities offer payments that are constant in nominal terms. Graded annuities increase at a predetermined percentage rate. Inflation-indexed annuities rise with the rate of inflation, thus preserving the purchasing power of the income. Variable annuity payouts are linked to an underlying portfolio of assets, and will rise and fall according to a predetermined relationship with that portfolio's value.

2 The Demand for Private Annuities

To illustrate the valuation of a life annuity, imagine a 65-year-old woman preparing to retire with a significant stock of accumulated assets, in a world without a Social Security system or a defined benefit pension plan. If this woman knew her date of death with certainty, it would be a fairly simple exercise for her to allocate her stock of wealth over her remaining years of life. But given uncertainty about the length of her life, determining how much to consume becomes a more difficult calculation. This is because she must consider two competing risks: *longevity* risk and *underconsumption* risk. The first refers to the chance that she will live far beyond her expected life span and thus run out of money. She could reduce this risk by consuming very conservatively, to protect against running out of money even if she lives to an extremely advanced age. For example, if she consumed only the interest on her wealth, and never drew on the principal, she would never run her wealth to zero. On the other hand, such an approach exposes her to the second risk—namely, that she will die with too much wealth left unconsumed. This second factor represents a risk since unconsumed wealth represents a forgone consumption opportunity. Assuming that the woman did not place any value on leaving a positive bequest, if she died with a positive amount of wealth, she could have consumed more in every period while alive, presumably making her better off.

The risks of outliving one's resources, and of underconsuming, arise from the substantial variation in length-of-life across people. In the United States, for example, an average 65-year-old man in the year 2000 can expect to live an additional 16.4 years to age 81, while a typical 65-year-old woman has a life expectancy of an additional 19.6 years. However, 12 per cent of men and 8 per cent of women will die prior to their 70th birthday, while 17.5 per cent of men and 31.4 per cent of women will live to age 90 or beyond. These large probabilities of living a long time underscore the significant uncertainty facing retirees when they seek to allocate their wealth across their remaining lifetimes.

A life annuity represents a solution to the retiree's wealth allocation problem. It allows her to exchange a stock of wealth for a guaranteed stream of income that will be paid as long as she is alive, and thus removes the risk of outliving her resources. In addition, an annuity avoids the problem of lost consumption opportunities. It provides the annuitant with a higher level of income than she could receive in the absence of annuitization, in exchange for making the receipt of this income contingent upon living. In short, the annuity provider (i.e., an insurance company, the retirement plan sponsor, or the government) uses the assets of those who die early to pay a higher rate of return to those who are still living.

To illustrate the value of an annuity more clearly, consider two identical 65-year-old men with $100,000 of accumulated retirement wealth. The first purchases an actuarially fair life annuity, which, with a nominal interest rate of 7 per cent, would pay the retiree $929.38 per month for as long as he lives. This estimate relies on the mortality rates for men born in 1935, as reported by the Social Security Administration (2000). The second man chooses not to annuitize, but tries to maintain the same living standard by consuming $929.38 per month while alive and keeping the balance of his wealth earning 7 per cent interest. He can do this for 13 years and 8 months, at which time he would run out of money with a 60 per cent chance of still being alive. Without annuitizing, the 65-year-old would have to consume only $623.85 per month (33 per cent less) in order to avoid running out of money by age 100, and even then there is a 1.2 per cent chance that he will still be alive.

Economists have long viewed annuities as an important component of any retirement portfolio because they protect against longevity risk. In fact, some early theoretical results suggested that life-cycle consumers who faced an uncertain date of death should annuitize all of the retirement wealth that they wished to dedicate to future consumption. Their only nonannuitized wealth would be that which they planned to leave as a bequest. Some of the results that we present in the subsequent chapters suggest that for a hypothetical lifecycle consumer, access to an actuarially fair annuity market raises utility as much as a 50 per cent or greater increase in wealth. Fair annuities are very valuable to individuals who otherwise have no means to insure against their own longevity.

The models that suggest the great value of annuities simplify the actual decision problem confronting retirees, and hence they omit some factors that might lead people to annuitize less than their full wealth. Such factors might include uncertainty about uninsured medical and long-term care needs or other potential expenditures, a desire for liquidity and control, and various capital market imperfections. Also, in many countries, the Social Security system provides retired households with a significant guaranteed annuitized benefit stream, and, in practice, total payouts from Social Security are much greater than individual annuity payouts.

The finding of substantial potential welfare gains from purchasing private annuities would suggest a substantial and active private market for these products. However, the private immediate annuity market in the United States is rather small. In 1999, premiums for individual immediate annuities totaled $7 billion. By comparison, individual life insurance premiums were $94 billion, and purchases of individual deferred variable annuities totaled $109 billion. The American Council of Life Insurers (2000) reports that there were 1.63 million individual annuity policies in a "payout phase" in 1999. Even these statistics may overstate the number of true annuity policies, since a significant fraction consists of the insurance policies that are labeled "individual annuities" are fixed-term annuities that simply provide their purchasers with a prespecified stream of payouts over a fixed number of years. These policies are essentially bonds, and they do not offer insurance against longevity risk.

In noting the small size of the individual annuity market in the United States, it is important to recognize that individual annuities represent only a small fraction of the annuity payouts received by U.S. households. Payments from group annuities, which are typically provided by defined benefit pension plans, tend to be far larger. Data from September 1994 Health and Pension Benefit Supplement to the Current Population Survey suggest that of the 17.4 million individuals over the age of 55 who were retired from private sector jobs, 7.2 million (or 41 per cent) were receiving annuity income from a private pension. The mean annual annuity payment for this group was $9,714, and total amount of annuity income was $69.9 billion (in 1994 dollars).

The small size of the individual immediate annuity market in the United States, and its limited recent growth, may be contrasted with the dramatic recent growth in the market for individual deferred "variable annuities." This market grew from only $2 billion in annual premiums in 1988 to $63 billion in 1999. During the accumulation phase, a variable annuity is similar to a mutual fund in that an individual's contributions are invested in a portfolio of assets. Tax on the income from these assets is deferred until withdrawal. Variable annuities usually differ from mutual funds in offering some form of implicit or explicit insurance, such as a guaranteed return of principal in the event of the insured's death, that is based on the mortality experience of the buyer. Variable annuities are also unique in offering a life annuity payout, either fixed or variable, as a distribution option. Nearly all of the extant variable annuities are deferred annuities that are still in the accumulation phase. If the accumulations in these annuities are eventually used to generate life-contingent payout streams, this will substantially boost annuity income. In 1996, however, the ACLI (1997) reports that only about $382 million was being paid on a periodic basis from variable annuities, while almost $40 billion in premiums was going into variable annuity contracts.

Economic researchers have tried to explain the disparity between the theoretical prediction that annuities should be an important part of most retirement plans and the empirical finding that the private annuity market is still small. There are a number of potential explanations for why people might choose not to purchase individual annuities with the assets that they accumulate by their retirement date. One is that individual annuities are "expensive," in the sense that the expected payouts from purchasing an individual annuity are low in comparison to the cost of such an annuity. Several subsequent chapters consider this possibility.

Another potential explanation is that older persons may have important bequest motives, intending to leave substantial sums to children or other heirs. As a result, they might not be willing to transfer large amounts to an insurance company in return for a payment stream that terminates with their death. This explanation becomes particularly powerful when combined with the observation that Social Security, and in some cases defined benefit pension plans, already provides annuitized payouts to nearly all of the retired population. For some individuals who are already substantially annuitized, bequest motives may be strong enough to outweigh the risk of low consumption levels associated with living longer than expected. They may therefore reasonably decide not to purchase individual annuities with their remaining liquid assets.

While the individual annuity market in the United States is currently small, there are several reasons to expect that it may grow in the future. One, noted above, is the rising proportion of older persons holding substantial assets in variable annuities that might someday be annuitized. A second and perhaps more important reason is the recent growth of defined contribution pensions such as 401(k) plans. Between the early 1980s and the late 1990s, the number of participants in 401(k) plans grew from several thousand to nearly 35 million. Projections of future growth presented in Poterba, Venti, and Wise (2000) suggest that the average 401(k) balance for individuals retiring in 2030 will be very close to the present discounted value of Social Security benefits, assuming the continuation of current law. In the late 1990s, the value of 401(k) assets was roughly one tenth as large as the value of Social Security wealth.

How people will draw down their 401(k) balances is an open question, because the majority of covered workers have not yet reached retirement age. They might choose to take lump sum distributions from the plans, thereafter managing the asset decumulation process without any formal arrangement insuring against longevity risk. But the growth of the number of households with substantial financial resources in 401(k) plans at the time of retirement seems likely to expand the demand for structured financial products that draw down these assets—and annuities are the natural product for this purpose.

3   "Mandatory Annuitization" and Social Security Reform

Current developments in defined contribution pension markets, particularly the growth of 401(k) plans, seem likely to stimulate future annuity demand. In addition, however, ongoing Social Security reform discussions in the United States and other nations also have the potential to increase the demand for private annuities. These reforms, if enacted, could also substantially affect the structure of the annuity marketplace.

The existing Social Security system in the United States is a pay-as-you-go defined benefit plan in which workers make payroll tax contributions to the system when young and receive retirement benefits in the form of a mandatory life annuity. Social Security benefits are indexed to the Consumer Price Index so the system promises retirees a real benefit flow for the length of their lifetimes. Under a regime of this sort, longevity and inflation risks are pooled across employers, workers, and taxpayers as a whole, as well as intertemporally.

In the United States and many other nations, analysts have noted with concern the possibility of Social Security system financial insolvency, if promised benefits come to exceed system revenue. This problem already plagues the underfunded defined benefit systems of many European and Asian nations. In some nations, it has given rise to a move toward fundamental restructuring in favor of an accumulation-based defined contribution retirement scheme. Whether run as a centralized program (e.g., a national Provident Fund) or as a decentralized system of individual accounts, as in the United Kingdom or Chile, a national defined contribution program typically specifies program contributions and requires that these contributions be invested until retirement.

National defined contribution programs typically offer little or no risk sharing among participants prior to retirement. Members accumulate their own funds in their individual accounts. These programs typically offer no longevity insurance at retirement, instead giving people access to their fund as a lump sum. As a result, participants in these plans will confront the need to manage their asset balances between their retirement and their date of death in a way that ensures a dependable flow of retirement income.

If national Social Security programs shift toward defined contribution structures, some are concerned that retirees may be under-annuitized. Some retirees who had accumulated substantial assets by retirement might end up poor in old age, possibly necessitating tax-financed poverty support. This could arise if individuals were not fully aware of the potential for outliving their assets, perhaps because they underestimate their remaining life expectancy, or if individuals intentionally retire early and overspend, knowing that they will be bailed out by antipoverty programs. Mandatory annuitization of defined contribution retirement plan assets may be offered as a partial means to correct these problems.

Mandatory annuitization is also sometimes advocated as a potential solution to adverse selection in the annuity market. Because an annuity pays for life, it is most attractive to those who expect to live a long time and less attractive to those who suspect that they will die prior to their life expectancy. As a result, when annuitization is voluntary, those who purchase annuities are likely to have a longer life expectancy than those who do not. If an insurance company were to price annuities based on the average mortality in the population as a whole, but only sell them to individuals who were longer-lived than average, then the company would lose money. To avoid this, insurers must charge more for annuities sold in a voluntary purchase market. They must lower the monthly payout they provide for a given annuity premium. Raising the annuity price makes annuities attractive to fewer and fewer individuals, thus potentially "unraveling" the market. This can lead to some annuity transactions not taking place even though they might be mutually beneficial to insurers and purchasers in the presence of full and symmetric information.

In this light, mandating annuitization for all participants in a national defined contribution system pools all risk classes together. Consequently, insurers can price their annuities using average mortality characteristics, and thereby offer greater payouts for a given premium amount. This is the rationale for the United Kingdom requirement that at least a portion of workers' Personal Pensions be converted to a mandatory annuity at retirement. In later chapters, we argue that mandatory annuitization in the United States could raise average annuity payouts by as much as 10 per cent relative to their current level in the private annuity market.

While there are several powerful arguments supporting a role for mandatory annuitization, it is important to recognize that mandatory annuitization may have costs as well. Some may feel they are forced to overannuitize, compared to what they would prefer because of poor health or a strong bequest motive. Mandatory annuitization can also have undesirable distributional consequences, making some retirees worse off. This may be of relatively little concern in some cases. For example, a healthy retiree could undo excessive annuitization and leave a bequest by buying life insurance. However, annuities that ignore individual or group characteristics could cause large transfers from high-mortality risk groups to low-mortality risk groups. Brown (2000) shows that mandating a single life inflation-indexed annuity, for example, would produce substantial transfers from men to women, from blacks to whites and Hispanics, and from lower education groups to higher ones. The size of these expected transfers could be reduced by using joint and survivor annuities, using period certain or refund options, or "front-loading" annuity payments, though these mechanisms also lower the flow of retirement income.

While the precise direction of Social Security reform in the United States and other nations may be difficult to predict, most proposals that involve increased reliance on defined contribution-style accounts are likely to result in increased attention to the operation of private annuity markets. Many such proposals could substantially increase the volume of annuity sales.

4   Overview of the Current Volume

This balance of this book is divided into six chapters, five of which have been previously published in professional journals or edited volumes. We first describe the history of annuity markets. Chapter 2 summarizes the development of annuity products in the United States during the twentieth century. It illuminates the dual role of annuity products, particularly deferred annuities, as both saving vehicles and products that offer insurance against mortality risk. Chapter 3 offers a more detailed analysis of the pricing of annuity products since 1919 through 1984. This chapter also introduces the concept of the expected present discounted value of payouts from annuity products, and it tracks this payout over several decades, relative to the purchase price of immediate annuities. The findings suggest that there is substantial variation over time in the average "cost" of an annuity. This variation may be caused by many factors including the overall condition of financial markets, the portfolio structure of insurance company general accounts, and the perceived risk of substantial changes in mortality patterns.

Chapter 4 offers more recent estimates of the cost of annuity products, as well as evidence on the expected utility gains potentially available for purchasers of annuity products. Here we evaluate the expected present discounted value of payouts, relative to the premium cost, for the average individual annuity product available in the mid-1990s. This chapter also develops a framework for analyzing the lifetime expected utility of those who can, and who cannot, purchase individual annuity products. This framework enables us to develop estimates of the amount that hypothetical consumers would be willing to pay to purchase annuity products.

In chapter 5 we build on the analysis of the utility gains from annuity purchase by studying the potential role of nominal annuities, real annuities, and stock market linked variable annuities in providing retirement security. Though there is a limited market for inflation-indexed annuities in the United States, these products are widely available in other nations, notably the United Kingdom, Australia, and Israel. We devote substantial attention to assessing the effective cost of U.K. annuity products, and then present numerical results regarding the potential welfare gains from participation in various types of annuity markets. The analysis suggests that equity-linked annuities that offer payouts that vary with the level of the stock market may have substantial economic value.

In chapter 6 we tackle a specific concern that arises in discussions of how a private-accounts Social Security system might operate, namely the mechanics of annuitization. In particular we focus on the potential gain from purchasing annuity contracts in a group rather than an individual setting. We examine the Thrift Savings Plan available to employees of the U.S. federal government, and TIAA-CREF retirement plans available to employees of nonprofit institutions. These are both plans that offer annuity options to their participants. These systems are generally able to offer their participants annuity rates that are substantially more attractive than those available in the retail, individual, market. The experience of these group programs provides insights regarding the feasibility of purchasing annuities with the balances of individual accounts in a national defined contribution program.

In the final chapter, chapter 7, we take up several tax issues that arise with respect to annuity payouts from retirement plans. We explain the rules that currently apply to U.S. annuity purchases and lump-sum distributions from nonqualified retirement plans, and present numerical results that suggest that that these rules do not substantially affect the private demand for annuity products. This chapter also sketches the complex tax rules that govern payouts from qualified accounts in which individuals have accumulated resources for retirement. It focuses in particular on the minimum distribution requirements that apply to these distributions, and on alternatives to their current structure.

5 Methodological Issues

The individual chapters in this volume address a wide range of issues concerning the operation of annuity markets. Nevertheless, they are linked by the use of a common set of valuation calculations. One is a *money's worth* calculation designed to compare the costs and payouts from annuity policies. The second is a *utility-based* calculation directed at measuring the welfare gains associated with annuitization. In this section we explain the logic of the two calculations and the inputs that are needed to make them.

5.1 Money's Worth

The *money's worth* of an annuity is defined as the ratio of the expected discounted value of its future payments to its initial purchase price, or policy premium. Calculations of this type depend on the annuity payout amounts available in the private market, as well as on mortality rates and interest rates. They are useful for determining the degree to which private market annuity prices deviate from their actuarially fair level. These calculations can also be used to decompose differences between a money's worth value of one, and the actual observed money's worth value, into a component attributable to administrative costs and a component due to differences between the life expectancy of annuitants and that of the general population (adverse selection).

The money's worth calculations reported in this book all use the same fundamental methodology. We take actual market prices for annuities provided from various industry sources, and we calculate the expected present value of the payments associated with these annuities. The expected values are taken with respect to the probability that a hypothetical individual will be alive to receive the payment at each date in the future. Mortality rates are derived from actuarial life tables, which will be explained further below. The stream of expected payments is discounted to the present using a term structure of interest rates. The resulting expected present value of payouts is then divided by the cost of the policy (usually $100,000), and the resulting ratio is the money's worth. A money's worth of one means that an individual will, in expectation, receive a future payments with a present discounted value of a dollar for each current dollar spent on the annuity contract. A money's worth of less than one (for example, 0.9) means that the individual will expect to get back less than the cost of the policy.

While the money's worth approach is similar in all chapters, there are some differences across chapters with regard to assumptions about payout rates, interest rates, and mortality rates. In most chapters, we use publications by A. M. Best, an insurance industry rating agency, as the source of our annuity payout information. However, when we examine inflation indexed annuities in the United States and when we compare money's worth ratios for the United States and the United Kingdom, we use annuity payout information from alternative industry sources.

For interest rates, there are small methodological differences across chapters, reflecting a gradual evolution and improvement in our modeling of the term structure of interest rates. Chapter 2, the earliest work in the volume, presents historical information on annuity prices in the United States; money's worth calculations in that chapter assume a flat term structure. In the next chapter, a complete term structure of interest rates is calculated for government bonds. However, the chapter uses a term structure of corporate bond yields that was constructed by adding a constant term, equal to the difference in yields on long-term corporate and government bonds, to the term structure for government bond yields. In later chapters, a full corporate term structure is separately calculated using data on BAA corporate bond rates of various maturities.

For mortality tables, again many alternative choices are available. A first distinction is between mortality tables that reflect the mortality experience of the *general population* versus ones that reflect the mortality experience of *annuity purchasers*, or people who have chosen to purchase annuities in the private market. The former is known as a population mortality table, while the latter is an annuitant mortality table. Voluntary annuitants tend to have lower mortality at all ages than average individuals in the population. This is partly attributable to the fact that annuity purchasers tend to have more wealth, which is correlated with lower mortality, and partly to the voluntary purchase character of individual annuities. When individual annuity buyers have information about their mortality prospects that is not known to the insurance companies selling the annuities, those with longer life expectancies will find annuities more attractive than those with shorter life expectancies. The life expectancy of those who buy annuities will therefore be greater than that for the population as a whole.

Another difference across mortality tables is the extent to which they incorporate expected future mortality improvement. *Period* life tables represent a point-in-time snapshot of mortality rates for each age in a given year. For example, a year 2000 period mortality table for the general population shows the fraction of individuals at each age who will die in the year 2000. While such a mortality table is useful for cross-sectional purposes, it is not appropriate for valuing annuities because it does not incorporate forward-looking mortality improvement. For studying annuities, one needs a *cohort* life table that incorporates mortality improvement. It reports the probability that a member of a given birth cohort (e.g., men born in 1935) will die at each age. This type of mortality table accounts for expected mortality improvements over time.

To see the relationship between cohort and period mortality tables, consider a 65-year-old in the year 2000. The age 65 mortality rate in a year 2000 period table will be equal to the age 65 mortality rate for the

1935 birth cohort table because an individual in that cohort would turn 65 in the year 2000. The cohort table and the period table, however, will show different mortality rates at age 66. In the year 2000 period table, the age 66 mortality rate reflects the mortality probability for an individual who is age 66 in 2000. In contrast, the age 66 mortality rate in the 1935 birth cohort table shows the probability that a 66 year old will die *in 2001*. The difference in these two numbers reflects the mortality improvement that occurs between 2000 and 2001.

All of our calculations of money's worth values for the United States use cohort mortality tables. For the general population, we use mortality tables constructed by the Office of the Actuary at the Social Security Administration. We use different birth cohorts as appropriate for different annuity policies. For example, when we value an annuity for a 65-year-old in 1995, we use the 1930 birth cohort mortality table. When we value an annuity available to a 70-year-old in 1995, we use the 1925 birth cohort table mortality table.

We also use the mortality experience of actual annuity purchasers in evaluating the money's worth of annuities. In the United States, the Society of Actuaries has published annuitant life tables from time to time. For many years, the 1983 Individual Annuity Mortality Table (1983 IAM) was the industry standard. However, in the mid-1990s, a new "Annuity 2000" mortality table was produced to account for mortality improvement over the intervening seventeen years. Most important, both the 1983 and 2000 annuitant tables are period tables, meaning that they are meant to represent the mortality experience of annuitants at a point in time.

To convert the period mortality tables for annuitants into cohort tables, we modified them in two ways. First, we created a period table for the year of interest (e.g., 1995) by assuming a constant rate of mortality improvement between 1983 and 2000. This allowed us to interpolate and to create annuitant mortality tables for years in which the Society of Actuaries does not publish them. Second, we converted our interpolated period table into a cohort table by applying the age and year specific rates of mortality improvement that are implicit in the difference between the period and cohort mortality tables for the general population provided by the Social Security Office of the Actuary. In other words, we assume that future mortality improvement for annuitants will mirror that for the general population.

In table 1.1, we report eight sets of mortality statistics for an age-65 individual in the year 2000. In the first two columns, we report the deaths per 1,000 individuals in the 2000 period table that was used by Social Security Administration Office of the Actuary (2000). These mortality rates are provided separately for men and women. In the third and fourth columns, we report mortality rates for the general population cohort born in 1935, that is, for those who turn 65 in 2000. As previously discussed, the age 65 mortality rates will be the same in the period and cohort tables, since these represent the same individuals. However, for ages beyond 65, the mortality rates are lower in the cohort table, as a result of expected mortality improvements.

The fifth and sixth columns of table 1.1 report annuitant "period" mortality rates for 2000 as constructed for the Society of Actuaries by Johansen (1995). The last two columns show our constructed annuitant "cohort" mortality rates for individuals born in 1935, incorporating the same degree of mortality improvement for annuitants as the Social Security Administration tables incorporate for the population at large.

The mortality rates in the various columns of table 1.1 suggest several conclusions. First, the annuitant mortality rates are systematically lower than those for the general population. In some cases the annuitant mortality is less than 70 per cent of the population mortality. Second, the projected mortality rates at older ages in the cohort tables are lower than those in the period tables, as a result of ongoing reductions in age-specific mortality rates. Finally, there are large differences in the mortality experience of men and women, which is the source of differences in the annuity payouts, per premium dollar, for men and women.

5.2 Wealth Equivalence and Annuity-Equivalent Wealth

The second type of calculation that appears in several chapters is a utility-based analysis of how an annuity might be valued by a risk averse life-cycle individual or couple. The objective of these calculations is to gauge the economic value of annuitization by comparing utility levels with and without an annuity market. We report two slightly different utility-based measures of annuity value: "wealth equivalence" and "annuity equivalent wealth."

Wealth Equivalence (WE), which appears in several chapters, is defined as follows. Imagine that an individual starts off with $100,000 of wealth outside an annuity, and that he has no access to annuity markets and hence cannot purchase an annuity. The *wealth equivalence* is the fraction of this $100,000 that the individual would require to

Table 1.1
Comparison of mortality tables, 2000 (number of deaths per 1,000 persons)

Age	Population mortality table, 2000 (Period)		Population mortality table, 1935 birth cohort		Annuitant 2000 basic mortality table (Period)		Annuitant mortality table, 1935 birth cohort	
	Male	Female	Male	Female	Male	Female	Male	Female
65	21.497	13.265	21.497	13.265	10.993	7.017	10.993	7.017
66	23.703	14.619	23.440	14.593	12.188	7.734	12.053	7.720
67	25.830	15.945	25.290	15.902	13.572	8.491	13.288	8.468
68	27.796	17.199	26.946	17.128	15.160	9.288	14.696	9.250
69	29.726	18.456	28.520	18.331	16.946	10.163	16.258	10.094
70	31.872	19.874	30.274	19.668	18.920	11.165	17.971	11.049
71	34.367	21.531	32.359	21.225	21.071	12.339	19.840	12.164
72	37.144	23.385	34.714	22.954	23.388	13.734	21.858	13.481
73	40.251	25.467	37.401	24.890	25.871	15.391	24.039	15.042
74	43.742	27.817	40.482	27.063	28.552	17.326	26.424	16.856
75	47.648	30.540	43.989	29.579	31.477	19.551	29.060	18.936
76	52.043	33.632	47.990	32.406	34.686	22.075	31.985	21.270
77	57.016	37.013	52.572	35.418	38.225	24.910	35.246	23.837
78	62.627	40.682	57.771	38.575	42.132	28.074	38.865	26.620
79	68.887	44.744	63.577	41.982	46.427	31.612	42.848	29.661
80	75.784	49.398	69.964	45.899	51.128	35.580	47.202	33.060
81	83.312	54.730	76.922	50.418	56.250	40.030	51.936	36.876
82	91.501	60.687	84.506	55.472	61.809	45.017	57.084	41.149
83	100.363	67.310	92.793	61.157	67.826	50.600	62.710	45.975
84	109.924	74.689	101.848	67.629	74.322	56.865	68.862	51.490
85	120.212	82.926	111.676	75.015	81.326	63.907	75.551	57.810
86	131.250	92.111	122.237	83.381	88.863	71.815	82.761	65.009
87	143.052	102.312	133.469	92.745	96.958	80.682	90.463	73.138
88	155.621	113.574	145.310	103.100	105.631	90.557	98.632	82.206

Age								
89	168.951	125.919	157.720	114.431	114.858	101.307	107.223	92.064
90	183.033	139.355	170.688	126.736	124.612	112.759	116.207	102.548
91	197.852	153.882	184.216	140.013	134.861	124.733	125.566	113.491
92	213.386	169.491	198.318	154.275	145.575	137.054	135.295	124.750
93	229.612	186.163	213.018	169.530	156.727	149.552	145.400	136.190
94	246.504	203.876	228.340	185.792	168.290	162.079	155.889	147.702
95	263.477	221.841	243.483	202.037	180.245	174.492	166.567	158.915
96	280.376	239.830	258.267	217.988	192.565	186.647	177.380	169.649
97	297.038	257.592	272.486	233.342	205.229	198.403	188.266	179.725
98	313.290	274.858	285.960	247.782	218.683	210.337	199.606	189.617
99	328.955	291.349	298.488	261.008	233.371	223.027	211.757	199.801
100	345.403	308.830	311.563	274.956	249.741	237.051	225.273	211.050
101	362.673	327.360	325.225	289.645	268.237	252.985	240.540	223.839
102	380.806	347.002	339.488	305.134	289.305	271.406	257.915	238.659
103	399.847	367.822	354.389	321.447	313.391	292.893	277.762	255.965
104	419.839	389.891	369.954	338.652	340.940	318.023	300.430	276.229
105	440.831	413.284	386.206	356.782	372.398	347.373	326.253	299.882
106	462.872	438.081	403.175	375.891	408.210	381.520	355.563	327.359
107	486.016	464.366	420.908	396.027	448.823	421.042	388.697	359.079
108	510.317	492.228	439.423	417.259	494.681	466.516	425.959	395.463
109	535.832	521.762	458.771	439.639	546.231	518.520	467.674	436.907
110	562.624	553.068	478.968	463.233	603.917	577.631	514.121	483.806
111	590.755	586.252	500.074	488.096	668.186	644.427	565.619	536.531
112	620.293	620.293	522.126	514.309	739.483	719.484	622.453	596.552
113	651.308	651.308	545.152	541.941	818.254	803.380	684.888	668.477
114	683.873	683.873	569.252	569.252	904.945	896.693	753.271	746.402
115	1,000.000	1,000.000	1,000.000	1,000.000	1,000.000	1,000.000	1,000.000	1,000.000

Sources: U.S. Population Mortality Rates for Calendar Year 2000 (columns 2 & 3) and for the 1935 Birth Cohort (columns 4 & 5) are Alternative 2 Assumptions from the Year 2000 Social Security Trustees' Report. Period mortality rates for annuitants (columns 6 & 7) are from Johansen (1995, p. 239). The authors have constructed the "cohortized" annuitant mortality rates; see the later chapters for detail on underlying calculations.

achieve the same level of utility that he attains with his nonannuitized
$100,000, *if he instead devoted this fraction of his wealth to an annuity.*
Because annuities provide a valuable form of insurance to risk averse
individuals, the wealth equivalent is typically less than one. For
example, in chapter 4 we find that a 65-year-old man with risk
aversion of one (log utility) and no pre-existing annuity wealth would
have a wealth equivalence of between .65 and .75, depending on our
assumptions about inflation and interest rates. This means that he
would be indifferent between $100,000 of wealth held outside an
annuity, and with no opportunity to annuitize, and between $65,000
and $75,000 of fully annuitized wealth.

In the final two chapters, we develop and evaluate another measure,
one we term the *annuity equivalent wealth*, or AEW. This measure is
closely related to the WE although in some ways it reverses the question that produces the WE measure. The AEW assumes that an individual has $100,000 of fully annuitized wealth and then considers the
consequences of *closing* the annuity market. That is, it asks by how
much the individual's wealth would need to be multiplied in order to
generate the same utility level without annuities, as with them. Because
the option of annuitizing is valuable, the answer to this question will
be a number greater than one. For example, for a 65-year-old man with
log utility and no preexisting annuities, in chapter 5 we find that the
AEW for a real annuity is equal to 1.502. This means that the individual would be indifferent between $100,000 of annuitized wealth
and $150,200 of nonannuitized wealth.

When an individual in the AEW calculation has no wealth outside
the annuity that we consider eliminating, and the individual in the WE
calculation has no preexisting annuity wealth, then the AEW is the
reciprocal of the WE. This relationship does not hold when preexisting
annuities are available. In particular, when people are assumed to have
annuitized income streams from Social Security or from defined benefit
pension plans, there is no simple relationship between AEW and WE.

In all but the last chapter, the Wealth Equivalent and Annuity Equivalent Wealth calculations are based on population mortality tables. This
is because we are interested in how an average person in the population would value actuarially fair annuities if offered them. Such calculations are potentially relevant for policy discussions of Social Security
reform. In the last chapter, when we study how the tax treatment of
annuities affects those who purchase annuities, we also report annuity
equivalent wealth calculations using the annuitant mortality table. This

is the mortality table that applies to these buyers. The resulting AEW findings are smaller than those calculated in earlier chapters using population mortality, because the actuarially fair annuity payment for a pool of actual annuity buyers is lower than that for a randomly-selected group of individuals from the population. The higher mortality rate of the latter group enables insurers to offer higher annuity payouts.

6   Lessons from the Annuity Market

The next six chapters present a wide range of institutional and empirical findings about the operation of annuity markets. Three key lessons emerge, however, from our analysis. First, individual annuity markets have the potential to assist people on the verge of retirement and in retirement to allocate their resources over an uncertain lifetime. Even when the expected present discounted value of annuity payouts is less than the premium cost of the annuity policy, individuals may be able to raise their expected utility by annuitizing at least part of their wealth. Second, while the expected present value of annuity payouts is less than the premium cost of these policies for people in the population at large, a substantial fraction of this divergence, perhaps half, is due to differences between the mortality experience of annuitants and those who do not buy annuities. The important role of adverse selection in explaining annuity prices suggests that policy reforms that increase participation in the annuity market might have significant effects on the pricing of annuities. This is particularly true if annuities can be purchased within a "group program," thereby reducing both the transactions costs and the adverse selection costs associated with annuity purchase.

Finally, a broad range of annuity products can contribute to retirement security. While virtually all of the annuities currently sold in the United States are nominal annuities with payout streams unaltered by consumer prices or by the returns on various securities, other products may also substantially enhance consumer welfare. Other nations have annuity markets that provide consumers with a somewhat richer menu of annuity products, including inflation-indexed annuities. It is possible that as experience with inflation-indexed bonds in the United States develops, similar inflation-linked annuity products will develop as well. Annuities are most valuable when they protect the real consumption stream that retirees receive until they die, and various types of "indexed annuities" may achieve that goal better than simple nominal annuities.

References

American Council of Life Insurers. 2000. *Life Insurers Fact Book*. Washington, D.C.: ACLI.

American council of Life Insurers. 1997. *Life Insurers Fact Book*. Washington, D.C.: ACLI.

Brown, Jeffrey R. 2000. "Differential Mortality and the Value of Individual Account Retirement Annuities." NBER Working Paper No. 7560, February 2000.

Johansen, Robert J. 1995. "Review of Adequacy of 1983 Individual Annuity Mortality Table," *Transactions of the Society of Actuaries* 47:211–249.

Poterba, James M., Steven F. Venti, and David A. Wise. 2000. "Saver Behavior and 401 (k) Retirement Wealth," *American Economic Review* 90 (May 2000):297–302.

Social Security Administration, Office of the Chief Actuary. 2000. "United States Life Table Functions and Actuarial Functions based on the Alternative 2 Mortality Probabilities." Unpublished data constructed for the 2000 Annual Report of the Board of Trustees of the Federal Old-Age and Survivors Insurance and Disability Insurance Trust Funds.

Warshawsky, Mark. 1984. "Aspects of Insurance Markets." Ph.D. dissertation. Harvard University.

2

A Brief History of
Annuity Markets

James M. Poterba

Annuities are contracts that provide periodic payments for an agreed-upon span of time. They include annuities certain, which provide periodic payouts for a fixed number of years, and life annuities, which provide such payouts for the duration of one or more persons (the annuitants') lives. The principal insurance role of annuities is to indemnify individuals against the risk of outliving their resources.

Annuities solve the problem of planning consumption in a world with uncertain lifetimes. In return for an initial capital payment, an annuitant is assured of receiving a constant income stream for the remainder of his life. The annuity provider can pool mortality risk across similar individuals and by can use the principal left behind by those who died sooner than expected to insure those who live unexpectedly long. As a result, the annuitant's payout from the annuity contract can, in theory, exceed what the income he could earn if he invested his annuity premium in a financial asset, such as a bond.

The annuity payout rate depends on both the annuitant's prospective mortality risk and on the rate of return that the annuity provider can earn on invested assets. Younger individuals, because they are expected to receive payments for a longer time period, receive lower annuity payouts than older annuitants for a given amount of capital invested. Higher rates of return generate greater income per dollar of capital for the insurance company, and therefore permit higher payout rates to annuitants.

Annuities are sometimes referred to as "reverse life insurance." With life insurance, the policyholder pays the insurer each year until he or she dies, after which the insurance company pays a lump sum to the insured's beneficiaries. With annuities, the lump-sum payment is from the annuitant to the insurance company before the annuity payout begins, and the annuitant receives regular payouts from the insurer until death.

Most annuity contracts have an accumulation phase and a liquidation phase. During the accumulation phase, capital builds up; this capital is dispersed during the liquidation phase. In the case of the single-premium immediate annuity, there is no accumulation phase. Annuitants make lump-sum payments of the accumulated capital that they wish to draw down to the annuity provider. During the liquidation phase, the annuitants receive payouts contingent upon their survival or in accord with other terms specified in the annuity contract. In some annuity contracts, payouts are specified as a guaranteed minimum, with the opportunity for a dividend if mortality experience or rates of return on insurance company investments prove better than expected. Many annuity products exhibit long accumulation phases, so they operate in part as saving vehicles. Although annuities are unique in their provision of income streams contingent on remaining alive, they compete with other financial products as a means for asset accumulation.

Annuities have historically been offered by insurance companies, which pool the mortality risk across many individuals and thereby achieve a more predictable cash flow than if they offered an annuity to only one person. The same principles that underpin risk reduction in life insurance sales apply to the provision of annuity payouts. The annuity supplier must have sufficient capital and be sufficiently long lived to ensure that annuity payouts will still be paid if the annuitant lives for many years.

This paper describes the historical evolution of the annuity market in the United States. It is divided into six sections. The first provides a short history of annuities, focusing primarily on individual annuities. It also describes the regulatory setting in which annuities are traded. The next section describes the structure of individual annuity contracts, as well as the evolution of the market for these contracts in the last few decades. Section 3 considers group annuity plans, and describes their significance in the insurance marketplace. The fourth section considers variable annuities, which have grown very rapidly in the last decade. Section 5 examines annuities in their role as investment vehicles. There is a brief conclusion.

1   The History of Annuities: Ancients through the Current Day

Since uncertainty about length of life is a ubiquitous source of risk, financial contracts similar to annuities have a long history. James (1947) reports that ancient Roman contracts known as *annua* promised an individual a stream of payments for a fixed term, or possibly for life, in return for an up-front payment. Speculators who dealt in marine and other lines of insurance offered such contracts. A Roman, Domitius Ulpianus, compiled the first recorded life table for the purpose of computing the estate value of annuities that a decedent might have purchased on the lives of his survivors.

Single-premium life annuities were available in the Middle Ages, and detailed records exist of special annuity pools known as *tontines* that operated in France during the seventeenth century. In return for an initial lump-sum payment, purchasers of tontines received life annuities. The amount of the annuity was increased each year for the survivors, as they claimed the payouts that would otherwise have gone to those who died. When the second-to-last participant in a tontine pool died, the sole survivor received the entire remaining principal. The tontine thus combined insurance with an element of lottery-style gambling.

During the 1700s, governments in several nations, including England and Holland, sold annuities in lieu of government bonds. The government received capital in return for a promise of lifetime payouts to the annuitants. Murphy (1939) provides a detailed account of the sale of public annuities in England in the eighteenth and early nineteenth centuries. Annuities initially were sold to all individuals at a fixed price, regardless of their age or sex. As it became clear over time that mortality rates for annuitants were lower than those for the population at large, a more refined pricing structure was introduced.

In the United States, annuities have been available for over two centuries. In 1759, Pennsylvania chartered the Corporation for the Relief of Poor and Distressed Presbyterian Ministers and Distressed Widows and Children of Ministers. James (1947) explains that it provided survivorship annuities for the families of ministers. In Philadelphia in 1812, the Pennsylvania Company for Insurance on Lives and Granting Annuities was founded. It offered life insurance and annuities to the general public and was the forerunner of modern stock insurance companies.

During the nineteenth century, the market for annuities grew slowly while that for life insurance grew quickly. This disparity in part reflects the different risks that these insurance products address. Individuals who, if they died unexpectedly, would leave dependents in need of income support provide the traditional market for life insurance. Individuals who have no dependents or relatives to provide support if they outlive their resources provide the natural market for annuities. Extended families, common in the nineteenth century, provided and informal alternative to structured annuity contracts. The falling incidence of multigenerational households in the early twentieth century contributed to the growing demand for annuity products. Murphy (1950) notes that families and other informal arrangements provided some insurance against longevity; Kotlikoff and Spivak (1981) explore related issues conceptually.

Today, annuities represent an important line of business for U.S. insurance companies. Tables 2.1, 2.2, and 2.3 describe the significance of annuities in the U.S. insurance market during recent decades. Table 2.1 presents the value of insurance company payouts on life insurance policies and on annuities over the period 1940–99, converted to 1994 dollars using the Consumer Price Index. Although annuities represented less than 10 per cent of the combined payouts on life insurance and annuities in the period before World War II, they grew more rapidly than life insurance in the five decades tracked in the table. By the early 1990s, annuity payouts constituted nearly 40 per cent of combined payouts. They remained at this level throughout the 1990s.

Table 2.2 reports the premium income received by insurance companies for annuity policies over the 1951–99 period. The table shows both the substantial growth of real annuity premiums, particularly between 1951 and the mid-1960s, and the breakdown of annuity premiums between individual and group policies. Although premiums on group policies were three to five times greater than the premiums on individual policies throughout the 1950s and 1960s, individual annuities grew more rapidly from the 1970s until the mid-1990s. In 1994, premium income from individual annuities exceeded that from group annuities. In the last few years, group annuity premiums have again exceeded those from individual annuities. The long-term growth of individual relative to group annuity premiums reflects both the decline in the growth of defined benefit pension plans and the rapid expansion of individual annuity products, particularly variable annuities.

Table 2.1
Annuity vs. life insurance payouts (millions of 1994 dollars)

Year	Life insurance payouts	Annuity payouts	Annuity payouts as percentage of total [(2)/((1) + (2))]
1940	26,355	1,864	0.07
1945	20,194	1,779	0.08
1950	20,947	2,012	0.09
1955	27,015	2,772	0.09
1960	36,514	4,158	0.10
1965	47,630	6,120	0.11
1966	49,760	6,557	0.12
1967	51,932	7,095	0.12
1968	53,827	7,474	0.12
1969	54,976	7,758	0.12
1970	54,767	8,102	0.13
1971	54,384	8,513	0.14
1972	56,574	9,323	0.14
1973	57,717	10,130	0.15
1974	54,450	10,080	0.16
1975	52,018	10,102	0.16
1976	52,627	11,517	0.18
1977	51,868	12,889	0.20
1978	51,748	13,335	0.20
1979	50,734	15,418	0.23
1980	50,118	18,348	0.27
1981	51,331	19,611	0.28
1982	54,064	19,692	0.27
1983	57,021	20,196	0.26
1984	60,690	25,566	0.30
1985	62,367	29,300	0.32
1986	61,710	30,629	0.33
1987	61,454	31,715	0.34
1988	60,706	32,173	0.35
1989	60,777	35,141	0.37
1990	63,277	36,933	0.37
1991	59,810	39,838	0.40
1992	60,733	39,662	0.40
1993	61,176	41,356	0.40
1994	67,618	40,412	0.37
1995	71,665	47,100	0.40
1996	75,723	48,260	0.39
1997	74,445	50,839	0.41
1998	79,046	54,913	0.41
1999	84,099	55,612	0.40

Source: American Council on Life Insurance (2000), pages 100–101. Consumer Price Index values are used to convert entries to 1994 dollars. Annuity payouts excludes "surrender values under annuities," which is only published in years after 1994. Life insurance payouts include payments to beneficiaries, surrender values under life insurance, policy dividends, matured endowments, and "other payments."

Table 2.2
Annuity premium income of life insurance companies (millions of 1994 dollars)

Year	Individual annuity	Group annuity
1951	1,209	4,272
1952	1,377	4,722
1953	1,433	5,152
1954	1,296	5,370
1955	1,317	5,810
1956	1,254	5,796
1957	1,177	6,254
1958	1,180	6,127
1959	1,203	6,411
1960	1,268	5,451
1961	1,399	5,471
1962	1,478	5,785
1963	1,871	6,572
1964	2,129	7,018
1965	2,580	8,060
1966	2,756	8,268
1967	3,024	8,836
1968	3,307	9,448
1969	3,455	11,747
1970	3,669	10,553
1971	4,420	13,559
1972	5,176	14,347
1973	5,598	17,018
1974	5,788	17,486
1975	7,343	20,677
1976	9,677	26,712
1977	11,140	25,505
1978	10,131	27,033
1979	10,164	26,480
1980	11,331	29,035
1981	16,788	28,206
1982	23,353	29,887
1983	20,850	24,629
1984	22,418	38,756
1985	28,793	45,493
1986	35,307	77,861
1987	44,039	71,624
1988	54,887	74,581

Table 2.2 (continued)

Year	Individual annuity	Group annuity
1989	59,089	78,444
1990	60,845	85,487
1991	56,220	78,251
1992	64,800	75,309
1993	78,957	81,491
1994	80,832	73,016
1995	75,204	80,253
1996	79,443	87,155
1997	83,247	99,089
1998	86,403	122,206
1999	102,903	137,586

Source: American Council on Life Insurance and author's calculations.

The data in table 2.2 may understate the actual significance of annuity contracts. Murphy (1950) notes that virtually all permanent life insurance contracts other than term life accumulate cash value. This accumulated value can be used to purchase an annuity. Such policies are classified as life insurance policies, but they can also be viewed as partly annuity products. Provisions regarding withdrawals and annuity conversions are almost always specified in the life insurance policy at the time of purchase.

The growth in annuity products shown in the premium data of table 2.2 is also reflected in the reserves held by insurance companies. Table 2.3 presents detailed information on reserves for both annuity policies and life insurance policies. These data, from the American Council on Life Insurance (2000), suggest that total annuity reserves were less than half of life insurance reserves in the mid-1960s. They have nevertheless grown more rapidly than life insurance reserves, so that by the 1990s, annuity reserves were more than twice the value of life insurance reserves. In part, this reflects the growth of term life insurance, for which reserve requirements are lower than for other types of life insurance. Within the annuity market, individual annuities have grown more rapidly than group annuities.

Annuities are sold in regulated markets. Until 1850, there was little regulation of the insurance industry in the United States. Several insurance scandals led to pressure for regulation, and in 1850, New

Table 2.3
Life insurance company reserves for annuities and life insurance policies (millions of 1994 dollars)

Year	Individual annuity	Group annuity	Supplemental annuity	Life insurance
1967	25,508	116,300	15,465	444,469
1968	26,694	121,171	15,384	447,073
1969	25,651	126,128	14,810	444,662
1970	26,564	129,289	14,241	441,238
1971	28,031	139,607	14,299	445,211
1972	30,366	152,373	14,003	455,036
1973	31,671	153,036	13,581	449,880
1974	31,618	147,019	12,562	426,009
1975	34,296	159,786	11,798	413,649
1976	39,999	182,328	11,494	412,735
1977	46,330	190,061	11,167	409,369
1978	52,442	224,436	10,806	404,284
1979	55,363	237,858	10,183	384,389
1980	56,768	252,717	9,386	356,109
1981	63,299	262,653	8,751	337,690
1982	78,378	294,906	8,689	328,539
1983	96,276	330,137	8,745	329,012
1984	109,879	363,388	8,323	322,440
1985	133,646	417,640	8,188	325,066
1986	163,772	480,935	8,494	340,718
1987	203,647	511,994	8,818	360,516
1988	242,971	543,920	9,200	375,954
1989	286,545	566,810	9,495	387,706
1990	319,874	584,803	9,659	395,437
1991	357,231	596,454	9,706	404,841
1992	402,096	591,271	9,912	425,056
1993	450,632	617,236	10,206	447,457
1994	482,172	612,394	22,989	468,469
1995	557,513	601,343	24,551	496,712
1996	587,801	652,506	26,078	525,546
1997	639,649	703,281	26,246	559,578
1998	693,866	768,254	28,135	596,289
1999	777,432	807,391	28,781	627,651

Source: American Council on Life Insurance and author's calculations.

Hampshire became the first state to appoint a commissioner of insurance. Many other states followed suit in the next two decades, and by the early 1870s the insurance industry in virtually all states operated under regulatory control, as described by Trieschmann and Gustavson (1995). The primacy of state regulation of insurance markets was confirmed when the U.S. Congress passed the McCarran-Ferguson Act in 1945. State insurance regulations are not uniform, and this can affect the scope of annuity products available to consumers in different places. Greene (1977) attributes the slow early growth of variable annuities, after their introduction by TIAA in 1952, in part to the requirement that such products receive regulatory approval in each state.

Insurance regulation arose historically in part because of the complexity of insurance products and the relative lack of sophistication on the part of many insurance buyers. Most annuities, like whole life insurance, involve investment decisions as well as decisions about mortality risk. Insurance regulation restricts the types of policies that can be offered, determines how policies can be explained to potential buyers, and sets limits on what constitutes an acceptable expense. There are also regulations on the capital that insurance companies must have and on the types of investments that they can purchase with assets that are held against future policyholder claims. Insurance regulations are designed to increase the safety and security of income streams purchased by policyholders.

Black and Skipper (1994) discuss the investment regulations that affect insurance companies, in particular the presence of "legal lists, " which describe the set of securities that insurers may invest in and the fraction of their assets that may be held in different securities. These regulations have implications for the rates of return that insurance companies can offer on fixed annuity products, since they typically restrict the amount of high-risk (and potentially high-return) securities in insurance portfolios. The foregoing regulations apply to fixed annuities. Group fixed annuities are subject to additional regulations from the provisions of ERISA, largely concerning the structure of contract terms for these products.

Variable annuities are regulated differently than fixed annuities, with insurers maintaining separate asset pools as reserves against variable annuities. This prevents poor returns on the variable annuity portfolio from affecting the capital base for other insurance company products. Variable annuities, because of their investment component, are also regulated in part under the federal securities law. These products are subject to provisions of the Securities Act of 1933, the Securities Exchange Act of 1934, and the Investment Company Act of 1940.

2 Individual Annuities

Understanding the growth of the individual annuity market requires recognizing the range of annuity products available to individuals and the risks the products are designed to insure against. Individual annuity products differ in their provisions for asset accumulation and in the terms under which the accumulated principal is dispersed during the liquidation phase. This section describes the primary types of individual fixed annuities and summarizes the growth of the individual annuity market in the United States.

2.1 Typology of Individual Annuities

Annuities can be categorized along many dimensions, including the number and timing of premiums, the number of lives covered, the nature of the payouts, and the date at which benefits begin. There are several methods of paying premiums: single premium, fixed annual premium, and flexible premium annuities are all available. Annuities can insure a single life, or they can insure multiple lives (joint life annuities). They can begin payouts immediately after the premium is paid (immediate annuities), or after some waiting period, sometimes involving many years (deferred annuities). The payouts may take the form of a life annuity without refund, they may offer a guaranteed minimum payout, or they may offer the annuitant a flexible structure of periodic withdrawals.

The simplest individual annuity contract is a single-premium immediate annuity. In return for a single premium payment, the annuitant receives a guaranteed stream of future payments that begin immediately. These payments can end when the annuitant dies (a simple life annuity), when both the annuitant and a coannuitant, such as a spouse, have died (a joint life survivorship annuity), or at the later of a fixed number of years or the date of death of the annuitant (life annuity with stipulated payments certain).

These different annuities address different insurance needs. A simple life annuity is primarily designed to insure annuitants against outliving their resources; a joint life survivorship annuity addresses this risk and also provides retirement income for dependents. The "payout certain" annuity is often attractive because potential annuitants are unwilling to turn over a capital sum to an annuity provider and risk dying shortly thereafter without receiving many annuity payments. The "fixed payments certain" product overcomes this inhibition by ensuring that payments will be made to the annuitants' beneficiaries for at least a fixed period. The level of the annuity payout associated with a "fixed payments certain" contract is lower than that for a simple life annuity.

In addition to the immediate annuities described above, there are also deferred annuities. A single-premium deferred annuity, for example, includes a waiting period between the premium payment and the beginning of annuity payouts. The promised stream of payments for a given premium is greater for a single-premium deferred annuity than for a single-premium immediate annuity, since the premium is invested and earns returns between the date when it is paid and the date when the payouts begin.

A variant on such an annuity, one that provides for multiple premium payments, could represent a saving plan for an individual who plans to use an annuity to draw down accumulated resources. This is known as an annual-payment annuity. It specifies a stream of premiums that the policyholder will pay during the policy's accumulation phase. At the conclusion of this phase or possibly some years afterward, the policy enters its liquidation phase and the annuitant and beneficiaries begin to receive payouts from the accumulated principal. While these products are available, single-premium deferred annuities have been the dominant contract in the individual annuity market for the last few decades.

One of the most popular annuity products is the flexible-premium deferred annuity, which permits annuitants to make cash contributions at times of their choosing and allows the accumulated value of these premium contributions to be converted to an annuity at some future date or specified age of the annuitant.

2.2 The Growth of the Individual Annuity Market

While the earlier discussion noted that annuities have a long history, the annuity business was a small share of the insurance market until the Great Depression. Data compiled by the Temporary National Economic Commission (TNEC) (1941) suggest that, over the period 1866–1920, annuity premiums averaged only 1.5 per cent of life insurance premiums received by U.S. insurance companies. The Great Depression, and the associated financial panic and bank failures, led many investors to seek reliable investment vehicles for their savings. Individual annuities, many offered by insurance companies with long and stable financial histories, were such vehicles, and they grew rapidly during the 1930s. TNEC (1941) data show that 68 per cent of all annuity premiums received between 1913 and 1937 were received between 1933 and 1937. In 1934–36, the premium income on newly issued individual annuities exceeded that on newly issued ordinary life insurance for the 26 large companies studied by the TNEC.

As a share of payouts, reserves, or total premium income, annuities were still a small part of the insurance business in the 1930s. TNEC (1941) data suggest that they accounted for 1.79 per cent of all insurance company disbursements over the 1929–38 period, compared with 24.3 per cent for death claims and 23 per cent for policy surrender values. Annuities accounted for a greater share (8.56 per cent) of premium income during this period, and individual annuities accounted for 80 per cent of annuity premiums. In 1938, annuity reserves were $2.67 billion, compared with $16.83 billion in life insurance reserves.

Although the individual annuity market grew rapidly in the 1930s, it represented only a small fraction of the insurance industry at the end of this period. Many firms that had sold policies during that decade subsequently experienced losses on their annuity contracts, for two reasons. First, the rate of return earned on insurance reserves fell during the early 1930s. Long-term interest rates on Moody's AAA corporate bonds averaged 4.68 per cent between 1928 and 1932 but 3.45 per cent between 1933 and 1940. The real interest rate was much greater than the nominal rate in the early 1930s. The consumer price index fell 20.3 per cent between 1928 and 1932, raising the real return to lenders. Long-term interest rates fell below 3 per cent in the late 1930s. Because annuities had been sold assuming that prevailing interest rates from earlier periods would remain in force, the drop in rates led to investment earnings below what was needed to service these contracts. Campbell (1969) reports that the net earnings rates of life insurance companies reached a high of 5.05 per cent in 1930 but declined for nearly two decades afterward, falling to 2.88 per cent in 1947. This was reflected in the poor profitability of annuity contracts.

A second factor in annuity losses was the longevity of annuitants relative to the assumptions that insurance companies used in pricing their annuity contracts. Gilbert (1948) and the TNEC (1941) explain that the mortality tables that life insurance companies used to price annuities were revised several times during the 1930s to reflect the lower mortality risk for annuitants than for the general public. The life tables in use particularly overstated the mortality experience of female annuitants at the beginning of the 1930s.

Gilbert (1948) compares the 1868 American Experience Table of Mortality, long a standard reference in the insurance industry, and the "expectation" table adopted in 1938 for annuity purposes. The tables show large gains in life expectancy at extreme ages, especially for women. The 1868 table combined both men and women to yield a life expectancy of 8.48 years at age 70. In contrast, the 1938 table shows a life expectancy of 15.62 years for female annuitants at age 70. The inappropriately high mortality assumptions built into annuities sold at the beginning of the 1930s contributed to the losses on these products later in the decade.

The annuity contracts that grew in popularity during the 1930s emphasized the role of annuities as retirement savings and investment vehicles. Annual-premium retirement annuities—contracts the allowed individuals to make premium contributions each year, to accumulate a capital fund, and then to choose from a number of payout options at the date of their retirement or another advanced age—expanded particularly rapidly. Retirement annuities were attractive retirement saving vehicles for several reasons. They offered returns that were often greater than those available elsewhere for small investors. They provided an option to purchase an immediate single-premium annuity at a future date, typically at terms specified at the beginning of the accumulation period, if the participant decided that was the best way to decumulate assets. Perhaps most important, annuities were supplied by secure financial institutions. Gilbert (1948) notes that even though surrender charges could sharply reduce the return on these products for those who redeemed them before maturity, this did not prevent the rapid expansion of the deferred annuity market in the 1930s.

Annuity premiums for a given payout steam increased during the 1930s. Gilbert (1948) reports that in 1930 Aetna Life Insurance Company would sell a $100 immediate annual annuity to a 65-year-old man (woman) for a premium of $925 ($1,040). By 1940, the premiums had increased to $1,220 ($1,435).

The individual annuity market expanded throughout the postwar period. As the data in table 2.2 show, individual annuity premium payments increased almost every year. However, comparing these premium payments with a yardstick for the size of the economy, such as gross domestic product, can be more revealing. Individual annuity premiums were 0.064 per cent (six one-hundredths of 1 per cent) of GDP in 1951. They declined to 0.053 per cent in 1961, then began to increase: to 0.110 by 1971, 0.339 per cent in 1981, 0.903 per cent in 1991, and 1.2 per cent in 1999. The early 1960s thus marked the beginning of the growth phase for individual annuities, with much of the growth concentrated in the period since the late 1970s, and much of the growth in the 1990s in the market for variable annuities.

2.3 Characteristics of Annuity Buyers

Survey data on the owners of nonqualified annuity products, such as the information collected and reported in Gallup (1996), provide some insight on the individuals who purchase these policies. In 1993, the average age of individual annuity holders was 63, and half of these policyholders were retired. Less than one-quarter were under the age of 54, so annuities are primarily a product that attracts buyers who are at or near retirement age. More than three-quarters of the annuity policyholders had annual incomes of less than $75,000 per year. The majority of those with annuities reported that they planned to use their annuities for retirement income.

The characteristics of annuity products that attract current buyers vary. Roughly three-quarters cite tax benefits associated with annuities as a primary reason for purchasing their policy. Another two-thirds per cent cite the safety and reliable income associated with an annuity, and more than half indicate that the long-term saving plan associated with an annuity product was an important attraction. A substantial fraction, nearly half, of all annuity holders report than they used a one-time income receipt, such as an inheritance, to purchase their annuity.

3 Group Annuity Plans

The Metropolitan Life Insurance Company pioneered the group annuity market, which is linked to corporate defined benefit pension plans, in the early 1920s. James (1947) explains the early growth of this business. Life insurance companies began underwriting group life, health, and disability policies for large corporations in the years after

World War I. Providing life annuities to retirees was a natural extension of this business.

Most early corporate pensions were financed on a pay-as-you-go basis, with the firm making payments to beneficiaries from current earnings. In 1921, Metropolitan began to write small contracts to manage corporate pension programs, collecting contributions while workers were employed and, in return, paying out benefits when they were retired. Metropolitan introduced its own retirement pension program in 1925 and began actively marketing group annuities, the name for structured pension programs, in 1927. In the first year of operation, Metropolitan sold only 30 contracts for group annuities, covering fewer than 40,000 individuals.

The group annuity market suffered from the same difficulties as the individual annuity market in the early 1930s, with low investment returns leading to losses on group annuity contracts. This experience, coupled with the passage of the Social Security Act of 1935 and the associated promise of a minimal retirement benefit for workers, led to slow growth of group annuities. By 1941, James (1947) reports, only 269,101 individuals were covered by group annuity policies with Metropolitan Life Insurance Company.

The typical policy in the early 1940s, which Dublin (1943) describes, required employer and employee contributions during the employee's active service. The employee was eligible to receive an annuity beginning at age 65, with some provisions for retirement at other ages. At retirement, the employee could typically choose between a lump-sum payout of his total contributions, and the "paid-up option" in which these contributions were used to purchase a life or joint life annuity. Employer contributions were usually applied to purchase an annuity. The goal of most group annuity plans was to provide, in conjunction with individual benefits from Social Security, a retirement income that replaced between 40 and 60 per cent of the retiree's earnings from employment.

The group annuity business grew rapidly in the late 1940s and throughout the 1950s. In 1958, 3.9 million workers were covered in various types of group annuity plans. This number grew to 38 million by 1988. It declined to about 31.1 million by 1999. At one time essentially all group annuities were associated with defined benefit pension plans, though not all defined benefit plans were administered through group annuities. In more recent years, group annuities have also been used in conjunction with defined contribution plans. Hoffman and

Mondejar (1992) provide data on the assets of insured and noninsured private pension funds. In 1950, insured pension fund assets were 40 per cent of the total assets of private pension funds; this fraction declined gradually to 31 per cent by the end of the 1980s. The broad trends in this ratio are sensitive to the mix of defined benefit and defined contribution pension plans.

3.1 Typology of Group Annuity Products

Group annuity contracts take several forms. The first type to achieve popularity was the *deferred group annuity contract*. An employer purchasing such a contract makes periodic payments to an insurance company, which applies these payments to the purchase of deferred annuities for covered workers. The purchase price of these annuities is specified by the employer's contract with the insurance company, so the insurer indemnifies the employer against changes in rates of return, mortality risk, or other factors that could alter the pricing of deferred annuities. Maclean (1962) reports that such policies were often structured so that the employer received a dividend from the insurance company if mortality experience or investment returns proved to be more favorable than the initial contract anticipated. The employer did not pay more, however, if supplying deferred annuities turned out to be more expensive than the insurance company had originally anticipated. This type of contract covered 71 per cent of the individuals with group annuity contracts in 1950 but declined to only 48 per cent a decade later.

A key attraction of deferred group annuity contracts is that employees know they have a certain pension income, which is guaranteed by the insurance company writing the annuity contract. Managers in turn know that they have met their future pension obligations in full. Because some workers will not remain with the firm long enough to collect pension benefits, however, fully funded deferred group annuity contracts require the employer to set aside funds for future pension liabilities that may not materialize. These contracts also give employers little flexibility in choosing the funding level for their pension.

A second type of group annuity contract, the *deposit administration contract*, grew in popularity during the 1950s. This type of contract offers more flexibility in the timing of employer contributions and a more direct link between employer cost and the mortality or turnover experience of employees than does the deferred group annuity contract. The insurer holds contributions to the deposit administration plan in an unallocated fund. The insurer promises a minimum return on this fund. When an employee retires, the insurer withdraws an amount sufficient to purchase an immediate fixed annuity for the amount /of the retiree's assured retirement benefit from the fund account. The insurer does not indemnify the employer against changes in the price of fixed annuities. Although the insurance company bears all risks of mortality and rate-of-return fluctuations for retired employees, the employer bears these risks for employees who have not yet reached retirement.

The employer may be able to contribute less to the reserve fund than the required contributions under a deferred group annuity contract. Deposit administration plans expanded very rapidly in the 1950s, from covering only 10 per cent of all individuals in insured pension plans in 1950 to covering 31 per cent by 1959.

A third class of group annuity contract, first offered in 1950 and one of the most popular in subsequent years, is the *immediate participation guarantee* (IPG) contract. This is a variant of the deposit administration contract, with a fund account maintained by the insurer but with even more direct links between the mortality experience of covered employees, returns on investment, and the pension costs of the employer. With an IPG plan, if the employer maintains a fund account balance large enough to fund the guaranteed annuities for all retirees, then the employer's account is credited with the actual investment experience of the insurer, and the actual payments to retirees are withdrawn from this account. In this way the employer is essentially self-insuring the mortality experience of retirees and receiving actual rather than projected investment returns. If the employer's fund balance drops below the amount needed to fund the required guaranteed annuities, however, then the plan becomes a standard deferred annuity contract, and the insurer uses the account balance to purchase guaranteed individual annuities for all participants in the pension plan. Provided the account balance is high enough, the employer bears the investment and mortality risks associated with the plan. The insurer assumes these risks if the account balance falls below the threshold.

The rules governing an employee's participation in defined benefit private pension plans vary from employer to employer, with corresponding effects on participation in associated group annuity programs. Several common features nevertheless deserve comment. First, when firms introduce these plans, they typically purchase deferred annuities for the pension liabilities associated with prior service of current employees. Second, if employees vested in a pension plan die before the plan's retirement age, their contributions will be returned, in most cases with interest; the employer's contributions to the pension plan will not be returned. Third, an employee who leaves the firm before reaching retirement age may choose to withdraw the current value of his or her pension benefit as a lump sum or to receive the benefits due at retirement age. With the advent of Individual Retirement Accounts and other self-directed retirement income accounts in the early 1980s, workers who were leaving the firm were able to roll over their accumulated pension wealth into another retirement saving account.

3.2   Group Annuities and Pension Policy in the United States

Group annuity contracts grew rapidly during the 1950s and 1960s. They were originally linked to defined benefit pension plans. These plans typically offer a retirement benefit specified by a formula depending on years of service and salary history. Their growth continued as employment at firms with defined benefit pension plans increased and as various legislative changes raised the fraction of the workforce at these firms that was covered by a pension. For a variety of reasons, however, the growth of defined benefit plans slowed and then reversed during the 1980s. Defined contribution plans, which permit employers to make contributions to an investment account maintained on behalf of the worker but which do not promise any particular stream of post-retirement benefits, have grown rapidly. In the late 1990s, the rate at which defined benefit plans were created fell sharply, while defined contribution plans continue to be created. This implies a changing role for group annuities, and prospectively greater use of these policies in conjunction with defined contribution plans.

Table 2.4 shows substantial changes in the relative flows of contributions to defined benefit and defined contribution pension plans during the 1980s. The table shows the number of defined contribution and defined benefit pension plans, participants in these plans, and contributions to these plans, during the period 1975–96. The number of defined contribution plans more than doubled between 1975 and 1982 and then rose another 50 per cent between 1982 and 1989. The number of defined benefit plans increased during the 1975–82 period, but the increase was slower than that for defined contribution plans. Between 1982 and 1991, however, the number of defined benefit plans actually *declined*, with the 1991 number more than 40 per cent below the peak. The number of participants peaked in 1984, and the number of active participants (those who were not retired) peaked in 1981. In contrast, the number of defined contribution plan participants increased throughout the 1980s, although more slowly than the number of plans.

The last column in table 2.4 tracks contributions to defined contribution and defined benefit pension plans. The disparity between the contribution series is even more dramatic than that between the number of participants or the number of plans. In constant 1989 dollars, defined contribution plan contributions increased from $35.4 billion in 1980 to $89.7 billion in 1991 and $143.9 billion in 1996. Much of this growth reflects rising contributions to voluntary retirement saving programs, such as 401(k) plans. Contributions to defined benefit plans, however, peaked at $64.1 billion in 1980 and 1981 and then declined. Their level has fluctuated during the last decade, with a high of $52.1 billion in 1993, and a low of $23.0 billion in 1990. Defined benefit contribution levels are affected by fluctuations in asset values. When asset values in existing plans rise, the amount that firms need to contribute to cover their future liabilities declines, so contributions may also decline.

The shift from defined benefit to defined contribution pension plans was the result of several coincident developments, including regulatory changes and a shift in employment growth from industries that historically offered such plans (manufacturing) to industries that did not (services and trade). The changing regulatory treatment of defined benefit and defined contribution pension plans began with the Employee Retirement and Income Security Act of 1974 (ERISA). ERISA imposed minimum plan standards for participation, vesting, and retirement, as well as requirements for funding past service liability. It also established the Pension Benefit Guaranty Corporation (PBGC) to insure pension benefits to employees in defined benefit plans and financed this insurance program with taxes on existing plans. ERISA placed a lower regulatory burden on defined contribution plans, which were subject only to the same minimum plan standards that affected defined benefit plans. Post-ERISA legislation has raised PBGC premiums, required faster funding of liabilities, and penalized employers for claiming excess assets of terminated defined benefit plans.

Table 2.4
Trends in pension plans, participants, and contributions

Year	Plans	Participants	Contributions
Defined contribution plans			
1975	207.7	11.5	29.5
1976	246.0	13.5	30.9
1977	281.0	15.2	32.5
1978	314.6	16.3	35.0
1979	331.4	18.3	35.4
1980	340.8	19.9	35.4
1981	378.3	21.7	38.7
1982	419.5	24.6	40.0
1983	426.6	29.1	44.9
1984	435.4	32.9	51.8
1985	462.0	35.0	61.3
1986	545.0	36.7	66.0
1987	570.0	38.3	66.0
1988	584.0	37.0	68.0
1989	599.0	36.5	73.2
1990	599.2	38.1	79.9
1991	597.5	38.6	89.0
1992	619.7	42.4	105.9
1993	618.5	43.6	118.3
1994	615.9	44.8	125.9
1995	623.9	47.7	144.3
1996	632.6	50.6	143.9
Defined benefit plans			
1975	103.3	33.0	55.8
1976	114.0	34.2	62.1
1977	121.7	35.0	63.8
1978	128.4	36.1	52.5
1979	139.5	36.8	69.3
1980	148.1	38.0	64.1
1981	167.3	38.9	64.1
1982	175.0	38.6	62.2
1983	175.1	40.0	57.6
1984	168.0	41.0	56.3
1985	170.2	39.7	48.4
1986	172.6	40.0	37.6
1987	163.1	40.0	32.5
1988	146.0	40.7	27.6
1989	132.5	40.0	24.7

Table 2.4 (continued)

Year	Plans	Participants	Contributions
1990	113.1	38.8	24.2
1991	101.8	39.0	30.1
1992	88.6	39.5	39.8
1993	83.6	40.3	60.7
1994	74.4	39.7	46.6
1995	69.5	39.7	50.9
1996	63.7	41.1	45.3

Note: The number of plans is measured in thousands, participants in millions, and contributions in billions of 1989 dollars, converted from current dollars using the Consumer Price Index. Data are drawn from U.S. Department of Labor (2000) and earlier issues of the same publication.

4 Variable Annuities

Both the individual and group annuity markets have changed over time, from markets primarily for fixed annuities to markets with growing use of variable annuities. Fixed annuities provide a guaranteed nominal payout during their liquidation phase. They distribute a given principal across many periods, but in most cases they do not provide a constant real (i.e., adjusted for inflation) payout stream if the price level changes. Inflation-indexed annuities have been marketed in the United States by some insurance companies, since the U.S. Treasury issued inflation-indexed bonds in 1997. When inflation is low, the real value of the annual distribution will not vary much over the liquidation period. But even modest inflation rates, if they persist throughout the liquidation period, can lead to substantial erosion in the real value of annuity payouts. At an inflation rate of 3 per cent per year, for example, the real value of annuity payouts in the first year of an annuity liquidation period is more than twice that of the same nominal payout 24 years later. At an inflation rate of 6 per cent per year, the real value of payouts is halved in only 12 years.

Variable annuities provide one way of addressing the risk of purchasing power erosion that is associated with fixed nominal annuities. Unlike fixed annuities that promise a constant nominal payout, variable annuities provide an opportunity to select a payout that bears a fixed relation to the value of an asset portfolio. If these assets tend to rise in value with the nominal price level, then the payout on the variable annuity will adjust to mitigate, at least in part, the effects of inflation. Because variable annuities are defined in part by the securities that back them, they are more complex contracts than fixed annuities. In spite of their complexity, however, they have become one of the most rapidly growing annuity products in recent years.

Variable annuities are structured to have both an investment component and an insurance element. During the accumulation phase, premium payments are used to purchase "investment units," the price depending on the value of the variable annuity's underlying asset portfolio. For example, if this portfolio consists of common stocks and if share prices are high when a premium payment is made, then this payment will buy relatively few units, and vice versa. During the accumulation phase, variable annuities resemble mutual funds in many respects, although there are differences. Mutual fund providers explicitly manage the assets in many recent variable annuity products. The dividends, interest, and capital gains on the assets that underlie the investment units are reinvested to buy additional investment units.

When the accumulation phase of the variable annuity ends, the accumulated value of the investment units is transformed into "annuity units." This transformation occurs as if the accumulation units were cashed out and used to purchase a hypothetical fixed annuity. The annuitant does not receive a stream of fixed annuity payments, but this hypothetical annuity plays an important role in computing actual payouts. The payout amount for the hypothetical annuity is used to credit the annuitant with a number of annuity units. Many variable annuities also allow annuitants the option of choosing a fixed annuity stream, or some combination of a fixed stream and a variable stream of payouts.

The actual variable annuity payout in each period depends on the number of annuity units that the annuitant is credited with, and, over some range of asset returns, on the value of the assets in the variable annuity's underlying portfolio. If the value of this portfolio rises by more than the increase implicit in the assumed interest rate, after the annuitant has converted to annuity units, for example because of rising nominal prices, then the payout will rise during the payout phase. If the value of the underlying assets falls, however, the value of the payout will also decline. The variable annuity's possibility of fluctuating payments is both an attraction (it provides potential protection against rising consumer prices) and, for some potential buyers, a disadvantage (the nominal payout stream is not certain).

Several product innovations during the last two decades have expanded the menu of investment options available for variable annuities. First, the range of portfolio investments that can be held through variable annuity policies has increased. Although the first variable annuities focused exclusively on diversified common stock portfolios, policies now offer variable annuities tied to more specialized portfolios of equities as well as to bonds or other securities. Variable annuities typically allow policyholders to move their assets among various policy sub-accounts, usually with different investment objectives, without fees or penalties. Second, virtually all variable annuities now offer lump-sum withdrawal options after the policy has reached a specified maturity date, as well as the possibility of withdrawing the principal in a set of periodic lump-sum payments. These features make it possible to use variable annuities as an asset accumulation vehicle without necessarily purchasing an annuitylike payout stream when the accumulation phase is over. This is because variable annuity contracts contain a purchase rate guarantee. Finally, some no-load mutual fund families have begun offering variable annuities in conjunction with some insurance companies in recent years. Schultz (1995) reports that investment management expenses for funds associated with variable annuities that invest primarily in diversified U.S. equity portfolios average 0.76 per cent per year, which combines with the 1.23 per cent average annual insurance expenses on these variable annuity products for a total expense ratio of 1.99 per cent. Variable annuities and other investment alternatives are compared in more detail below.

Variable annuities were introduced in the United States by the Teachers Insurance and Annuities Association-College Retirement Equity Fund (TIAA-CREF) in 1952. The first variable annuities were qualified annuities that were used to fund pension arrangements. Variable annuities grew slowly during the next three decades—in part, as Green (1977) explains, because of the need to obtain regulatory approval for these products from many state insurance departments. Because variable annuities are usually backed by assets, such as corporate stocks, that do not guarantee a fixed minimal payout, the reserves that back these policies are maintained in separate accounts from the other policy reserves of life insurance companies. Maclean (1962) notes that no major insurance company other than TIAA-CREF had issued a variable annuity policy as of 1960, primarily because state laws prohibited insurers from supplying a new class of products backed by common stock assets that were segregated from the insurer's other assets. Campbell (1969) provides a detailed account of the introduction and growth of variable annuity products, with particular attention to the regulatory hurdles that had to be cleared to market these products.

The slow growth experienced in 1950s and 1960s has been reversed in recent years. The growth rate of variable annuity premiums during the last decade has been second only to health insurance premiums among insurance products. Between 1989 and 1993, individual annuity premiums (measured in 1994 dollars) increased from $58.6 to $71.8 billion, largely as a result of growth in variable annuity sales. Since 1993, the growth has accelerated. The annual average percentage growth rate of variable annuity sales over the 1989–1999 period was an astonishing 32.8 per cent.

Table 2.5 chronicles the growth of the number of variable annuity policies. Although the number of policies has risen quickly, most of these policies are not yet mature, so payouts have not increased commensurately. Most variable annuity policies are currently in the accumulation phase. One open question is whether a substantial fraction of the assets currently accumulating in variable annuity contracts will ultimately be used to purchase life annuity contracts, or whether it will be withdrawn as lump sums or in other forms.

Table 2.5 shows only 670,000 contract owners in variable annuity policies in 1977, compared with 3.7 million in individual fixed annuity policies that year. By 1993, the number of variable contract owners had increased to 5.25 million, and the number of fixed contract owners had grown to 21.5 million. Both variable and fixed annuities grew rapidly between the late 1970s and late 1980s. In more recent years, variable annuities have grown faster than fixed annuities as table 2.5 illustrates. By 1999, the number of variable annuity policies was 17.5 million, compared with 26.2 million fixed annuity policies.

Both individual and group variable annuity policies have grown during the 1990s. Table 2.6 presents information on the reserves held for variable annuity policies. The early growth of variable annuity policies was concentrated in group policies. As recently as the late 1960s, more than 95 per cent of the reserves for variable annuity policies were held in group policies. Individual variable annuity policies, however, have grown more quickly than group policies during the last two decades. The policy reserves for individual variable annuity policies surpassed those for group policies in 1987; by 1996, individual variable annuity reserves were more than twice those for group policies.

Table 2.5
Fixed and variable individual annuities in force, 1977–1999 (millions)

	Fixed	Variable
1977	3.68	0.67
1978	4.24	0.69
1979	4.49	0.72
1980	5.40	0.76
1981	6.11	0.80
1982	7.69	0.90
1983	8.55	1.03
1984	9.47	1.20
1985	10.00	1.46
1986	10.88	1.91
1987	12.07	2.29
1988	14.16	2.73
1990	16.31	2.91
1991	17.34	2.84
1992	19.29	3.93
1993	21.50	5.25
1994	23.83	6.49
1995	23.06	7.64
1996	23.87	8.16
1997	28.90	7.40
1998	25.96	14.60
1999	26.20	17.46

Source: American Council on Life Insurance, *Life Insurance Fact Book*, various issues. Statistics exclude supplementary contracts.

5 Annuity Products as Investment Vehicles

Different types of annuities are designed to achieve different objectives, and there are trade-offs in the comparison of annuity products with other investment and insurance vehicles. Variable annuities are the annuity products that compete most directly with other investment alternatives. The central trade-offs that investors must evaluate are the insurance benefits that annuities offer, the costs of potential annuity surrender charges, the potential tax advantages to investing through annuities, and the different transaction costs and investment options associated with various financial products. Several features of annuities, such as their management expenses, their surrender charges, and

Table 2.6
Life insurance company variable annuity reserves (millions of 1994 dollars)

Year	Group policies	Individual policies
1970	9,223	581
1971	11,069	1,311
1972	12,790	2,239
1973	13,400	2,849
1974	12,303	2,960
1975	15,911	4,377
1976	18,184	5,958
1977	19,042	6,431
1978	18,230	7,094
1979	15,976	8,144
1980	17,920	8,673
1981	17,683	9,445
1982	17,547	10,481
1983	19,617	13,252
1984	22,449	14,370
1985	25,589	20,559
1986	30,166	28,105
1987	30,726	35,612
1988	33,619	41,469
1989	37,275	49,867
1990	38,239	54,141
1991	41,170	57,984
1992	43,239	79,512
1993	56,052	114,534
1994	65,639	145,523
1995	80,744	196,109
1996	107,423	233,273

Source: American Council on Life Insurance, *Life Insurance Fact Book* (various issues) and author's calculations. Data for years after 1996 are not reported in a format comparable to the earlier years.

their tax treatment, affect their attractiveness from the standpoint of investors.

The management expenses associated with variable annuities typically average between 100 and 150 basis points per year, substantially higher than the comparable expenses for many mutual funds. Variable annuities are therefore most attractive to individuals who value the insurance associated with them and who are prepared to pay for this insurance, or who value the tax-deferred "inside build-up" associated with these accounts.

Surrender charges illustrate the complex pricing of annuities. These charges, found in many but not all deferred annuity contracts, stipulate that an annuitant who decides to cancel the policy before its maturity date (typically five or ten years) must pay a fee to the insurer. Insurers justify these provisions as needed to recover the commission and other production costs associated with annuity products. When assets are held in an annuity product for a long period until the maturity date, the insurer can cover these costs through the annual management fees and expenses of the annuity. When the annuity contract is terminated prematurely, however, the total collected from such management fees is reduced, and the insurer collects a surrender charge to compensate for these lost fees.

The combination of surrender charges and income tax penalties for premature withdrawal of annuity assets makes long-term investors who do not expect to need their invested assets in the short term the natural market for deferred annuities. Black and Skipper (1994) report a standard surrender charge of 5–10 per cent of the accumulated value, typically with a declining schedule and ceasing after a fixed period of years. These charges can substantially reduce the rate of return on annuity assets for those who terminate their contract prematurely. In addition, annuity holders under the age of 59 who make premature withdrawals from either qualified or nonqualified annuities face a 10 per cent federal income "penalty tax" on their withdrawals. This tax applies only to the income that has been accumulated in the annuity contract. These withdrawal penalties, which are very similar to those on early withdrawals from qualified retirement plans, further encourage annuity investors to accumulate for the long term and reduce the return earned by those who withdraw their assets.

Surrender charges were more prevalent in the 1930s and 1940s than at present. In fact, some annuity products marketed in recent years do not include surrender charges. Pallay (1995) estimates that approximately one-fourth of annuity reserves are currently accounted for by annuities with no surrender charges, although some of this includes contracts on which surrender charges have expired.

At a time when surrender charges were more prevalent, Gilbert (1948) illustrated their effect on the returns earned by those who terminate their annuity contract before maturity. He focused on a typical deposit annuity in the 1940s, which imposed a loading charge as well as an early surrender charge. If the annuitant could directly earn the 3 per cent rate of return assumed in the annuity, then the capital fund an investor could build by contributing premium contributions to a personal account would grow faster than the surrender value of the annuity. In each of the first 11 years of a typical annuity policy, Gilbert (1948) showed, the surrender value was less than the sum of the nominal premiums that the annuitant had paid. Whether an individual can match the return promised in annuity contract depends on existing investment opportunities and the degree to which the insurance firm offering the annuity provides valuable investment direction.

It should be noted that annuities are not the only products with surrender fees. Some mutual funds impose a special charge on investors who withdraw their assets before a specified holding period. The nature of surrender charges and their effect on the investment return for these products are important factors to consider in comparing annuities with other financial products.

The tax treatment of annuities is an attractive feature that has undoubtedly contributed the most to their recent growth. The income on assets held in a deferred annuity account is not taxed until the payout phase, which can be many years after the income accrues. Annuities therefore afford an opportunity for asset accumulation at the pretax rate of return.

People planning for retirement may purchase annuities with pretax or after-tax dollars. As with qualified pension plans, annuities that are part of a qualified retirement plan may be purchased with pre-tax dollars; "nonqualified" annuities are purchased with after-tax dollars.

Between the time the annuity is purchased and the time the contract owner receives payouts, no taxes are due on the dividends, capital gains, or interest earned on the assets in the annuity portfolio. When payouts are received, taxes are due on the difference between the annuity payouts and the annuitant's policy basis. The key tax principle is the derivation of an exclusion ratio, an estimate of the ratio of the annuitant's investment in the contract to the total expected payouts on the contract. The exclusion ratio is multiplied by the annuity payout in each period to determine the part of the payout that can be excluded from taxable income.

The opportunity to defer taxes on the investment income from assets held in annuities is a powerful tool for building asset balances. Consider, for example, a 35-year-old evaluating various retirement saving options, with retirement beginning at age 65. Assume further that this individual plans to invest in an asset with an expected return of 7 per cent per year and that investment income faces a marginal tax rate of 28 per cent.

Under these assumptions, an investment of $10,000 at age 35 will cumulate to $45,356 (= $10,000*e^{.07*30}$) at age 65, assuming that each year's asset income is fully taxed and that the after-tax income is reinvested. If the same $10,000 were invested in a way that permits tax deferral on asset income, for example in an annuity product, and if the pretax rate of return on this investment equaled that on the taxable investment, then the principal would cumulate to $81,662 at age 65. Assuming that the withdrawals from this account would be taxed at the 28 per cent marginal tax rate and that they would be taken as a lump sum at retirement, rather than spread over the annuitant's remaining life (which would permit further asset appreciation), the after-tax value of this account would be $61,596 = 10,000 + (1 − 0.28)*(81,662 − 10,000). This amount is 35.8 per cent greater than the amount in the after-tax investment. If the annuitant faces a marginal tax rate that is lower after retirement than while working, the implied rate-of-return advantage on the tax-deferred annuity vehicle will be even greater.

Table 2.7 presents additional comparisons between the return to investments that offer tax deferral and investments that do not. It considers individuals with four different return horizons (10, 20, 30, and 40 years) and assumes four different rates of return (3, 5, 7, and 9 per cent per year). The table reports the percentage increase in the value of an investment for an individual in the 28 per cent marginal tax bracket, the 39.6 per cent tax bracket, and a 20 per cent marginal tax rate on investment income. The latter category might be representative of an investor who received investment income primarily in the form of capital gains during a period when capital gains tax rates were substantially lower than ordinary income tax rates.

The entries in table 2.7 correspond to the 35.8 per cent figure reported above. They are the additional value, in percentage terms, which an

Table 2.7
Comparison of rates of return on tax-deferred and taxable investments

Rate of return	Time horizon			
	10 years	20 years	30 years	40 years
Marginal tax rate = 28%				
3%	0.9%	3.3%	7.3%	12.6%
5%	2.4	8.9	19.0	32.7
7%	4.5	16.8	35.8	61.4
9%	7.3	26.8	57.3	99.4
Marginal tax rate = 39.6%				
3%	1.1%	4.2%	9.3%	16.3%
5%	2.9	11.4	25.4	45.2
7%	5.6	22.2	49.9	90.3
9%	9.3	36.5	83.7	155.8
Marginal tax rate = 20%				
3%	0.7%	2.6%	5.5%	9.4%
5%	1.8	6.7	14.0	23.4
7%	3.4	12.4	25.5	42.2
9%	5.5	19.4	39.6	65.6

Source: Author's calculations. Each entry shows the value of $100*(1 + (1 - \tau)(e^{rT} - 1))/$ $e^{r(1-\tau)T}$. The numerator reflects the value of an asset that accumulates at a pretax rate of return r for a period of T years, and is taxed at maturity at a rate τ on the difference between its maturity value and initial investment. The denominator is the value of an asset that grows at an after-tax rate of return $r(1 - \tau)$ for T years.

investor who invested in a tax-deferred rather than taxable format would have at the end of the investment horizon. The disparities are largest when the investment horizon is long, when the rate of return is high, and when the marginal tax rate is high. In some cases, particularly those with long investment horizons and high assumed tax rates and rates of return, the principal at retirement from investing in a tax-deferred account can be more than double that of investing through a taxable account.

6   Conclusion

Annuities were a small share of the U.S. insurance market until the 1930s, when two developments contributed to their growth. Flexible-payment deferred annuities, which include a saving component as well as an insurance component, expanded rapidly as concerns about the stability of the financial system drove investors to products offered by long-standing and reputable insurance companies. In addition, the group annuity market for corporate pension plans began to develop in the 1930s; it became the largest part of the U.S. annuity market in the years following World War II. The market for individual annuities expanded in the 1970s and early 1980s. The most recent development in the annuity marketplace was the expansion of variable annuities in the late 1980s and 1990s. These products, which combine the investment features of many mutual funds with certain insurance elements and which qualify for the tax deferral accorded to investment income on life insurance products, have attracted a substantial and growing volume of premiums in recent years.

The demand for annuity products is concentrated at advanced ages. The Gallup (1996) survey data show that more than three-quarters of nonqualified annuity buyers are at least 55 years old. Growing attention to these products is suggested by the aging of the U.S. population: the proportion of the U.S. population over the age of 65 has grown from 6.8 per cent in 1940 to 11.3 per cent in 1980, and is projected at 12.2 per cent in 2000 and 16.2 per cent in 2020. A central issue for the future is how prospective changes in federal programs that affect the well-being of the elderly, notably Medicare and Social Security, will alter private financial arrangements. Whether potential reductions in these "annuitized" benefit streams will lead to increased private demand for annuity contracts remains an open issue.

References

Abel, Andrew. 1986. "Capital Accumulation with Adverse Selection and Uncertain Lifetimes." *Econometrica* 54: 1079–1098.

Black, Kenneth J., and Harold D. Skipper, Jr. 1994. *Life Insurance*. 12th edition. Englewood Cliffs, NJ: Prentice-Hall.

Campbell, Paul A. 1969. *The Variable Annuity: Its Development, Its Environment, and Its Future*. Hartford: Connecticut General Life Insurance Company.

Covaleski, John M. 1994. "Baby Boom's Explosion in Annuities." *Best's Review: Life and Health* (November), 45–111.

Dublin, Louis I. 1943. *A Family of Thirty Million: The Story of the Metropolitan Life Insurance Company*. New York: Metropolitan Life Insurance Company.

Friedman, Benjamin, and Mark Warshawsky. 1988. "Annuity Prices and Saving Behavior in the United States." In *Pensions in the U.S. Economy*, ed. Zvi Bodie, John Shoven, and David Wise. Chicago: University of Chicago Press, 53–77.

Gallup Organization. 1994. "Survey of Non-Qualified Annuity Owners." Princeton, N.J.: Gallup Organization.

Gentry, William M. 1994. "Annuity Markets and Retirement Saving." In *Proceedings of the National Tax Association-Tax Institute of America*. Columbus: National Tax Association, 178–183.

Gentry, William M., and Joseph Milano. 1994. "Taxes and the Increased Investment in Annuities." Mimeo, Duke University Department of Economics.

Gifford, Donald W. 1974. "A Note on Loading Charges for Variable Annuities: Comment." *Journal of Risk and Insurance* 41: 523–526.

Gilbert, E. Albert. 1948. *Insurance and Your Security.* New York: Rinehart and Co.

Greene, Mark R. 1973. "A Note on Loading Charges for Variable Annuities." *Journal of Risk and Insurance* 40: 473–478.

Greene, Mark R. 1977. *Risk and Insurance.* 4th edition. Cincinnati: South-Western Publishers.

Harwood, E. C., and Bion H. Francis. 1942. *Life Insurance from the Buyer's Point of View.* Cambridge: American Institute for Economic Research.

Hoffman, Arnold J., and John P. Mondejar. 1992. "Pension Funds and Financial Markets, 1950–1989." In *Trends in Pensions 1992*, ed. John A. Turner and Daniel J. Beller. Washington: U.S. Government Printing Office.

James, Marquis. 1947. *The Metropolitan Life: A Study in Business Growth.* New York: Viking Press.

Kotlikoff, Laurence J., and Avia Spivak. 1981. "The Family as an Incomplete Annuities Market." *Journal of Political Economy* 89: 372–391.

LIMRA International. 1994. *U.S. Individual Annuities: Third Quarter 1994.* Hartford: LIMRA International.

Lonkevich, Dan. 1994. "Greenspan's Stance Worries Insurers." *Best's Review/Life and Health* 95 (November): 51–55.

Maclean, Joseph B. 1962. *Life Insurance.* 9th edition. New York: McGraw Hill.

Murphy, Ray D. 1939. *Sale of Annuities by Governments.* New York: Association of Life Insurance Presidents.

Murphy, Ray D. 1950. "Significant Annuity Developments." In *Life Insurance Trends at Mid-Century*, ed. David McCahan. Philadelphia: University of Pennsylvania Press, 84–99.

Pallay, Gary S. 1995. "Outlook Remains Good for Variable Annuities." *Best's Review: Life/Health* 96 (January): 50–53.

Schultz, Ellen E. 1995. "With Annuities, One Golden Egg Doesn't Mean Snap Up the Carton." *Wall Street Journal*, 5 October 1995, p. R13.

Temporary National Economic Commission. 1941. *Concentration of Economic Power.* Washington: U.S. Government Printing Office.

Trieschmann, James, and Sandra Gustavson. 1995. *Risk Management and Insurance.* 9th edition. Cincinnati, Ohio: South Western College Publishing.

U.S. General Accounting Office. 1990. *Tax Treatment of Life Insurance and Annuity Accrued Interest*. Washington: U.S. General Accounting Office.

U.S. Department of Labor. 2000. *Private Pension Plan Bulletin: Abstract of 1996, Form 5500 Annual Reports*. Washington: U.S. Department of Labor, Office of Research and Economic Analysis.

Variable Annuity Research and Data Service. 1994. *The VARDS Report* (January).

Warshawsky, Mark. 1988. "Private Annuity Markets in the United States, 1919–1984." *Journal of Risk and Insurance* 40 (September): 518–528.

3   Private Annuity Markets in the United States: 1919–1984

Mark J. Warshawsky

This study examines the pricing of individual life annuities over an extended historical period. It attempts to identify and examine the factors relevant to annuity pricing: the roles that adverse selection of mortality risks, the use of portfolio yields, and transaction costs play in the determination of load factors on individual annuity contracts. The claim by Abel (1986) that the cost of adverse selection increased with the introduction of Social Security and pension plans is also briefly examined.

Empirical evidence on private annuity markets may help to broaden and inform current discussions in the economics literature concerning the life cycle hypothesis of savings and the impact of the introduction of Social Security on steady-state wealth and social welfare. Relying on simulation work, Davies (1981) attempts to reconcile the life cycle hypothesis with the observed slow dissaving of marketable assets by the retired. He claims that it is unnecessary to resort to a bequest motive for explanation because plausible parameters of the utility function and the absence of private annuity markets can adequately explain the slow dissaving of assets by the aged in the face of an uncertain lifetime. Abel (1985) employs this scenario to demonstrate that the introduction of a Social Security system alleviates the need for precautionary saving and therefore leads to a reduction in steady-state wealth. Eckstein, Eichenbaum, and Peled (1985) demonstrate how particular schemes for the introduction of a Social Security system lead unambiguously to a Pareto improvement in social welfare in the absence of private annuity markets. The results of these theoretical analyses, however, are suspect because of the strong and incorrect assumption that private

From the *Journal of Risk and Insurance* 55, no. 3 (September 1988): 518–528. Reprinted by permission of the American Risk and Insurance Association.

annuity markets are nonexistent. The more relevant questions which researchers should instead pose are: (a) whether observed load factors on annuity contracts are sufficient to account for the lack of participation in private annuity markets and the slow dissaving of assets by the aged; and (b) whether a private annuity market with load factors would increase or decrease social welfare when compared to a social annuity program like the Social Security system. It is hoped that the empirical evidence on private annuity markets produced in this chapter will enable researchers to pose these questions.

1 Overview

1.1 Measures of Level of Activity

The extent of activity in private annuity markets in the United States has always been limited. Crobaugh (1933), for example, reported that in 1928 there were 119,000 annuity policies outstanding. Assuming one annuity per individual over age 65, less than 2 per cent of the elderly population owned an annuity in 1928. The vast majority of annuity policies were issued to elderly females. Crobaugh (1933) and Harwood and Francis (1935) uniformly attributed Americans' traditional lack of participation in private annuity markets to investment preferences. They claimed that most Americans preferred more speculative (equity) investments. This claim is consistent with increased annuity purchases during the Depression years; by 1933, according to Crobaugh, there were 300,000 annuities outstanding, representing 4 per cent of the over-65 population. The increased activity was attributed to the widespread perception that insurers were safe havens for investment in the aftermath of the stock market crash of 1929 and the ensuing bank panics. In addition, it was emphasized by analysts that insurers credited policies with higher rates of interest than were generally available in the market at the time.

A measure of activity in private annuity markets, annuity premium income earned by life insurers, also indicates that activity increased during the Depression. This activity again increased following World War II, but dropped off in the late 1940s. Unfortunately, aggregate statistics are unavailable for more recent years. The Retirement History Survey, however, indicates that only 2 per cent of the elderly population in recent years owns individual annuities of any sort; see Friedman and Sjogren (1980). More recent informal discussions with insurers confirm the observation of a relatively inactive private annuity market.

1.2 Prices of Annuities: 1919–1984

The per-annuity-dollar premiums for nonparticipating single-premium immediate annuities issued in the United States during 1919–1984 to 65-year-old males are presented in Figure 1. Values are also available for 65-year old females; because females have longer life expectancies than males, they are charged higher premiums. The premiums are compiled from successive annual issues of *Spectator's Handy Guide* and *A.M. Best's Flitcraft Compend*.

The line in Figure 3.1 labeled "large company mean" indicates the mean premium charged on this basic annuity contract by ten large U.S. life insurers. These data are probably the most relevant for measuring economy-wide annuity premiums. The large insurers usually do business in all regions of the country, so that the typical 65-year-old has

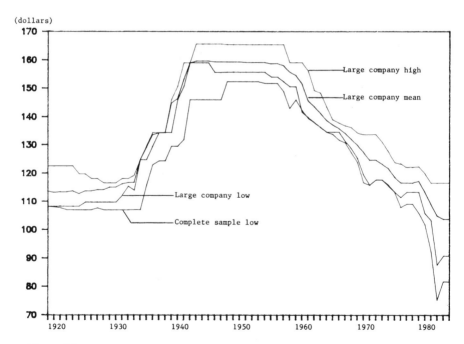

Figure 3.1
Premiums for $1 monthly anuity, 65-year-old males

access to annuities at this mean premium with minimal search costs. The annuity premium for these companies rose in the 1930s and early 1940s and has fallen continuously since the late 1950s as the general level of interest rates fell and rose, respectively. (As will be noted in the next section, there is an inverse relationship between annuity premiums and interest rates.) Increasing life expectancy has tended to buoy premiums throughout the period.

The remaining lines of Figure 3.1 illustrate the dispersion of premiums charged by different insurers for this basic contract. The lines labeled "large company high" and "large company low" show data for the highest and lowest premiums charged for this contract by any of the ten large insurers. Presumably most 65-year-olds have access to the lowest premium in this group at only modest search cost. The line labeled "complete sample low" shows the lowest premium charged for this contract by any of the fifty-odd insurers in the samples. Because the smaller companies in the sample do not necessarily maintain sales forces in all parts of the country, however, there is no presumption that the typical 65-year-old has ready access to this premium. The dispersion of premiums was lowest in the early 1960s when interest rates were stable and widened somewhat in the early 1980s when interest rates became very volatile. This dispersion may reflect search costs. If so, it indicates potential returns to search by consumers. Alternatively, it could reflect aspects of nonprice competition, differences in mortality costs or the relative riskiness of the asset portfolios of different insurers. More recently, the use by some insurers of market yields in pricing annuities combined with the continued use by others of portfolio yields may have caused increased dispersion of premiums in the early 1980s.

2   Actuarial Present Value of Annuities

The extent to which and why gross premiums of immediate annuities deviate from net premiums may be measured by calculating the actuarial present value of these annuities under various assumptions. The two key ingredients in such calculations are the assumed structure of mortality probabilities and the assumed interest rate. The equation for the value of an immediate annuity with annual $1 payments, issued in year T to an individual aged x is:

$$a_x^T = \sum_{t=1}^{w-x-1} (1+r^T)^{-t}\,{}_tP_x^T \tag{1}$$

where w is the assumed maximum length of life (generally taken to be 120 years), r^T is the relevant interest rate, and ${}_tP_x^T$ is the sex-specific probability that an individual of age x in year T will survive to age x + t. The calculation for an annual payment annuity is then converted to a monthly payment annuity.

Annual calculations of actuarial present value of annuities issued to 65-year-old males are shown in Figure 3.2. It is assumed that the mortality probabilities for the years 1919 through 1980 are straight-line interpolations from the mortality tables of general population for 65-year-old males as reported in the U.S. Life Tables for the decennial years 1910 through 1980. The interpolated probabilities for the years 1981 through 1984 are also based on the Social Security Administration mortality probability forecast for 1990.[1] It is also assumed for each calculation that long-term interest rates will remain at levels prevailing in year T.

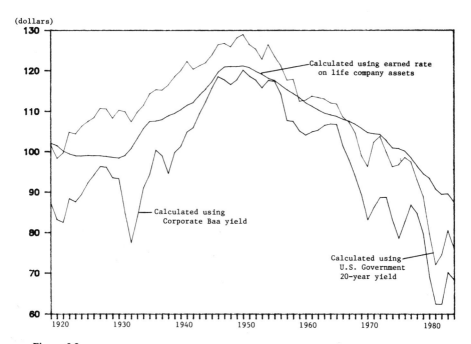

Figure 3.2
Present expected value of $1 monthly, 65-year-old males—general population

If all individuals had identical mortality probabilities, the actuarial present values shown in Figure 3.2 would be the only relevant estimates of net premiums. In fact, many individuals have information that leads them to expect either a shorter or a longer lifetime than the population-wide average. Insurers generally, however, do not gain that mortality information and charge a uniform premium to all individuals of the same age and sex. Individuals expecting longer or shorter than average lifespans will therefore perceive life annuities as more or less attractively priced, and hence will be more or less likely to buy them. This adverse selection will lead to losses if the insurer continues to charge a premium based on the mortality probabilities of the population as a whole. The sub-population who choose to buy annuities therefore will have a greater survival probability than the general population and annuities are likely to be priced based on this probability.[2] Calculations of actuarial present value based on alternative mortality probabilities, compiled from the actual company experience on individual life annuity contracts issued in the United States ("annuity purchasers") during years 1913, 1923, 1943, 1963, and 1973 are reported in Figure 3.3.[3]

Figures 3.2 and 3.3 report annual calculations of actuarial present values based on three different interest rates: the average yield on seasoned Baa corporate bonds, the U.S. government bond yield, and the net rate of interest earned on assets of life insurance companies reported to the National Association of Insurance Commissioners (portfolio rate). Which of the three interest rates is most relevant depends upon the perspective taken in the analysis. From the standpoint of an investor in a fund that holds medium-grade corporate bonds, the seasoned corporate Baa yield may be the correct rate to choose. The fund incurs default and call risks on most corporate bonds held in portfolio, however, and therefore the lower yield on U.S. government bonds may be the appropriate approximation to the risk-adjusted rate relevant to an average investor. Insurers, however, (until the early 1980s) universally used the portfolio rate in pricing newly issued life insurance and annuity contracts. The portfolio rate, therefore, is the appropriate rate with which to examine how investment products sold by the insurance industry are priced and with which to investigate the influence of the level of interest rates on load factors.[4]

The six calculations shown in Figures 3.2 and 3.3 (as well as six others for females) provide estimates of the net premium of a $1 monthly annuity issued to 65-year-olds under various assumptions about

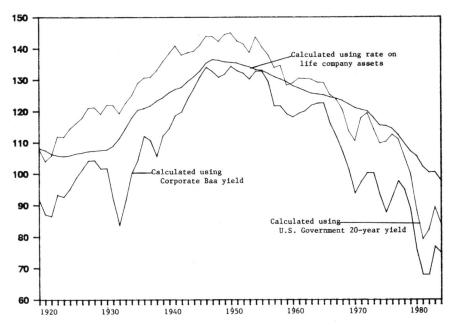

Figure 3.3
Present expected value of $1 monthly, 65-year-old males—annuity purchasers

mortality probabilities and interest rates. Because corporate bonds always bear higher yields than do government bonds, the values calculated using this yield are smaller than the corresponding values calculated using the government bond yield. The actuarial present value calculated using the portfolio rate is higher (lower) than the value calculated using the government bond yield when the portfolio rate is lower (higher) than the government yield. In similar fashion, due to the greater life expectancy of annuity purchasers, the values shown in Figure 3.3 are uniformly greater than the corresponding values shown in Figure 3.2, based on the same three interest rates but on mortality probabilities of the general population. Of course, actuarial present values for females are higher than those in Figures 3.2 and 3.3 due to the longer life expectancy of females.

3   Load Factors

A comparison between the gross premiums charged and the actuarial present values indicates the load factor on individual annuities. One hundred forty-four load factors (not shown) were calculated for this

Table 3.1
Sources of load factors on life annuities issued to 65-year-old males

| | Load factor | | |
Source	1919–1940	1941–1962	1963–1984
Mortality probability			
General population	$ 1.104	$ 1.289	$ 1.282
Annuity purchasers	−1.002	−1.132	−1.129
Cost of adverse selection	$ .102	$ .157	$ .153
Interest rate			
Government bond	$ 1.002	$ 1.132	$ 1.129
Portfolio rate	−1.076	−1.189	−1.063
Fee (Rebate) for use of portfolio rate	−$.074	−$.057	$.066

study.[5] For the three time periods, 1919–1940, 1941–1962, and 1963–1984, each of four premiums (as shown in Figure 3.1) were compared to each of the twelve actuarial present value calculations using three interest rate assumptions and two mortality assumptions for the two sexes. The periods were chosen to measure, very roughly, any impact of the introduction of extensive Social Security and pension coverage after 1940. The average load factors (not shown) have a wide range.

Given the wide range of load factors, it is helpful to focus on the most relevant ones, as shown in Tables 3.1 and 3.2. From the perspective of an average individual contemplating the purchase of an annuity or of government officials formulating policy, that is for welfare analysis, the most relevant factors are probably the mean premiums charged by the ten large insurers compared to the actuarial present value based on government bond yields and mortality rates for the general population. The load factors in Table 3.1 of $1.104, $1.289, and $1.282 may be interpretated as the net cost to a 65-year-old U.S. male randomly selected from the population, for whom the government bond yield represented the opportunity cost of capital for each $1.00 of expected present value when he purchased a life annuity in the periods 1919–1940, 1941–1962, and 1963–1984, respectively. The comparable factors for a female are $1.15, $1.26, and $1.21, as shown in Table 3.2.

It is possible to trace the source of these load factors to adverse selection, the use of portfolio rates, and transaction costs. The costs of adverse selection may be derived by comparing load factors calculated

Table 3.2
Sources of load factors on life annuities issued to 65-year-old females

	Load factor		
Source	1919–1940	1941–1962	1963–1984
Mortality probability			
General population	$ 1.150	$ 1.260	$ 1.210
Annuity purchasers	−.991	−1.103	−1.129
Cost of adverse selection	$ .159	$ .157	$ .081
Interest rate			
Government bond	$ .991	$ 1.103	$ 1.129
Portfolio rate	−1.073	−1.167	−1.055
Fee (Rebate) for use of portfolio rate	−$.082	−$.064	−$.074

using the same interest rate but different mortality rates. As already noted, the load factors computed from mortality probabilities of the general male population are $1.104, $1.289, and $1.282. Among the longer-lived sub-population who actually purchased life annuities, the load factors based on the government bond yield are $1.002, $1.132, and $1.129. Hence, the existence of adverse selection has led to increases in annuity premiums of 10.2 cents, 15.7 cents, and 15.3 cents during 1919–1940, 1941–1962, and 1963–1984, respectively. For the general population of females, 15.9 cents, 15.7 cents, and 8.1 cents represents the cost of adverse selection. The evidence supports Abel's (1986) claim that private annuity premiums, even prior to the introduction of Social Security, contained load factors and that the cost of adverse selection is an important, if not major, part of the explanation. The evidence, however, is somewhat inconsistent with the conjecture of Abel (1986) that the cost of adverse selection would progressively increase (private annuity markets would worsen) with the introduction in 1939 and expansion of Social Security coverage.[6] The cost of adverse selection increased somewhat and then declined slightly for males, while it steadily declined for females.

The cost or subsidy implicit in the use by insurers of portfolio yields in pricing policies may be derived by comparing load factors using the same mortality assumptions but different interest rates, namely the government bond yield and the portfolio rate. For those individuals whose opportunity cost is the government bond yield and who have annuity purchasers' mortality probabilities the relevant load factors were $1.002, $1.132, and $1.129. To an annuities-issuing insurer who credited policies with the portfolio rate, however, the load factors earned were $1.076, $1.189, and $1.063 for each $1.00 of actuarial present value. In other words, −7.4 cents, −5.7 cents and +6.6 cents represented an implicit fee or rebate charged or paid by insurers when they issued annuities with yields lower or higher than the yield on new investments in government bonds in 1919–1940, 1941–1962, and 1963–1984. Similar results are shown in Table 3.2 on load factors on annuities issued to females. The first period of analysis includes the late 1920s and early 1930s when the portfolio rate substantially exceeded the government bond yield. These observations are consistent with Crobaugh's 1933 claim that annuities were more popular during the Depression years because they were good investments. For individuals with the mortality probability of annuity purchasers, only 0.2 cents of the factor was paid by the individual: 7.4 cents represented a rebate paid by the insurer. In the last time period of analysis, however, these individuals were charged 12.9 cents in load factor, of which 6.6 cents was due to insurers crediting a lower rate than generally available on market instruments. A second consideration in explaining load factors on annuities, therefore, is the use of portfolio rates. It remains as a subject for further research why insurers used (and to some extent, still use) portfolio rates in pricing policies.

The remaining portion of the load factors, after deduction of the cost of adverse selection and the portfolio yield rebate (fee), largely represents various transaction costs. A 3 cent to 4 cent commission is generally paid to agents for annuity sales, 0.5 cent cover administrative fees, some amount, roughly estimated from 0.5 to 4 cents, pays federal taxes (an amount which fluctuated with changes in the tax law for life insurers) and an unspecified residual is added to the profits of stock company shareholders or the surplus of mutual companies.[7] These estimates of transaction costs completely exhaust the load factors for the first and last periods, while approximately 12 cents is left unaccounted during the 1941–1962 period.

4   Implications of the Load Factors

Knowledge of the size of load factors on life annuities is relevant to the questions for consumption-saving behavior implicitly raised by Davies (1981) and Abel (1985). Is an average load factor of 29 cents sufficient to account for the twin observations of slow dissaving of assets by the aged and the small participation in the individual life annuity market in the United States? In short, have most elderly retired people chosen not to consume out of their wealth, and therefore left unintentional bequests, merely because they were reluctant to pay $1.29 for every $1.00 of actuarial present value of annuities?

A formal approach to this issue is taken by Friedman and War-shawsky (1985a,b) (F-W) in simulation models of annuity demand and savings behavior. In deducing the relative weight of a bequest motive and a load factor in explaining the lack of participation in private annuity markets, F-W used load factors calculated from premiums charged during the years 1968–1983. Their conclusion was that a modest bequest motive and a load factor in the range of $1.40 can explain empirical observations about savings behavior. Using the generally lower load factors calculated in this study, their simulations would strengthen the bequest motive as an explanation of saving behavior in the United States.

While load factors of $1.29 would not prevent individuals from purchasing private annuities (in the absence of a bequest motive), such load factors are large when compared to the net administrative expenses of the Social Security program. In 1950, net administrative expenses for Social Security were 7.8 per cent of benefit payments; in 1984 these expenses were 1 per cent of benefit payments.[8] From the perspective of load factors alone, therefore, annuities in the form of Social Security benefits seem to be preferable to alternatives in the private market. Of course, the implicit returns available from pay-as-you-go systems may be so low under certain demographic scenarios as to offset the cost of load factors present in a private system. Additionally, the extensive cross-subsidization between groups in a given cohort makes social welfare analysis of the current Social Security system a very difficult problem.

Notes

1. See Warshawsky (1987) for further details.

2. See Rothschild and Stiglitz (1976) for an analysis of the economic principles underlying adverse selection. Since the insurer cannot observe the purchase by individuals of annuities from other insurers or other financial information, the appropriate equilibrium concept is pooling. An alternative explanation for the differences in mortality probabilities between the general population and annuity purchasers relies on transactions costs instead of asymmetric information. Rational agents with short life expectancies will fail to annuitize their wealth if the transaction costs (narrowly defined) of doing so are very high.

3. Actual company experience is reported periodically in the *Transactions of the Society of Actuaries*. See Warshawsky (1987) for further details.

4. See Warshawsky (1985) for an analysis of the pricing of cash-value life insurance.

5. See Warshawsky (1987) for further details.

6. Abel (1986) claims that the introduction of Social Security benefits leads all types of retired individuals to reduce their demand for private annuities. Individuals with high mortality probabilities, however, reduce their annuity demands more than do individuals with low mortality probabilities. Furthermore, since high probability individuals begin with a lower demand for annuities than low probability individuals, the percentage reduction in annuity demand is greatest for high probability individuals. Since it is the annuities sold to the high probability individuals on which insurers expect positive profits, this shift in the composition of annuity holders away form the profitable (high probability) individuals leads to a reduction in expected profits. In order to restore expected profits, insurers must increase premiums. The cost of adverse selection should increase with the introduction of Social Security coverage where that cost is calculated by comparing load factors based on the mortality probability of the general population to those based on the mortality probability of annuity purchasers. One possible explanation for the observed failure of Abel's hypothesis is that, even prior to Social Security, most elderly individuals did not hold private annuities.

7. Hunter (1920) assumes a sales commission of 5 cents (which he notes is higher than generally allowed), taxation of 2 cents, and other expenses of 0.5 cent. Recent informal discussions with insurers suggest 3 cents sales commission, 4 cents taxation and 0.5 cent administrative expenses, similarly adding to 7.5 cents. Also see Tilley (1979).

8. *Social Security Bulletin*, July 1986, p. 30.

References

Abel, Andrew (1985), "Precautionary Saving and Accidental Bequests," *American Economic Review*, Vol. 75, No. 4, pp. 777–91.

———, (1986), "Capital Accumulation with Adverse Selection and Uncertain Lifetimes," *Econometrica*, Vol. 54, pp. 1079–98.

Crobaugh, Clyde (1933), *Annuities and Their Uses*, (Boston: Clyde Crobaugh).

Davies, James (1981), "Uncertain Lifetime, Consumption, and Dissaving in Retirement," *Journal of Political Economy*, Vol. 89, No. 3, pp. 561–77.

Eckstein, Zvi, Eichenbaum, Martin, and Peled, Dan (1985), "The Distribution of Wealth and Welfare in the Presence of Incomplete Annuity Markets," *Quarterly Journal of Economics*, Vol. 100, No. 3, pp. 789–806.

Friedman, Benjamin and Warshawsky, Mark (1985a), "The Cost of Annuities: Implications for Saving Behavior," National Bureau of Economic Research Working Paper No. 1682.

———, (1985b), "Annuity Prices and Saving Behavior in the United States," National Bureau of Economic Research Working Paper No. 1683; to appear in Bodie, Zvi, Shoven, John, and Wise, David (eds.), *Pensions in the U.S. Economy*, University of Chicago Press, 1988.

Friedman, Joseph and Sjogren, Jane (1980), "Assets of the Elderly as They Retire," mimeo, Social Security Administration.

Harwood, E. C., and Francis, B. H. (1935), *Insurance and Annuities From the Buyer's Point of View* (Cambridge: American Institute for Economic Research).

Hunter, Arthur (1920), "Mortality Among American Annuitants and Premiums Based Thereon," *Transactions of the Actuarial Society of America*, pp. 157–77.

Rothschild, Michael and Stiglitz, Joseph (1976), "Equilibrium in Competitive Insurance Markets: An Essay on the Economics of Imperfect Information," *Quarterly Journal of Economics*, Vol. 90, No. 4, pp. 629–49.

Social Security Administration, *Social Security Bulletin*, July 1986.

Tilley, James (1979), "The Pricing of Nonparticipating Single Premium Immediate Annuities," *Transactions of the Society of Actuaries*, Vol. 31, pp. 11–52.

Warshawsky, Mark (1985), "Life Insurance Savings and the After-tax Life Insurance Rate of Return," *Journal of Risk and Insurance*, Vol. 52, No. 4, pp. 585–606.

———, (1987), "Private Annuity Markets in the United States: 1919–1984," Research Papers in Banking and Financial Economics No. 96, Board of Governors of the Federal Reserve System.

4

New Evidence on the Money's Worth of Individual Annuities

Olivia S. Mitchell,
James M. Poterba,
Mark J. Warshawsky, and
Jeffrey R. Brown

> *[I]f you observe, people always live forever when there is any annuity to be paid them.
> . . . An annuity is a very serious business; it comes over and over every year, and there
> is no getting rid of it.*

Jane Austen (1962, pp. 10–11)

As baby boomers near retirement, policy analysts have begun to ask how this cohort will handle the process of drawing down its retirement saving. One mechanism for doing this is the life annuity, an insurance product that pays out a periodic sum for life in exchange for a premium charge. The main appeal of the life annuity is that it offers retirees the opportunity to insure against the risk of outliving their assets by pooling mortality experience across the group of annuity purchasers.

The market for individual life annuities in the United States has historically been small. Previous researchers working in the context of the standard life-cycle model, notably Benjamin Friedman and Warshawsky (1988, 1990), have argued that it is puzzling that so few people avail themselves of the private market for annuities. This market has recently begun to attract substantial attention from those considering proposals to replace part of Social Security with private retirement saving accounts, because one way individuals might choose to spread the payouts from these accounts over their retirement years is by purchasing individual annuity contracts.

The standard explanation for the limited size of the individual annuity market is adverse selection. As the foregoing quotation from Austen suggests, those who voluntarily purchase annuities may tend

From *American Economic Review* 89 (December 1999): 1299–1318. Reprinted by permission of the American Economic Association.

to live longer than average; insurance premiums therefore must be set high enough to compensate insurers for the longer life expectancies of purchasers. The extent to which adverse selection reduces the attractiveness of life annuities for potential annuitants is an empirical question.

In this chapter, we present new data on the value of individual life annuities that were available in the private market in 1995. We develop a more sophisticated algorithm for annuity valuation than that in previous work. We value single-life annuities for a wider range of ages than previous studies, and we also value joint-and-survivor annuities. We allow for a term structure of interest rates instead of using a single long-term interest rate to value payouts, thereby obtaining a more accurate measure of the present value of payouts, and we consider the special federal tax treatment of income paid from annuities. We also recognize the impact of uncertain inflation on the subjective valuation of nominal annuities. We apply our algorithm to annuity policies that were available in 1995, as well as to policies that were offered in 1985 and 1990. Previous studies of annuity valuation relied on data from more than a decade ago, and many factors have changed in the intervening years, including a sharp decline in nominal interest rates and a general increase in life expectancies at older ages. Even without our methodological improvements, there is a substantial rationale for revisiting the question of annuity valuation.

We present several empirical findings. First, the prices charged for a single-premium immediate life annuity vary widely. For policies with the same initial cost, the difference in annuity payouts between the ten highest-payout and the ten lowest-payout insurance companies is close to 20 per cent. The dispersion varies by age and by sex of the insured.

Second, we find that the expected present discounted value of annuity payouts per dollar of annuity premium averages between 80 and 85 cents for an individual chosen at random from the population, and between 90 and 94 cents for an individual chosen at random from the pool of individuals who purchase annuities. This implies that a typical retiree with average mortality prospects faces a significant "transaction cost" if he purchases an individual annuity from a commercial insurance carrier. The differential between the premium cost and the expected payouts must cover marketing costs, corporate overhead and income taxes, additions to various company contingency reserves, and profits, as well as the cost of adverse selection. The expected present discounted value of payouts per premium dollar generally declines as the age of the annuity purchaser increases and, regardless of age, is typically higher for annuities issued to women and joint-and-survivors than for those issued to men.

Third, we compare current annuity values with those found in the early 1980's. The pay-out value-per-premium dollar has risen by roughly 13 percentage points during the last decade and a half. This suggests that the effective transaction costs to participating in the individual annuity market have declined during this period.

Fourth, we find that incorporating the specialized income tax liabilities that are associated with annuity income does not significantly affect the expected present discounted value of annuity payouts. This is because the tax rules governing annuity products approximately offset the tax burdens on alternative investments that retirees might make.

Finally, we compute the expected utility that a consumer with a random lifetime and an additively separable utility function would derive from following an optimal intertemporal consumption plan in the absence of annuity markets, and the same individual's utility if he can purchase an actuarially fair nominal annuity. We then calculate the fraction of his initial, nonannuitized wealth that this individual would be prepared to pay to gain access to such an annuity market. This fraction is of the same order of magnitude as the "transaction cost" that we observe in the current annuity market. We perform these calculations assuming certain, as well as random, inflation, and find that our results are not very sensitive to the presence of random price fluctuations.

The chapter is divided into six sections. The first provides an overview of the market for individual annuity products. Section 2 describes the expected present discounted value approach that we use to value the stream of payouts from annuity products. Section 3 describes our key data inputs. The fourth section presents our results on the present value of individual annuity payouts relative to their premium cost. Section 5 explores the gain in expected utility from purchasing an individual annuity instead of following the optimal postretirement consumption strategy in the absence of annuity contracts. It considers nominal annuities in a setting with positive, but certain, inflation, and also allows for uncertain inflation. Section 6 concludes by indicating a number of directions for future research and by discussing the relevance of this research to national retirement policy concerns.

1   Overview of the Private Annuity Market

Annuities are contracts between an insurance company and an insured person or persons in which the insured receives a monthly or annual sum as long as he lives, in exchange for a one-time premium payment or flow of premium payments. The date at which level payouts begin can be different from, and in some cases many years later than, the premium payment date(s). The annuity protects the individual against the risk of outliving his saving, given uncertainty about his remaining lifetime.

The annuity contract generally specifies what happens during two distinct phases. These are the *accumulation phase*, when the premium is paid and capital accumulates, and the *decumulation phase* when the benefits are paid out.[1] There are many different paths for building up the annuity capital. One approach is to deposit a single-premium lump sum with the insurer; another is to gradually accumulate capital over a long period. A defined benefit pension plan can in some ways be viewed as an example of a slowly accumulating annuity. The annuity's payout path can also vary a great deal. Popular options include a life annuity with payments over the annuitant's lifetime, a joint-and-survivor annuity with payments to the annuitant and to his survivor, and a "years certain" annuity in which payments to the annuitant or his heirs are guaranteed to continue for at least a certain number of time periods, even if the annuitant dies before this number of periods has elapsed. Historically, most annuities offered periodic payouts and accumulations fixed in nominal terms, but variable annuities in which accumulations and/or payouts are linked to the returns on an underlying asset such as stocks have become increasingly popular in recent years.

The annuity market, including fixed as well as variable annuities and individual as well as group annuity contracts, has grown sharply in the last decade. In the mid-1990's, individual annuity sales were nearly as large as group annuity purchases, the latter mainly from defined benefit pension plans. The American Council on Life Insurance (1996) reports that there were roughly 23 million individual annuity policies in force in 1995. The Life Insurance Marketing Research Association International (LIMRA International, 1996) reports that reserves to cover promised payments for individual annuity benefits stood at $792 billion.

Variable annuities account for the bulk of current annuity sales, and they account for most of the growth of the annuity market in recent years. Although assets held in variable annuity contracts can be withdrawn in annuity form, they can also be withdrawn in other ways, for example with a stream of lump-sum payouts. Because most variable annuity contracts have not yet reached their payout phase, it remains to be seen whether many variable annuity purchasers will choose the annuitization payout option. This underscores the fact that aggregate data on "annuity purchases" often include many insurance products other than life annuities. We do not include variable annuities in our analysis because they typically do not provide any guarantee of principal or return. Valuing the expected payout from a variable annuity therefore requires forecasting the future returns on various types of securities in a way that valuing a fixed annuity does not.

There are two primary types of premium payment in the individual annuity marketplace: flexible premium and single premium. Flexible-premium payments are in turn divided into first payments for newly purchased annuities, and renewal payments for existing annuity contracts. The single-premium category is divided into single-premium deferred annuities (SPDA) and single-premium immediate annuities (SPIA). LIMRA International (1996) reports that SPIAs accounted for only $6.2 billion of premium payments in 1995, while SPDAs accounted for $46.3 billion. Moreover, not all SPIA contracts provide payouts that are life contingent. Some SPIAs provide for a stream of fixed periodic payments, and therefore do not provide "life length insurance" of the type traditionally associated with annuity products. The small volume of SPIA purchases suggests that the recent growth of the aggregate annuity market has not resolved the long-standing puzzle, discussed for example in Friedman and Warshawsky (1990), of why individuals do not choose to annuitize their wealth.

The remainder of this paper focuses on the market for SPIAs. Surveys of annuity buyers provide some information on the nature of this market. According to LIMRA International (1996), the average SPIA premium in 1995 was $79,600. An unpublished LIMRA International 1993 survey of 26 companies selling SPIAs found that 55 per cent of individual annuities were sold to men.[2] Most SPIAs (74 per cent) were not part of a tax-qualified retirement plan such as an individual retirement account.[3] The modal purchaser is between the ages of 66 and 70 and nearly three SPIA buyers in four are between the ages of 61 and 80.

2   The Money's Worth Framework

The centerpiece of our analysis is a calculation of the expected present discounted value (EPDV) of payouts for immediate annuities in relation to the premium cost of the annuity. The expected present discounted value depends on three inputs: the *amount* of the annuity payout, the *interest rate* that is used to discount future payouts, and the *mortality rates* used to compute the probability that the representative annuity purchaser will still be alive at a given future date.

The most straightforward component of the EPDV calculation is the amount of the annuity payout (A). Data are available on the monthly payout to an individual purchasing an immediate single-life annuity for a set of initial purchase prices, most commonly $100,000. This amount varies across annuity policies, but for the policies we will consider, it remains fixed in nominal terms for the life of the annuity contract.

To discount nominal cash flows received j periods into the future, we make two alternative assumptions about the term structure of future short-term nominal interest rates. First, we use the term structure of yields on Treasury bonds to estimate the time series of expected, future, nominal short-term interest rates.[4] We use i_k to denote the nominal short rate k periods into the future. The present discounted value today of one dollar paid j periods in the future is therefore $1/[(1 + i_1)* \ldots * (1 + i_j)]$. In addition to this term structure for riskless interest rates, we also consider a term structure of interest rates for risky bonds. We compute the difference between the average yield on BAA corporate bonds, and the yield on a Treasury bond with ten years to maturity; let v denote this yield differential. Then, we assume that this risk premium is constant at all maturities, and we construct a term structure of interest rates on risky bonds using nominal future short-term rates of $i_k + v$. We label the two term structures "Treasuries" and "Corporates" in what follows.

Estimating anticipated future mortality rates represents the most complex step in our EPDV calculation. We let $q_{a,t}$ denote the probability that an a-month-old individual who is alive at the beginning of month t will die during that month. To illustrate this notation, consider an individual whose 65th birthday is this month, and normalize this month to be calendar month one. The probability that this individual will die this month is $q_{780,1}$, where $780 = 12*65$. The probability that this individual will be alive at the end of the current month is $1 - q_{780,1}$, and the probability that this individual will still be alive in two months is $(1 - q_{780,1})*(1 - q_{780,2})$. We summarize future mortality experience by defining P_j as the probability that someone who is 65 years old at the time when he purchases an annuity survives for at least j months:

$$P_j = (1 - q_{780,1})*(1 - q_{781,2})*\ldots*(1 - q_{780+j-1,j}).$$ (1)

We set $P_{600} = 0$, which imposes the restriction that no one lives beyond age 115 years.[5] To compute the EPDV of an annuity that a 65-year-old person might purchase in 1995, we need to forecast this individual's *future* mortality rates. We consider this issue in the next section.

We use $V_b(A)$ to denote the EPDV of a life annuity with monthly payout A purchased by an individual of age b. The expression we evaluate in our "before-tax" calculations, which differs from that in Friedman and Warshawsky (1988, 1990) and Warshawsky (1988) primarily in our allowance for a term structure of interest rates, is:

$$V_b(A) = \sum_{j=1}^{600} \frac{A*P_j}{\prod_{k=1}^{j}(1 + i_k)}.$$ (2)

In calculations not reported in this paper, we have recomputed our key findings under the assumption that the term structure is flat, with the discount rate given variously by the 10-year Treasury bond yield, the 30-year Treasury bond yield, and the BAA corporate bond yield. Allowing for slope in the term structure, as we do, does not account for an appreciable share of the difference between our findings and those in earlier studies using older data.

Taxes are not included in the foregoing valuation expression, even though after-tax annuity payments determine the consumption opportunities of individual annuity purchasers. The federal tax treatment of annuities is governed by a specialized set of rules which are described by the U.S. General Accounting Office (1990) and James Trieschmann and Sandra Gustavson (1995), among others. For any annuity contract, the Internal Revenue Service (IRS) specifies the expected number of years over which the annuitant can expect to receive benefits. We label this expected payout period T'; it is determined by the IRS using the 1983 Individual Annuitant (Unisex) Mortality Table and the individual annuitant's age at the time when payouts begin. Using T', the tax law prescribes how to calculate an *inclusion ratio* (λ), which determines the share of annuity payments in each period that must be included in the recipient's taxable income. The inclusion ratio is designed to measure the fraction of each annuity payout that reflects the capital income on the accumulating value of the annuity premium.

For an annuity policy with a \$100,000 premium, during the first T' years of payouts, the inclusion ratio is defined by:

$$\lambda = 1 - \frac{100,000}{A*T'}. \tag{3}$$

After T' years, all payouts from the annuity policy are included in taxable income. Assuming that the annuitant faces a combined federal and state marginal income tax rate of τ, the tax-adjusted expression for annuity value (V_b') is:

$$V_b'(A) = \sum_{j=1}^{12*T'} \frac{(1-\lambda*\tau)*A*P_j}{\prod_{k=1}^{j}(1+(1-\tau)*i_k)} + \sum_{j=12*T'+1}^{600} \frac{(1-\tau)*A*P_j}{\prod_{k=1}^{j}(1+(1-\tau)*i_k)}. \tag{4}$$

In the after-tax calculation, the appropriate interest rate is the after-tax interest rate facing the annuitant. We report both the before-tax and after-tax calculations, V_b and V_b', in our analysis below. Because virtually all annuity purchasers are taxable individuals, we focus on the after-tax case. We also consider annuity policies that are offered to individuals at age 55, 65, and 75; the money's worth framework described above generalizes easily to different ages.

3   Data on Annuity Premiums and Mortality Projections

This section describes the data that we collect on annuity premiums and the algorithm that we use to project future mortality rates. These are important inputs to our analysis of the expected present discounted value of annuity payouts.

3.1   The Purchase Price of Individual Annuities

We assume that an individual is contemplating the purchase of a *nonparticipating, single-premium, immediate, individual life annuity* from a commercial life-insurance company. "Nonparticipating" means that the benefit payment is fixed and guaranteed, and does not reflect the insurance company's subsequent unanticipated experience with mortality, investment returns, or expenses.[6] "Single-premium immediate" means that the investor pays a one-time premium and then begins receiving annuity payments within the next month, quarter, or year, depending on the payment frequency chosen. "Individual" means that the annuity is purchased directly from an insurance company, generally via an agent or broker, for the named investor, and is not obtained through a group annuity owned by an employer-sponsored pension plan.[7] A "life" annuity means that payments are promised to continue for the investor's lifetime.[8] "Commercial life-insurance companies" include U.S. mutual and stock companies of all sizes, domiciles, and financial strength classifications, but exclude most of the life-insurance organizations, generally nonprofit, that have memberships in specialized industrial, religious, or professional groupings.

Premiums for life annuities are reported periodically in numerous publications issued by A. M. Best. We gathered data on annuity policies offered by a wide range of life-insurance firms in 1985, 1990, and 1995. We collected data for single-life annuities, as well as joint-and-survivor annuities. For 1985 and 1990, we drew reported annuity premiums from Best's *Flitcraft Compend*, which is the source used by Warshawsky (1988) in his analysis of annuity prices over the period 1919 through 1984. For premiums charged in 1995, we used data from the July 1995 issue of *Best's Review*, where Best's reports the results of its annual survey of insurance companies issuing single-premium immediate annuities.[9] The Best's data correspond to single-premium annuities with a $100,000 premium; we do not have any information on how the ratio of annuity payouts to the premium varies as the size of the premium changes. TIAA is not included in the Best's data because its policies are not available to the general public and because it does not offer single-premium nonparticipating immediate annuities.

The number of companies in the Best's annuity data base varies over the years. Large life insurers with a national presence and immediately recognizable names are almost always included, along with many small companies with apparently regional customer footings or firms that emphasize special insurance product lines. In 1985, for example, there were 47 companies in the A. M. Best's database; in 1990, 133 companies appeared, and in 1995, 100. For 1995, we gathered annuity premiums charged to men, women, and couples purchasing these products at ages 55, 65, and 75, respectively. For the comparative analysis over time, we collected data only on premiums for annuities issued to 65-year-old men using the 1985 and 1990 publications. In all cases,

the premiums published are gross of state premium taxes, as well as
federal and state income taxes that apply to the annuity payouts.

To provide illustrative information on annuity policies, Table 4.1
indicates the monthly income payment per $1,000 of premium for
annuities issued in 1995 to single men and women, and to couples, of
different ages. The first panel in the table records the average monthly
annuity payment offered by all companies in the data base. For
example, a 65-year-old man purchasing a typical $100,000 single-
premium annuity at age 65 would receive a monthly payment of $794,
or $9,528 per year, for life. Because women live longer than men on
average, a 65-year-old woman paying the same $100,000 premium

Table 4.1
Immediate monthly annuity payouts per $1,000 premium, by age and sex, 1995

	Age 55	Age 65	Age 75
All companies, average			
Men	6.64	7.94	10.52
Women	6.24	7.17	9.22
Joint and survivor	5.78	6.48	7.94
Ten highest payouts, average			
Men	7.38	8.72	11.61
Women	6.88	7.76	9.99
Joint and survivor	6.39	7.07	8.60
Ten lowest payouts, average			
Men	5.98	7.25	9.45
Women	5.59	6.56	8.63
Joint and survivor	5.14	5.84	7.23
Twenty highest-rated firms, average			
Men	6.50	7.78	10.35
Women	6.09	7.07	9.09
Joint and survivor	5.72	6.40	7.82
Ten largest annuity firms, average			
Men	6.72	7.98	10.43
Women	6.31	7.21	9.14
Joint and survivor	5.84	6.43	7.79

Source: Annuity payout data provided in *Best's Review*, July 1995. Each entry indicates
the monthly income based on the purchase of a $100,000 single-premium immediate life
annuity policy. The $100,000 purchase price is inclusive of policy fees, but excludes state
annuity premium taxes.

would receive about 10 per cent less, $717 per month, or $8,604 per year. A 65-year-old couple buying a joint-and-survivor annuity would receive $648 monthly, about 18 per cent less than a single male.

Monthly annuity payments also increase with the age of the individual or couple to whom the annuity is issued. For example, a 75-year-old man paying $100,000 for an annuity would receive a payout of $1,052 per month, almost one-third more than his counterpart ten years his junior. For women, aging also raises the value of the annuity payout, but by less: a 75-year-old woman receives only 28 per cent more than a woman a decade younger. Table 4.1 also shows that the male/female annuity payout differential changes with age. At age 55 men receive annuity payouts that are 6 per cent higher than those for women, but by age 75, the monthly payout to men is 14 per cent higher than that for women. The joint-and-survivor benefit payments also change with age. At age 55, the couple receives a monthly benefit 13 per cent below that paid to a single man, but by age 75, the couple's annuity amount is 25 per cent lower. These payment patterns reflect differential mortality patterns for the various types of annuity purchasers.

The next two panels in Table 4.1 suggest the rather wide range of benefits paid by companies in Best's database. The range of payouts between the ten highest-payout annuity contracts and the ten lowest-payout policies, all conditional on a $100,000 premium payment, is 18 per cent for 65-year-old men $[(8.72 - 7.25)/0.5*(8.72 + 7.25)]$. A 65-year-old man might receive from $725 to $872 monthly depending on the identity of the company from which he purchased the annuity. The all-firm average for such a purchaser was $794. The range of payouts for 65-year-old men is slightly lower than the range for 75-year-old men (about 20 per cent), and slightly higher than that for 65-year-old women (about 16 per cent). These data suggest that the benefits of "shopping around" for an annuity policy vary by age and by sex.[10] Our finding of substantial price variation in the annuity market supports earlier studies such as Bev Dahlby and Douglas West (1986) and G. Frank Matthewson (1983) that find price dispersion in automobile- and life-insurance markets.

A possible explanation for the variation in annuity payouts across firms is differences in the financial stability of the insurance companies selling the annuities. It is conceivable that insurers rated as more stable would pay lower annuity amounts, while companies rated as riskier might be forced by the market to pay higher monthly benefits to attract investors. One way to judge whether this is true is to examine the fourth panel of Table 4.1, which sets out average annuity payments made by the 20 highest-ranked companies according to Joseph Belth's (1995) index of financial strength.[11] The results are similar to those in the top row of Table 4.1, and they suggest that annuity investors do not pay a substantially higher price when purchasing an annuity from a firm with an above-average financial rating.

The final panel of Table 4.1, which shows payments made by the ten insurance companies with the largest market share in the individual annuity market as reported by A. M. Best's, suggests a similar conclusion with respect to firm size. The average price for the large firms is similar to that for all firms.

3.2   Current and Projected Mortality Rates

Valuing an annuity stream requires estimates of the relevant mortality probabilities facing an individual annuitant or couple. Since future mortality probabilities are not known, it is necessary to use available data on past mortality rates to forecast future rates.

There are two relevant types of mortality probabilities. The first set reflects the expected mortality experience of the *general population*, based on mortality tables created by the Office of the Actuary at the U.S. Social Security Administration. These tables are used in the annual Social Security Trustees Reports to project the future financial position of the nation's major social insurance systems. The second set reflects expected mortality probabilities of the subset of the population that purchases *individual annuities*. Annuitant mortality data are based on tables made available by the Society of Actuaries, and are consistent with data actually used or proposed for use in the calculation of life-insurance company reserves for individual annuity products.

Mortality probabilities for the general population and for individual annuity purchasers differ significantly. The mortality probabilities for both men and women in the general population at every age are higher than the mortality probabilities for annuity purchasers. This difference may be due to two nonexclusive factors. First, individuals with higher-than-average net worth may live longer than those without substantial assets, and these individuals may be represented disproportionately in the annuity-buying population. Second, *conditional* on net worth, the individuals who purchase individual annuities may live longer, on average, than those who do not.

With respect to the link between wealth and annuitant mortality, it is likely that the individuals and couples who demand an annuity stream beyond that given by Social Security and many private pension plans have higher-than-average net worth. Recent research including Gregory Pappas et al. (1993) and Orazio Attanasio and Hilary Hoynes (1995) suggests that individuals with higher-than-average net worth actually live somewhat longer than the population at large. With respect to other types of adverse selection, it is possible that individuals with higher-than-average mortality risk, such as those with serious illnesses, conclude that their shortened life expectancy makes annuities too expensive. In this case, the mortality probabilities of the group that decides to purchase annuities are truncated. Insurance companies, of course, price annuities with this truncation in mind. Such pricing is the cornerstone of the analysis of equilibrium in competitive insurance markets developed by Michael Rothschild and Joseph Stiglitz (1976) and Charles Wilson (1980).

In addition to deciding whether to use general population or annuity purchasers' life tables, one must also decide whether to use *period* or *cohort* life tables to project mortality rates for annuitants. A period table represents the mortality experience of a group of people during a relatively short period of time, usually a year.[12] A cohort or generation table represents lifetime mortality experience of a cohort of persons born during a particular year.[13] For cohorts that are no longer alive, cohort tables can be compiled from past period tables. For currently living cohorts, however, constructing a cohort table requires blending information from past as well as projected future period tables.

When calculating annuity values, it seems natural to use cohort tables because they reflect the probabilities that a rational forward-looking individual would likely apply in making his decision concerning the purchase of an annuity. Note that the projected age-specific mortality rate for individuals in a given cohort may change over time as a result of new information on trends in individual mortality patterns and life expectancy. For example, the 1960 cohort mortality table for individuals born in 1930 would show a different projection for the mortality rate of this group when it reached age 70, in the year 2000, than would the 1990 cohort mortality table for the same cohort. The 1990 table would presumably show a lower projected mortality rate as a result of the substantial unpredicted mortality rate declines in the three decades between 1960 and 1990.

We use two different types of mortality probabilities in the EPDV calculations below. Our first approach uses projected cohort mortality tables for the general population as compiled by the Social Security Administration Office of the Actuary in 1995. These mortality tables are based on unpublished statistics used for the 1996 Social Security Trustees' Report projections for each relevant birth cohort.[14] For valuing annuities offered to 65-year-olds in 1995, we use the 1930 birth cohort probabilities. For 55-year-olds in 1995, we use data for the 1940 birth cohort, and for 75-year-olds, we use probabilities from the 1920 birth cohort. In each case we rely on SSA's 1995 projections of the future mortality experience for these cohorts, because such projections should be based on the same information about aggregate mortality trends that insurance companies use in pricing their annuities.

Our second approach uses period tables for the annuitant population, in conjunction with the SSA cohort tables, to construct estimates of the 1995 cohort mortality table for individual annuitants. Cohort tables are unavailable for the annuity purchasing population, so we must make adjustments to the period tables for annuitants in order to mimic the desirable forward-looking properties of a cohort table. In our 1995 calculations, for example, we use information from the unpublished "basic" Annuity 2000 period table to estimate the cohort mortality patterns for individual annuitants.[15] The Annuity 2000 life table is designed to reflect projected annuitant mortality experience in the year 2000; it was recently issued by a committee of the Society of Actuaries.[16] To construct a cohort-like table for 1995 annuitants, we first interpolate between the basic Annuity 2000 table and the 1983 Table A reported in the Committee to Recommend a New Mortality Basis for Individual Annuity Valuation (1981). Then, the ratios of relevant mortality probabilities from the 1995 Social Security cohort table to the 1995 Social Security period table are applied to the 1995 annuity period table. This correction, which assumes that the prospective rate of mortality improvement for annuitants will be the same as that for the general population, yields a 1995 cohort-like annuitant mortality table.

Table 4.2 shows the resulting 1995 population and annuitant mortality rates by gender and age. It illustrates the lower mortality rates for the annuitant population. The differential is most notable, greater than one-third, at ages immediately following the traditional age of retirement.

To compare the expected discounted value of annuity payouts in different years, we also require cohort-like general population mortal-

Table 4.2
General population and annuitant mortality rates (per 1,000 persons), 1995

Gender and age	Life table for 1930 birth cohort general population	1995 individual annuitant life table
Men		
65	22.2	11.5
70	31.5	18.8
75	46.7	30.9
80	73.7	50.4
85	113.8	79.8
90	169.0	120.6
95	238.4	172.6
100	305.3	236.0
105	380.4	341.9
Women		
65	13.4	7.3
70	19.8	11.5
75	29.1	19.4
80	44.3	33.4
85	69.6	57.6
90	116.7	101.3
95	189.5	158.4
100	259.2	211.3
105	337.1	299.0

Sources: The first column is based on unpublished tabulations provided by the Social Security Administration, Office of the Actuary. The second column is drawn from mortality tables produced as part of the Society of Actuaries' Annuity 2000 project, adjusted to reflect mortality rates in 1995 rather than 2000.

ity probabilities for 1985 and 1990.[17] To carry out our analysis for 1990, we made the 1990 Social Security period table in Bell et al. (1992) into a cohort-like table by applying projected annual survival improvements of 0.75 and 1.00 per cent for men and women, respectively. These improvement rates were previously used by Friedman and Warshawsky (1988, 1990) and Warshawsky (1988), and they represent half the actual rates observed during the prior 15-year period. For 1985, we created a period table by interpolating between the 1980 Social Security period table appearing in J. Faber (1982) and the 1990 period table. The resulting 1985 period table was then made cohort-like by applying the same survival improvement rates.

We used a similar methodology to produce cohort-like annuitant mortality probabilities for earlier years. The 1983 Individual Annuity Mortality Basic Table A was brought forward to 1985 and 1990 by using general population survival improvement rates over the relevant periods to produce period tables. These period tables were then made cohort-like by applying the projected survival improvement rates mentioned above.

4   Empirical Findings: Money's Worth Results

We present our detailed findings for 1995, and then move on to present a restricted set of results for earlier years. Table 4.3 reports our estimates of the expected discounted value of annuity payouts using the all-company average payout rates from Table 4.1. It uses the after-tax valuation formula presented above.[18] The first two columns show calculations based on the 1995 *population* cohort mortality table, while the third and fourth columns use the 1995 *annuitant* cohort-like mortality

Table 4.3
Annuity values-per-premium dollar, 1995, after-tax calculations

	Population mortality table		Annuitant mortality table	
	Treasury yield curve	Corporate yield curve	Treasury yield curve	Corporate yield curve
Men				
Age 55	0.852	0.773	0.934	0.840
Age 65	0.814	0.756	0.927	0.853
Age 75	0.783	0.743	0.913	0.860
Women				
Age 55	0.880	0.791	0.937	0.838
Age 65	0.854	0.785	0.927	0.847
Age 75	0.846	0.796	0.919	0.861
Joint and survivor				
Age 55	0.889	0.792	0.930	0.824
Age 65	0.868	0.792	0.929	0.841
Age 75	0.846	0.791	0.922	0.857

Notes: Each entry shows the expected present discounted value of the annuity payouts per dollar of annuity premium. All calculations use the all-company sample average annuity payout rates to estimate the stream of payments associated with individual annuity contracts.

table in valuation. All annuity values are computed using both the term structure of short-term nominal interest rates implicit in the Treasury bond yield curve, and the related yield curve for BAA corporate bonds. We assume that the annuitant faces a 28-per cent combined federal and state tax rate.[19] In 1995, a married joint-filer household would have needed taxable income between $39,000 and $94,250 to face this tax rate. While the vast majority of older households have incomes below this range, the current set of individual annuity purchasers is substantially more affluent than the elderly population at large. In later sections, when we assess the demand for annuities among *all* elderly households, we use a lower marginal tax rate (15 per cent). This difference can be thought of as divergence between the "annuitant" and "population" tax rates.

4.1   Basic Results on Expected Present Discounted Values

Table 4.3 shows the expected present discounted value of annuity payments per premium dollar in 1995. When we use the general population mortality tables for a 65-year-old man, the value-per-premium dollar for a life annuity on an after-tax basis is 0.814 when we use the Treasury yield curve in valuation, and 0.756 when we use the corporate bond yield curve. For a woman of the same age the average values are higher, 0.854 and 0.785, respectively. In general, the fact that all value-per-premium dollar entries in Table 4.3 are well below 1.00 implies that a typical retiree with average mortality prospects would perceive a noticeable "transaction cost" when purchasing an annuity from a commercial insurance carrier. This transaction cost is equivalent to purchasing an actuarially fair annuity as determined from the general population mortality table, but having to give up roughly one-fifth of one's wealth before investing the remainder in this annuity product.

The results in Table 4.3 show that the higher the discount rate used in the valuation exercise, the lower the value-per-premium dollar. The expected discounted value of annuity payouts are systematically lower when we use BAA corporate interest rates to discount payouts than when we use the Treasury term structure. Table 4.3 also shows that for most combinations of mortality tables and interest rates that we consider, value-per-premium dollar declines with age. Values also vary by gender: controlling for age, value-per-premium dollar is lower for men than for women and couples.[20]

Table 4.3 focuses on annuity valuation using the after-tax valuation equation, equation (4). We show below that the differences between the before-tax and after-tax calculations are not large. There is weak evidence suggesting that annuities are more attractive on an after-tax than on a before-tax basis. This appears to derive from the fact the IRS has mandated the use of an old period mortality table, the 1983 Individual Annuitant Mortality table, in calculating the exclusion ratio.

The results in the last two columns of Table 4.3 show annuity value to premium ratios using annuitant mortality probabilities rather than general population mortality rates. Because annuitants have longer life expectancies than nonannuitants, the entries in this panel are uniformly higher than those in the previous panel. For example, a 65-year-old man using the annuitants' mortality table would assess the value-per-premium dollar as 0.927 on an after-tax basis using the Treasury yield curve. This compares to a ratio of 0.814 using general population survival rates. For a 65-year-old woman, the average value is also higher. The value using the annuitant table is 0.927, compared with 0.854 using the general population table.

The value-per-premium dollar figures vary substantially more as the discount rate changes from the Treasury yield curve to the corporate yield curve in the case that uses annuitant mortality probabilities than in that using general population mortality rates. This is because the effective duration of payouts is greater when the annuity policy is evaluated using the annuitant table. With a longer duration, the present-value calculations become more sensitive to differences in the discount rate.

Regardless of discount rate, and controlling for age, value-per-premium dollar in Table 4.3 is roughly comparable for men, women, and couples when we use the annuitant mortality tables. In the general population calculations, however, value-per-premium dollar is lowest for men. This result may be due to the fact that the ratio of life expectancies in the annuitant to the general population is higher for men than for women.

The results in Table 4.3 using the corporate term structure imply that annuity purchasers in the age ranges examined here would expect to receive payouts of between 82 and 86 cents per premium dollar. This set of calculations presumably represents the pure mortality and investment-related costs to the insurance companies of issuing life annuities, assuming that their typical portfolio investment is a BAA corporate bond. This implies that commercial insurance companies in

1995 allowed about 14–18 per cent of annuity premiums to cover commissions and other marketing costs, corporate overhead, income taxes, additions to various company contingency reserves, and profits.[21] These figures are smaller than the figure of 25 per cent computed for the 1970's and early 1980's by Friedman and Warshawsky (1988) and significantly smaller than the figure of 31 per cent for the early 1980's alone.[22]

We can calculate the cost of adverse selection in 1995 by comparing, for like age, gender and discount rate, the value-per-premium dollar ratios using the population and annuitant mortality tables. For example, for an annuity sold to a man aged 65 and using the Treasury yield curve, the cost of adverse selection is 11.3 percentage points (0.927–0.814). For the 1970's and early 1980's, the cost of adverse selection was 9 per cent, similar to the current cost. For an average individual, adverse selection appears to explain roughly half of the disparity between the expected discounted present value of annuity payouts and the cost of an individual annuity.

4.2 Internal Rate of Return Calculations

Annuities can be compared to other securities—in our case, bonds—either by computing the expected present discounted value of annuity payouts, using the return on the other asset as a discount rate, or by comparing the internal rate of return on annuities with the yield on these alternative investments. Samuel Broverman (1986) describes this second approach in detail. The internal rate of return is the discount rate at which the present discounted value of annuity payouts will equal the cost of purchasing the policy. For the standardized $100,000 SPIAs that we consider, the internal rate of return is the value ρ^* for the no-tax case, or ρ^*_{at} for the after-tax case, that satisfies:

$$100,000 = \sum_{j=1}^{600} \frac{A*P_j}{(1+\rho^*)^j} \tag{5}$$

or

$$100,000 = \sum_{j=1}^{12*T'} \frac{(1-\lambda*\tau)*A*P_j}{\left(1+(1-\tau)*\rho^*_{at}\right)^j} + \sum_{j=12*T'+1}^{600} \frac{(1-\tau)*A*P_j}{\left(1+(1-\tau)*\rho^*_{at}\right)^j}. \tag{6}$$

Table 4.4 presents these internal rates of return for SPIAs that were available in 1995. The table shows that for a 65-year-old man, when we

Table 4.4
Internal rates of return (percentage points) on annuity contracts offered to men aged 65 in 1995

	Before-tax calculation		After-tax calculation	
	Population mortality	Annuitant mortality	Population mortality	Annuitant mortality
Men				
Age 55	5.46	6.35	5.17	6.46
Age 65	4.62	6.31	3.81	6.16
Age 75	3.17	6.03	1.39	5.31
Women				
Age 55	5.68	6.26	5.73	6.55
Age 65	5.13	6.09	4.91	6.24
Age 75	4.47	5.82	3.77	5.61
Joint and survivor				
Age 55	5.83	6.20	5.95	6.51
Age 65	5.44	6.15	5.33	6.36
Age 75	4.63	5.94	4.08	5.89

Notes: Each entry shows the internal rate of return that equates the expected present discounted value of payouts for an individual annuity, using the all-company sample average annuity payout rates, to the purchase price of the annuity.

base the calculation on the no-tax formula, the internal rate of return was 4.62 per cent when we use the population mortality table, and 6.31 per cent when we use the annuitant table. For women, the analogous internal rates of return are 5.13 per cent and 6.09 per cent. When we do the calculation recognizing the taxation of interest and of annuities, the internal rate of return is 3.81 per cent with the population mortality table, and 6.16 per cent with annuitant mortality. To place these returns in perspective, the yield on a Treasury bond with ten years to maturity was 7.09 per cent at the beginning of May 1995, and the yield on a 30-year Treasury bond was 7.35 per cent. BAA corporate bonds yielded an average of 8.57 per cent at this time. Thus the internal rates of return on the annuities we consider are between 100 and 200 basis points below the market returns available to fixed-income investors.

The internal rate of return on SPIA contracts appears to decline as the age at which the contract is purchased rises. For men, there is more than a 200-basis-point differential between the internal rate of return on an annuity contract purchased at age 55 and a contract purchased at age 75.

4.3   Comparisons of EPDV over Time

We now consider how the expected value of annuity products has changed over time, and for this purpose we return to our focus on the expected discounted value of annuity payouts. Table 4.5 shows the value-per-premium dollar calculations for annuities offered to 65-year-old men, using the Best's all-company average payout for 1985, 1990, and 1995. The table presents calculations using our no-tax as well as our tax-inclusive formula. We present results from calculations without any correction for income taxes to facilitate comparison with earlier studies, since earlier work did not consider annuity taxation.

It is clear that regardless of the discount rate, mortality table, or tax basis, value-per-premium dollar grew roughly 8 percentage points between 1985 and 1995.[23] The present estimates for 1985 are close to Warshawsky's (1988) calculations for 1984, confirming that our methodology is similar enough to generate comparable results for nearby years. We also note that our 1995 results are reminiscent of the high values-per-premium dollar that Warshawsky (1988) reports for several earlier periods, including the 1940's, early 1950's, and mid-1960's.

The fluctuations in annuity value-per-premium dollar raise questions about the determinants of annuity prices. These prices should be

Table 4.5
Values-per-premium dollar of annuity policies offered for men aged 65—1985–1995

	Before-tax calculation		After-tax calculation	
	Treasury yield curve	Corporate yield curve	Treasury yield curve	Corporate yield curve
Using population life tables				
1985	0.749	0.677	0.764	0.704
1990	0.814	0.746	0.812	0.757
1995	0.816	0.742	0.814	0.756
Using annuitant life tables				
1985	0.827	0.740	0.865	0.790
1990	0.912	0.828	0.926	0.856
1995	0.916	0.825	0.927	0.853

Notes: All entries show the present discounted value of annuity payouts per dollar of annuity premium, assuming a $100,000 single-premium immediate annuity purchase. See text for further details regarding calculations.

related to the level of real interest rates, but they may also be related to the level and variability of nominal interest rates. When interest rates are low and stable, insurance companies may be able to price nonparticipating annuities more competitively with other fixed-income investments. In contrast, when interest rates are high and variable, insurance companies may be reluctant to assume that current yields will be maintained for the duration of annuities issued in that year, and therefore they act more conservatively and require larger contingency funds in their annuity pricing. A particularly important question concerning the interpretation of the results in Table 4.5 is whether the increase in the expected present discounted value of annuity payouts per premium dollar is the result of a trend toward higher payouts, or an artifact of cyclical fluctuations in annuity pricing. We cannot resolve this issue with the available data.

5 The Insurance Value of Annuity Contracts

Our discussion of the expected present discounted value of annuity payouts neglects the important insurance value of annuities. To provide some insight on this issue, we invoke an explicit individual utility function and compare the expected *utility* of purchasing an annuity with that from alternative, nonannuitized methods of decumulating assets during retirement.[24] The alternative we consider is the optimal consumption path that results if the individual solves the dynamic stochastic optimization problem for lifetime consumption.

5.1 Analytical Framework

We consider an individual who purchases a fixed nominal annuity at age 65. This individual will receive an annuity payment in each year that he remains alive, and his optimal consumption path will be related to this payout. The after-tax annuity payout that the individual receives at age $a(A_a)$ depends on his wealth at the beginning of retirement (W_0), the annual annuity payout per dollar of premium payment (θ), and the tax rules that govern annuity income:

$$A_a(W_0) = \left[1 - \lambda * \tau * I_{a<65+T'} - \tau * I_{a\geq65+T'}\right] * \theta * W_0. \tag{7}$$

The variable $I_{a<65+T'}$ is an indicator variable set equal to one for ages less than the date at which all annuity income is included in taxable income, and zero otherwise. The other indicator variable is defined in complementary fashion.

We limit our analysis to annuity contracts that pay fixed nominal benefit streams. We begin our analysis by assuming a fixed inflation rate of 3.2 per cent per year, which corresponds to the historical average over the 1926–1995 period as reported in Ibbotson Associates (1996). This means that the nominal annuity is a real annuity with payouts that decline at the rate of 3.2 per cent per year.[25] In a later subsection we allow for a distribution of inflation outcomes.

We compute the actuarially fair annuity payout per premium dollar (θ) for a 65-year-old male, in 1995, using the Social Security Administration's cohort life table for men born in 1930. We find θ from the following equation:

$$1 = \sum_{j=1}^{50} \frac{\theta * P_j}{((1+r)(1+\pi))^j},$$ (8)

where P_j denotes the probability of a 65-year-old retiree remaining alive j years after retirement, r denotes the annual real interest rate, and π is the annual inflation rate. In distinction from our earlier analysis, we now focus on years rather than months in our annuity valuation, to simplify our dynamic programming calculations of optimal consumption paths. We continue to assume that no one survives beyond age 115, so $P_{50} = 0$.

We compute the expected discounted utility stream associated with the consumption stream generated by the annuity contract by assuming that individuals have additively separable utility functions of the following form:

$$U = \sum_{j=1}^{50} P_j^* \frac{\left(\left(\frac{C_j}{(1+\pi)^j}\right)^{1-\beta} - 1\right)}{(1-\beta)*(1+\rho)^j}.$$ (9)

The parameter β determines the individual's risk aversion and also the degree of intertemporal substitution in consumption. The nominal consumption flow is deflated by the price index, $(1+\pi)^j$.

We perform this calculation in two cases. The first assumes that all of the individual's resources at age 65 have been used to purchase the annuity contract. The other assumes that only half of the individual's resources can be used for such a purchase, and that the other half is already invested in a real annuity. We view this as a stylized characterization of the current Social Security system. We thus investigate whether the marginal gains from annuitization of private assets decline substantially when some wealth is already held in annuitized form. Comparing these two cases may provide some evidence on the time-series variation in annuity demand, since Alan J. Auerbach et al. (1992) observe that over time, the elderly have held a rising fraction of their assets in annuitized form.

We illustrate our procedure for computing the insurance value of purchasing an annuity contract by considering an individual who does not have any annuitized wealth. The generalization to the case with some annuitized wealth follows naturally. First, we find the optimal consumption path for someone with assets of W_0 at age 65, who does not have access to an annuity market, and who maximizes the utility function above over remaining lifetime by choosing a consumption path $\{C_a\}$. This maximization is carried out subject to the initial wealth constraint W_0 and the budget constraint

$$W_{a+1} = (W_a - C_a)*[1 + (r + \pi)(1 - \tau)]. \tag{10}$$

In this equation τ denotes the marginal income tax rate that applies to nominal interest income.[26] We solve for the optimal consumption path $\{C_a\}$ using stochastic dynamic programming, where the stochastic component of the problem arises from uncertainty regarding date of death. We then compute the value of the expected utility function (U^*) for this consumption stream.

In the second stage of our calculation, we ask what amount of wealth at age 65 (W_{EQUIV}) the individual would require to reach utility level U^* if he used this wealth to purchase an actuarially fair nominal annuity and thereby obtained a nominal income stream equal to $A_a(W_{EQUIV})$.[27] We use a standard dynamic programming algorithm to find the optimal consumption profile for an individual with an annuitized income stream, and then to find his expected utility level from implementing this consumption plan. This expected utility level is found by maximizing the utility function in (9) subject to the constraints $W_0 = 0$ and

$$W_{a+1} = (W_a + A_a(W_{EQUIV}) - C_a) \times [1 + (r + \pi)(1 - \tau)]. \tag{11}$$

$A_a(W_{EQUIV})$ denotes the annuity payout stream that can be purchased with an initial wealth of W_{EQUIV}. For a given value of W_{EQUIV}, denote the resulting value of the expected utility function by $U^{**}(W_{EQUIV})$. We normalize annuitizable first-period wealth at unity ($W_0 = 1$) and then apply a numerical search algorithm to find the value of W_{EQUIV} that yields $U^{**}(W_{EQUIV}) = U^*$. Since the longevity insurance provided by the annuity market makes the individual better off, W_{EQUIV} is less than W_0.

5.2 Results with Certain Inflation

Table 4.6 presents the resulting values of W_{EQUIV}/W_0 for two different assumptions about individual risk aversion ($\beta = 1$ and $\beta = 2$). The table includes results for several different assumptions about the level of real interest rates and individual time preference rates. The upper panel of the table describes the results that assume a fixed annual inflation rate. Because these calculations are designed to indicate the demand for annuities in the population at large, our after-tax calculations assume a marginal tax rate of 15 per cent, which is likely to apply to the majority of retired households.

The calculations in Table 4.6 suggest that, in the canonical life-cycle model with uncertain mortality, consumers would be prepared to give up substantial fractions of their wealth in order to purchase actuarially fair annuities. In the before-tax calculations, for example, we find that individuals would accept a reduction of between 30 and 38 per cent in their wealth at age 65 if they were able to purchase actuarially fair nominal annuities rather than pursue an optimal consumption strategy without annuity contracts. The amount of wealth that individuals would forgo is increasing in their risk aversion, and decreasing in the rate of return that they can earn on their own investments.

These results are similar to those presented by Laurence J. Kotlikoff and Avia Spivak (1981) for the case of private annuities and by R. Glenn Hubbard (1987) for the case of publicly provided annuities. In contrast, if half of an individual's wealth at retirement were held in an annuitized form (similar to Social Security), the share of nonannuitized wealth that he would be prepared to relinquish in order to obtain access to an annuity market declines. Depending on the real interest rate and discount rate assumptions, individuals would still forgo between 23 and 31 per cent of their discretionary wealth to obtain a nominal annuity.

5.3 Results with Uncertain Inflation

Some might argue that the results in the upper panel of Table 4.6 overstate the insurance value of nominal annuities, because they do not

Table 4.6
Wealth equivalence between annuitized and nonannuitized assets

	Before-tax calculation		After-tax calculation	
Parameter values	$\beta = 1$	$\beta = 2$	$\beta = 1$	$\beta = 2$
Certain inflation, $\pi = 0.032$:				
No Preexisting Real Annuity				
$r = 0.03$, $\rho = 0.01$	0.659	0.619	0.657	0.604
$r = 0.03$, $\rho = 0.03$	0.678	0.626	0.680	0.614
$r = 0.05$, $\rho = 0.01$	0.692	0.670	0.683	0.653
$r = 0.05$, $\rho = 0.03$	0.703	0.675	0.697	0.659
Preexisting Real Annuity Worth 50 Percent of Wealth at Retirement				
$r = 0.03$, $\rho = 0.01$	0.730	0.695	0.759	0.717
$r = 0.03$, $\rho = 0.03$	0.771	0.723	0.809	0.748
$r = 0.05$, $\rho = 0.01$	0.732	0.714	0.736	0.709
$r = 0.05$, $\rho = 0.03$	0.757	0.729	0.770	0.732
Uncertain inflation (mean $\pi = 0.032$):				
No Preexisting Real Annuity				
$r = 0.03$, $\rho = 0.01$	0.668	0.631	0.664	0.613
$r = 0.03$, $\rho = 0.03$	0.687	0.639	0.687	0.623
$r = 0.05$, $\rho = 0.01$	0.700	0.682	0.689	0.662
$r = 0.05$, $\rho = 0.03$	0.712	0.688	0.703	0.667
Preexisting Real Annuity Worth 50 Percent of Wealth at Retirement				
$r = 0.03$, $\rho = 0.01$	0.737	0.703	0.763	0.721
$r = 0.03$, $\rho = 0.03$	0.778	0.732	0.813	0.753
$r = 0.05$, $\rho = 0.01$	0.739	0.722	0.749	0.723
$r = 0.05$, $\rho = 0.03$	0.764	0.737	0.784	0.746

Notes: In the upper panel, the annual inflation rate is 3.2 percent. In the lower panel, the inflation rate is stochastic, drawn from a four-point distribution described in the text. In both panels, r denotes the real interest rate, and ρ is the individual's time preference rate. The SSA cohort life table for men born in 1930 is used for all calculations. The after-tax calculations assume a marginal income tax rate of 15 percent.

allow for the possibility that fluctuations in postretirement inflation will alter the utility value of the nominal annuity stream. To address this possibility, we modified our wealth equivalent calculations to allow for uncertain inflation. In lieu of a constant inflation rate of 3.2 per cent each year, we allowed the inflation rate in each "year" to take one of four values: −1.4 per cent, 1.8 per cent, 3.8 per cent, or 9.0 per cent. The respective probabilities of these inflation outcomes were 0.2, 0.3, 0.3, and 0.2. These inflation values correspond approximately to the 10th, 35th, 65th, and 90th percentiles of the annual inflation distribution for the years 1926–1995, and they imply an average annual inflation rate of 3.2 per cent.[28] The stochastic dynamic programming problem is substantially more complex in the presence of stochastic inflation and mortality than in the case of stochastic mortality alone, but the same basic approach can be used to find the wealth equivalent in this case.

The lower panel of Table 4.6 presents our wealth equivalents for the uncertain inflation case. Compared to our findings in the certain inflation case, a risk-averse individual would forgo less of his wealth to purchase a nominal annuity. The quantitative difference between the results in the upper and lower panels of Table 4.6 is small, however. In most cases, there is less than a 1-percentage-point difference in the fraction of wealth that an individual would be prepared to give up to purchase nominal annuities in the fixed and random inflation cases. Hence our findings suggest that uncertain inflation is not a key factor explaining the limited individual demand for nominal annuities.[29] These findings may also explain, in part, the relatively limited demand for U.S. Treasury Inflation Protection Securities (indexed bonds) since their debut over a year ago.

5.4   Implications

The findings in Table 4.6 imply that even if the EPDV calculations presented above yielded only 0.75 per dollar of premium payment, individuals with preferences such as those modeled here would still prefer to purchase the annuity rather than pursue an optimal consumption strategy without such insurance products. Thus in a simplified stochastic life-cycle model without bequest motives, the fact that the expected present discounted value of annuity payouts is less than the cost of these policies cannot explain the low demand for nominal annuities.

These calculations should be viewed as exploratory for at least three reasons. First, they ignore the possibility of bequest motives, even though a substantial literature suggests that some individuals behave in ways that are consistent with the presence of such motives.[30] Second, they do not recognize the possibility of large one-time consumption needs, for example for medical and long-term disability care, that might induce some individuals to prefer not to annuitize their assets. Finally, they do not consider the complex issues raised by annuitization decisions of married couples, where the expected time path of consumption needs may differ from the level nominal annuity offered by most insurance contracts.

6   Conclusions and Future Work

This chapter presents new evidence on the expected present discounted value of payments for annuity policies and compares these to the cost of purchasing an individual annuity contract. We find that the average annuity policy available to a 65-year-old man in 1995 delivered payouts valued at between 80 and 85 cents per dollar of annuity premium. There was substantial heterogeneity across annuity providers in the payouts per dollar of premium payment. We also find evidence that the expected present discounted value of annuity payouts relative to premium payments has increased by approximately 8 percentage points during the last decade. Thus, from the standpoint of potential purchasers, an individual annuity contract appears to be a more attractive product today than ten years ago.

These findings bear on a set of issues that arise in designing national retirement policy. Although the individual annuity market is currently quite small, it has attracted substantial interest from researchers and policy makers concerned with the evolving system of retirement income provision. In light of current discussions of Social Security reform and the shift from defined benefit to defined contribution private pension plans, we suspect that there may be increased interest in individual annuity products in the future. Current trends place greater emphasis on individual choice and self-reliance in planning for retirement. These developments may increase the demand for individual annuity products as retirees confront the problems of optimal decumulation of assets amassed in various retirement plans.

Valuation exercises such as those presented here are also important for assessing the extent of adverse selection in the market for individual annuities. This, in turn, is a key consideration in the policy debate regarding whether the government should intervene directly and mandate a national annuity pool, should the current Social Security system be partly replaced by a mandatory private saving system [see the discussion in Technical Panel on Trends in Income and Retirement Savings (TIRS), 1995].[31] These results provide an important input for this analysis, although they should be viewed with caution because a policy change of this magnitude could alter the set of individuals purchasing annuities and therefore affect the pricing of these products.

Our findings raise a number of questions for future research. The most important outstanding issue may be how to explain the differential between the expected present discounted value of annuity payouts and the premiums for these policies. This difference may be partly due to the corporate income taxes on the insurance companies offering annuity products. Our analysis has recognized the effect of annuitant-level taxes on the relative value of annuities and other financial products, but it has not tried to explain how taxes at the corporate level might affect the pricing of annuities. Another portion of the differential between the premium and the discounted benefit flow is attributable to the insurance company load, or charge levied to cover marketing and administration costs and normal profitability. There also may be company-to-company differences in underwriting, making the cross-firm premium variation reflective of specific risk pools that our overall correction does not fully capture. Nonetheless, the fact that the differential has diminished over time suggests that potential imperfections in the annuity business of two decades ago may be attenuated in today's insurance market.

Future research could usefully extend this analysis to consider the pricing and value of group annuity products. Because of the risk pooling inherent in the purchase of group annuities, for example through a pension fund, there is likely to be less adverse selection in the group market than in the individual annuity market. Hence we would expect to see smaller differences between the expected present discounted values and premium costs for the population, and for group annuitants, than we found in the individual annuity market.

It would also be interesting to expand our analysis to include other components of household portfolios. We have effectively assumed that the payouts from an annuity contract are certain, conditional on individual life length, and that riskless assets such as Treasury securities or investment-quality corporate bonds are the only alternatives to an annuity contract. If an individual's portfolio also included risky securities such as corporate equities, then the comparison between purchasing an annuity and holding other financial assets might change from the one we present. Yet another complexity arises from the recent introduction of government bonds with yields linked to changes in the Consumer Price Index. If such "indexed bonds" prompted the introduction of annuity contracts with fixed real payouts rather than fixed nominal payouts, this could also change the relative appeal of annuity products.

Notes

1. Poterba (1997) provides a typology of various annuity contracts, describing their provisions during both the accumulation and decumulation periods.

2. We thank Walter Zultowski of LIMRA for providing us with these unpublished data.

3. According to the 1993 survey, although the majority of SPIA annuitants had chosen a life annuity payout option, most selected some form of period certain or installment refund option as well: only 8 per cent chose zero refund and only 7 per cent elected a joint-and-survivor life option. The age distribution of annuitants clearly tends toward older ages. The relatively small group of young annuitants below age 50 may include substantial numbers of individuals receiving annuities in structured payment of legal settlements.

4. We use the nominal yields on Treasury bonds with fixed maturities of 1, 2, 3, 5, 7, 10, 20, and 30 years to estimate the term structure of expected short-term interest rates. We calculate the expected nominal short rate in each future period as the nominal short rate that would satisfy the expectations theory of the term structure for the two adjacent long-term bonds.

5. The calculations reported below are relatively insensitive to assumptions about the upper limit on lifespan. Assuming a value of 100 years instead of 115 years results in estimates of the expected present discounted value within 0.02 per cent of those reported below.

6. Participating annuities, in contrast, guarantee principal and minimum investment return payments and supplement those payments with dividends that depend on the insurance company's evolving investment, mortality, and expense experience. Because of a lessened need to maintain large contingency reserves to cover reinvestment and other risks, an insurer issuing participating contracts should be able to offer higher returns than one issuing nonparticipating contracts. With the prominent exception of TIAA, the nonprofit insurer issuing annuity contracts exclusively to workers in higher education and nonprofit research institutions, participating annuities are rare.

7. We also consider a "joint-and-survivor" life annuity purchased by a couple, where the level benefit payments continue as long as one member of the couple is alive.

8. We do not consider annuity contracts that guaranty payments for a "fixed-period certain," although it would be straightforward to extend our money's worth framework to analyze these contracts.

9. The Best's survey is conducted at the beginning of May, and we use the term structure of Treasury yields for the first week of May in calculating the discount factors that we use below.

10. We found substantial correlation in the relative payouts that different firms offered to annuitants of different ages. For example, eight of the ten firms that offered the highest payouts to 65-year-old male annuitants were also among the ten firms offering the highest payouts to 55-year-old male annuitants.

11. Belth's (1995) criterion focuses on firms receiving very high ratings from at least two of the four major private rating firms: Standard and Poor's, Moody's, Duff and Phelps, and Weiss.

12. This approach is taken in the Society of Actuaries' tables and some Social Security tables, as explained by Felicitie Bell et al. (1992).

13. This second approach is also sometimes used by the Social Security Administration (SSA).

14. We thank Felicitie Bell of the Social Security Administration for providing these data.

15. "Basic" in this context means a mortality table formed from industry experience without an additional margin for conservatism. The difference between a "basic" table and a table without this modifier is an implicit load for annuity pricing. The 1983 IAM Table A and the 1983 Individual Annuity Basic A tables, for example, differ by a 10-per cent load factor. Throughout our calculations, we use annuitant basic tables.

16. The Annuity 2000 table has an interesting history. The 1983 annuity table was based on actual annuitants' mortality experience in a large group of companies over the period 1971–1976, updated to reflect and project 1983 conditions. The Society of Actuaries' Individual Annuity Experience Committee (1991–1992) studied the annuity experience of a small group of companies over the period 1976–1986, and concluded that the 1983 table was adequate for the 1980's. More recent population mortality statistics from the Social Security Administration and the National Center for Health Statistics, along with evolving conditions in the group annuity market, however, convinced R. Johansen (1996), an actuary actively involved in the earlier studies, to call for a new individual annuity table. His call, although not his specific recommendations, was answered affirmatively and a Society of Actuaries committee was convened to consider the subject. Because there are no recent studies of industry-wide annuitant mortality experience, however, the committee decided simply to use the basic 1983 annuity table projected forward to the year 2000 using mortality improvement factors consistent with the recent experience of the general population as well as that of one company with substantial annuity business.

17. It was not possible to obtain the actual cohort tables used by the Social Security Administration in preparing the 1986 and 1991 Trustees' Reports.

18. Even when we ignore income taxes, we recognize premium taxes that some states impose on annuity purchases. According to Marci Castillo (1997), only 12 states impose taxes on annuity premiums; their average rate is 1.5 per cent. To get the national average state premium tax rate of 0.52 per cent, we weighted the individual state tax rates by the percentages of the U.S.-over-65-year-old population residing in each state.

19. Because many annuity income recipients may also be Social Security recipients, the marginal tax rate on annuity or interest income could exceed the combined federal and state tax rate if this income leads to inclusion of Social Security benefits in taxable income. We explored the sensitivity of our results to higher marginal tax rates, but did not find any substantial changes relative to the findings reported here.

20. We assume that couples evaluate joint-and-survivor annuities assuming that their individual mortality probabilities are independent. However, recent research by Edward W. Frees et al. (1996) suggests that the mortality of husbands and wives exhibits positive dependence. Canadian insurance data suggest that annuity values for couples should be reduced by about 5 per cent when using dependent mortality models, relative to the values computed using standard models that assume independence.

21. For insurance companies licensed to write business in New York State, direct marketing costs, which include commissions to agents and brokers and related direct expenses, are not allowed to exceed 7 per cent of the annuity premium.

22. They are also lower than the estimates of annuity payouts per dollar of premium payment in Canada, as reported in Moshe A. Milevsky (1998). Milvesky suggests payouts with EPDV values of between 0.91 and 0.96 per dollar of premium.

23. The dispersion of annuity prices has also declined over time. In 1985, for a 65-year-old man, the monthly income for the ten highest-payout policies averaged 1.152 times that for the entire sample of policies in the Best's data base, while the average payout for the ten lowest-payout companies was 0.885 times the sample average. In 1990, the analogous statistics were 1.097 and 0.892, and in 1995, 1.098 and 0.913.

24. For recent treatments of the question of whether individuals should purchase annuity contracts, see Agar Brugiavini (1993) and Milevsky (1998).

25. We have done some calculations comparing the utility levels afforded by these nominal annuities and alternative real annuity contracts. Even though the nominal annuities offer consumption streams that decline in real value, this deviation from the constant real consumption path that would be optimal from the annuitant's standpoint does not lead to a large reduction in utility. This is because the tilting of the real consumption profile takes place locally around the optimal path. The graded payment method for annuity payouts, first proposed by John H. Biggs (1969) and implemented by TIAA in 1982, allows for an increasing payout profile roughly in line with the rate of inflation.

26. In the analysis reported below, we consider cases with and without taxation ($\tau = 0$).

27. The individual could choose to consume the nominal annuity payout in each remaining year of life, but in general the optimal consumption path will in general not coincide with the annuity payout stream (see Tadashi Yagi and Yasuyuki Nishigaki, 1993). We assume that annuity recipients cannot borrow against future annuity income, but they can save and invest their annuity income at a return r.

28. We also examined other inflation processes that allowed for greater year-to-year inflation persistence, but did not find results substantially different from those reported in Table 4.6.

29. We have explored the sensitivity of the wealth equivalent calculations with random inflation to changes in the coefficient of risk aversion. More risk-averse individuals value a nominal annuity less when there is uncertain inflation. When we set $\beta = 6$, for example, we found differences of approximately 3 per cent in the wealth equivalent values under certain and uncertain inflation. These differences are larger than those reported in Table

4.6. Brown et al. (2000) discuss the availability of and demand for inflation-indexed annuities in more detail.

30. John Laitner and F. Thomas Juster (1996) and Mark Wilhelm (1996) represent recent contributions to the literature on bequest motives and provide references to earlier studies. Andrew B. Abel and Warshawsky (1988) discuss alternative specifications of the bequest motive that could be used to modify the calculations presented above. Alain Jousten (1998) explores the link between bequest motives, annuity markets, and optimal consumption profiles. Brown and Poterba (1999) explore annuity valuation for married couples purchasing joint-and-survivor annuities.

31. The potential for market failure in the individual annuity market has historically been advanced as one of the reasons for government provision of retirement income; see Peter A. Diamond (1977). Abel (1986) provides a formal analysis of the interactions between public retirement programs and private annuity markets. Warshawsky (1997) suggests a clearinghouse mechanism that could be put into place if individual accounts were to be set up under a partially privatized Social Security system.

References

Abel, Andrew B. "Capital Accumulation and Uncertain Lifetimes with Adverse Selection." *Econometrica*, September 1986, 54(5), pp. 1079–97.

Abel, Andrew B. and Warshawsky, Mark. "Specification of the Joy of Giving: Insights from Altruism." *Review of Economics and Statistics*, February 1988, 70(1), pp. 145–49.

American Council on Life Insurance. *1996 life insurance fact book*. Washington, DC: American Council on Life Insurance, 1996.

Attanasio, Orazio and Hoynes, Hilary W. "Differential Mortality and Wealth Accumulation." National Bureau of Economic Research (Cambridge, MA) Working Paper No. 5126, May 1995.

Auerbach, Alan J.; Kotlikoff, Laurence J. and Weil, David. "The Increasing Annuitization of the Elderly: Estimates and Implications for Intergenerational Transfers, Inequality, and National Saving." National Bureau of Economic Research (Cambridge, MA) Working Paper No. 4182, October 1992.

Austen, Jane. *Sense and sensibility*. New York: Harcourt Brace & World, Inc., 1962.

Bell, Felicitie; Wade, A. and Goss, S. "Life Tables for the United States Social Security Area 1900–2080." Actuarial Study No. 107, Social Security Administration, Office of the Actuary, 1992.

Belth, Joseph. "Special Ratings Issue." *Insurance Forum*, October 1995, 22(10), pp. 237–72.

Biggs, John H. "Alternatives in Variable Annuity Benefit Design." *Transactions of the Society of Actuaries*, November 1969, 21, pp. 495–517.

Broverman, Samuel. "The Rate of Return on Life Insurance and Annuities." *Journal of Risk and Insurance*, September 1986, 53(3), pp. 419–34.

Brown, Jeffrey R.; Mitchell, Olivia S. and Poterba, James M. "The Role of Real Annuities and Indexed Bonds in an Individual Accounts Retirement System," in J. Campbell and M. Feldstein, eds., *Risk Aspects of A Investment-Based R Social Security Reform*. Chicago: University of Chicago Press, 2001.

Brown, Jeffrey and Poterba, James. "Joint Life Annuities and Annuity Demand by Married Couples." National Bureau of Economic Research (Cambridge, MA) Working Paper No. 7199, June 1999.

Brugiavini, Agar. "Uncertainty Resolution and the Timing of Annuity Purchases." *Journal of Public Economics*, January 1993, *50*(1), pp. 31–62.

Castillo, Marci. "Essays on the State Taxation of the Life Insurance Industry." Ph.D. dissertation, Massachusetts Institute of Technology, 1997.

Committee to Recommend a New Mortality Basis for Individual Annuity Valuation. "Report (Derivation of the 1983 Table A)." *Transactions of the Society of Actuaries*, 1981, *33*, pp. 675–751.

Dahlby, Bev and West, Douglas. "Price Dispersion in an Automobile Insurance Market." *Journal of Political Economy*, April 1986, *94*(2), pp. 418–38.

Diamond, Peter A. "A Framework for Social Security Analysis." *Journal of Public Economics*, December 1977, *8*(3), pp. 275–98.

Faber, J. "Life Tables for the United States: 1900–2050." Actuarial Study No. 87, Social Security Administration, Office of the Actuary, 1982.

Frees, Edward W.; Carriere, Jacques and Valdez, Emiliano. "Annuity Valuation with Dependent Mortality." *Journal of Risk and Insurance*, June 1996, *63*(2), pp. 229–61.

Friedman, Benjamin, and Warshawsky, Mark. "Annuity Prices and Saving Behavior in the United States," in Z. Bodie, J. Shoven, and D. Wise, eds., *Pensions in the U.S. economy*. Chicago: University of Chicago Press, 1988, pp. 53–77.

————. "The Cost of Annuities: Implications for Saving Behavior and Bequests." *Quarterly Journal of Economics*, February 1990, *105*(1), pp. 135–54.

Hubbard, R. Glenn. "Uncertain Lifetimes, Pensions, and Individual Saving," in Z. Bodie, J. Shoven, and D. Wise, eds., *Issues in pension economics*. Chicago: University of Chicago Press, 1987, pp. 175–206.

Ibbotson Associates. *Stocks, bonds, bills, and inflation: 1996 yearbook*. Chicago: Ibbotson Associates, 1996.

Individual Annuity Experience Committee. "Report: Mortality Under Individual Immediate Annuities, Life Income Settlements, and Matured Deferred Annuities Between 1976 and 1986 Anniversaries." *Transactions of the Society of Actuaries: 1991–1992 Reports*, 1991–1992, pp. 65–116.

Jousten, Alain. "Essays on Annuity Valuation, Bequests, and Social Security." Ph.D. dissertation, Massachusetts Institute of Technology, 1998.

Johansen, R. "Review of Adequacy of 1983 Individual Annuity Mortality Table." *Transactions of the Society of Actuaries*, 1996, *47*, pp. 101–23.

Kotlikoff, Laurence J. and Spivak, Avia. "The Family as an Incomplete Annuities Market." *Journal of Political Economy*, April 1981, *89*(2), pp. 372–91.

Laitner, John and Juster, F. Thomas. "New Evidence on Altruism: A Study of TIAA-CREF Retirees." *American Economic Review*, September 1996, *86*(4), pp. 893–908.

LIMRA International. "The 1995 Individual Annuity Market—Sales and Assets." Hartford: LIMRA International, 1996.

Matthewson, G. Frank. "Information Search and Price Variability of Individual Life Insurance Contracts." *Journal of Industrial Economics*, December 1983, *32*(2), pp. 131–48.

Milevsky, Moshe A. "Optimal Asset Allocation Towards the End of the Life Cycle: To Annuitize or Not to Annuitize." *Journal of Risk and Insurance*, September 1998, *65*(3), pp. 401–26.

Pappas, Gregory; Queen, Susan; Hadden, Wilbur and Fisher, Gail. "The Increasing Disparity in Mortality Between Socioeconomic Groups in the United States, 1960 and 1986." *New England Journal of Medicine*, July 8, 1993, *329*(2), pp. 103–09.

Poterba, James M. "The History of Annuities in the United States." National Bureau of Economic Research (Cambridge MA) Working Paper No. 6003, March 1997.

Rothschild, Michael and Stiglitz, Joseph. "Equilibrium in Competitive Insurance Markets: An Essay on the Economics of Imperfect Information." *Quarterly Journal of Economics*, November 1976, *90*(4), pp. 629–49.

Technical Panel on Trends in Income and Retirement Savings (TIRS). *Final report to the Social Security Advisory Council*, U.S. Department of Health and Human Services, December 1995 [available at www.ssa.gov].

Trieschmann, James and Gustavson, Sandra. *Risk management and insurance*, 9th Ed. Cincinnati, OH: South-Western College Publishing, 1995.

U.S. General Accounting Office. *Tax treatment of life insurance and annuity accrued interest*. Washington, DC: U.S. General Accounting Office, 1990.

Warshawsky, Mark. "Private Annuity Markets in the United States." *Journal of Risk and Insurance*, September 1988, *55*(3), pp. 518–28.

———. "The Market for Individual Annuities and the Reform of Social Security." *Benefits Quarterly*, 1997, 3rd Qtr., pp. 66–76.

Wilhelm, Mark. "Bequest Behavior and the Effect of Heirs' Earnings: Testing the Altruistic Model of Bequests." *American Economic Review*, September 1996, *86*(4), pp. 874–92.

Wilson, Charles. "The Nature of Equilibrium in Markets with Adverse Selection." *Bell Journal of Economics*, Spring 1980, *11*(1), pp. 108–30.

Yagi, Tadashi and Nishigaki, Yasuyuki. "The Inefficiency of Private Constant Annuities." *Journal of Risk and Insurance*, September 1993, *60*(3), pp. 385–412.

5 The Role of Real Annuities and Indexed Bonds in an Individual Accounts Retirement Program

Jeffrey R. Brown,
Olivia S. Mitchell, and
James M. Poterba

It is better to have a permanent income than to be fascinating.
Oscar Wilde, *The Model Millionaire: A Note of Admiration*

The current U.S. Social Security system provides retirees with a real annuity during their retirement years. After a worker's primary insurance amount has been determined at the date of retirement, the purchasing power of Social Security benefits remains fixed for the balance of the individual's life. This is accomplished by indexing retirement benefits to annual changes in the consumer price index (CPI). Retirees are therefore insulated from inflation risk, at least as long as their consumption bundle is not too different from the bundle used to compute the CPI.

Several current reform plans propose to supplement, or partially replace, the existing defined-benefit Social Security system with mandatory individual defined-contribution accounts. These plans are discussed in Gramlich (1996), Mitchell, Myers, and Young (1999), and NASI (1998). In most "individual account" plans, retirees would be required to purchase an annuity with all or part of their accumulated account balances. Yet the existing market for individual annuities in the United States is small, the expected present value of annuity payouts is typically below the purchase price of the annuity, and virtually all annuities currently available offer nominal rather than real payout streams. This has led some to argue that individual account plans

From *Risk Aspects of Investment-Based Social Security Reform*, ed. John Y. Campbell and Martin Feldstein (Chicago: University of Chicago Press, 2001). © 2001 by the National Bureau of Economic Research. Reprinted by permission of the University of Chicago Press.

would expose retirees to inflation risk that they do not currently face. If individuals purchase nominal annuities with their accumulated funds and the inflation rate is positive during their payout period, then the real value of their annuity payouts will decline over time. Even if inflation was *expected* to be positive at the time of the annuity purchase, some individuals may not recognize this, and they may experience an unexpected decline in real payouts. This effect is distinct from the inflation risk that arises from differences between expected and actual inflation rates.

In this chapter, we explore four issues concerning real annuities, nominal annuities, and the inflation risks faced by prospective retirees, all of which are relevant to the prospects for individual accounts under social security reform. We begin by describing the annuity market in the United Kingdom. Annuitants in the United Kingdom can select from a wide range of both real and nominal annuity products. The U.K. annuity market demonstrates the feasibility of offering real annuities in the private marketplace. Moreover, the current U.K. annuity market may indicate the direction in which the U.S. annuity market will evolve since indexed bonds promising a fixed real return to investors have been available in the United Kingdom for nearly two decades. The availability of such bonds has made it possible for U.K. insurers to offer real annuity products without bearing inflation risk. Similar bonds have been available in the United States for only two years. Our evaluation of the U.K. annuity market includes an analysis of the relative prices of both real and nominal annuities, and we present estimates of how much a potential annuitant must pay to purchase the inflation insurance provided by a real annuity.

Next, we turn to the annuity market in the United States and investigate the availability of real annuities in this country. In early 1997, the U.S. government introduced Treasury inflation-protection securities (TIPS), and, since then, two products that might be described as *inflation-indexed annuities* have come to market. One, offered by the Irish Life Company of North America (ILONA), promises a constant-purchasing-power stream of benefits. Although this product offers buyers a real stream of annuity payouts, there have been no sales to date. The second, offered by TIAA-CREF, is a variable-payout annuity with payouts linked to returns on the CREF index-linked bond account. We describe the operation of the latter account in some detail and explain why, in practice, the TIAA-CREF variable annuity is not an inflation-indexed annuity. Our analysis of these two products suggests that no commercially significant real annuities are currently available in the U.S. annuity market.

We then consider whether a retiree could use a portfolio of stocks or bonds, in lieu of a portfolio of indexed bonds, to hedge long-term inflation risk. Specifically, we evaluate how much inflation risk annuitants would bear if, instead of purchasing nominal annuities, they purchased variable-payout annuities with payouts linked to various asset portfolios. We assess the potential inflation protection provided by different variable-payout annuities using historical correlation patterns between inflation and nominal returns on stocks, bonds, and bills.

The final portion of the analysis explores the expected-utility consequences of annuitizing retirement resources in alternative ways. A stylized model is used to calculate the expected lifetime utility of a retiree who could purchase a nominal annuity, a real annuity, and a variable-payout equity-linked annuity. In the first and third cases, the retiree would bear some inflation risk. We calibrate this model using available estimates of risk aversion, mortality risks, and the stochastic structure of real returns on corporate stock. Our results suggest that, for plausible values of risk aversion, retirees would not pay very much for the opportunity to purchase a real rather than a nominal annuity. This finding is sensitive, however, to assumptions regarding the stochastic process for inflation. Very high expected inflation rates, or very high levels of inflation variability, can reverse this conclusion.

We also find that a variable-payout annuity with payouts linked to the returns on a portfolio of common stocks is more attractive than a real annuity for consumers with modest risk aversion. This result rests on assumptions about the expected return on stocks relative to riskless assets and hence must be viewed with some caution since there is substantial prospective uncertainty about expected stock returns. The finding nevertheless illustrates the potentially important role of variable-payout annuities as devices for annuitizing assets from individual accounts.

The chapter is divided into five sections. Section 1 presents our findings on the real and nominal annuity markets in the United Kingdom. Section 2 describes two "inflation-linked annuities" offered in the United States. Section 3 reports our findings on the correlation between unexpected inflation and real returns on various financial assets and summarizes previous research on this relation. This section also presents evidence on the ex post real payout streams that would have been paid to retirees had they purchased variable-payout annuities at different dates over the last seventy years. Section 4 outlines our algorithm for evaluating the utility benefits of access to various types of annuity products. We link this work with the rapidly growing literature on lifetime portfolio allocation in the presence of risky asset returns and uncertain inflation. In a brief concluding section, we sketch directions for future work.

1   The Market for Real Annuities in the United Kingdom

We begin our analysis by describing the real annuity market in the United Kingdom since it provides important evidence on both the feasibility of providing real annuities through private insurers and the consumer costs of buying inflation insurance. We then calculate the expected present discounted value of payouts on real and nominal annuities currently available in the United Kingdom.

1.1   The Current Structure of the U.K. Annuity Market

Annuities providing a constant real payout stream are widely available in the United Kingdom. This is partly due to the fact that government-issued indexed bonds have been available in the United Kingdom for nearly two decades. Insurance companies holding these bonds can largely hedge the price-level risk that is associated with offering annuity payouts denominated in real rather than in nominal terms. (Payouts on indexed bonds in the United Kingdom adjust to past inflation with a lag, which results in some residual price-level exposure for insurance companies offering real annuities.) Blake (1999) reports that insurers offering nominal annuities typically back them by holding nominal government bonds while those offering real annuities hold indexed bonds.

There are two segments of the individual annuity market in the United Kingdom, defined according to where funds used to purchase the annuity have been accumulated. One market segment involves annuities purchased with tax-qualified retirement funds; the other is focused on annuities purchased outside such plans. Qualified retirement plans in Britain include defined-benefit occupational pension schemes and personal pension plans (PPPs). Most occupational plans are defined-benefit plans, and the annuities that are paid out to their beneficiaries are not purchased in the individual annuity market. PPPs, available since 1988, are retirement-saving plans that are broadly similar to individual retirement accounts in the United States. (Prior to 1988, a similar type of plan was available only to self-employed individuals.) Contributions to PPPs are tax deductible, and income on the assets held in such plans is not taxed until the funds are withdrawn. Budd and Campbell (1998) report that, in the early 1990s, roughly one-quarter or U.K. workers participated in a personal pension plan. These plans are likely to account for most of the purchases of qualified annuities since defined-contribution plans constitute a minority of U.K. occupation pensions.

Those who reach retirement age with assets in a defined-contribution occupational pension, or with assets in a personal pension plan, are legally required to annuitize at least part of their pension accumulation. For this reason, the U.K. market for annuities purchased with funds from qualified pension plans is known as the *compulsory annuity market*. In recent years, there has been some relaxation of the rules requiring annuitization. Currently, a retiree can withdraw up to one-quarter of a personal pension plan accumulation as a lump-sum distribution, and assets can be held in the PPP up to age seventy-five before they must be annuitized.

The U.K. annuity market also includes a second segment, which contains voluntarily purchased annuities. This is known as the "noncompulsory" market. In this second market segment, funds accumulated outside qualified retirement plans are used to purchase annuity products.

The demographic characteristics and mortality prospects of annuity buyers in the compulsory and noncompulsory markets are likely to differ. The set of people who purchase annuities in the voluntary market is likely to have better mortality prospects (i.e., longer life expectancies) than the U.K. population at large. In addition, workers who have PPPs or who are covered by defined-contribution occupation plans are probably not a random subset of the population. They may also have better longevity prospects than those of the population at large. Finkelstein and Poterba (1999) compare the U.K. compulsory and noncompulsory annuity markets and show that payouts as a fraction of premiums are somewhat lower in the noncompulsory market than in the compulsory market. This finding is consistent with the view that adverse selection among annuitants receiving employer pensions is less substantial than adverse selection among people buying individual annuities outside a retirement plan. Our analysis focuses on annuities offered in the "compulsory-annuity" marketplace.

The compulsory annuitization requirement for personal pension plans has created a substantial group of retirement-age individuals in the United Kingdom who must purchase an annuity. To service their needs, annuity brokers exist to help retirees obtain quotes on annuity products. We contacted several of these brokers and requested data on U.K. annuity prices and the terms of annuity contracts. We obtained data from a number of firms. While we have not established precisely how much of the annuity market our sample firms cover, our sample of insurance companies appears to include most of the major annuity providers.

To focus the discussion, we restrict our attention to nominal and inflation-liked single-life annuity products. Here, the term *nominal* is used to refer to values denominated in current pounds (or dollars), while *real* refers to inflation-corrected pounds or dollars. We analyze products offered by nine insurance companies offering retail price index (RPI)-linked single-life annuity policies and fourteen companies offering nominal single-life products. (By comparison, there are nearly one hundred insurance companies offering individual annuity products in the United States, according to A. M. Best's surveys.) We do not consider "graded" nominal annuity policies that offer a rising stream of nominal benefits over the life of the annuitant, with a pre-specified nominal escalation rate. Graded annuities provide annuitants with a way of backloading the real value of payouts from their annuities, but they do not insure against inflation fluctuations as real annuities do. We focus our attention on policies that were available in late August 1998, and we consider annuities with a £100,000 purchase price (premium).

Table 5.1 reports mean monthly payouts for both nominal and RPI-linked annuities for the firms in our sample. The first two columns show the sample average payout for each type of annuity. They indicate that the first-month payout on a real annuity is between 25 and 30 per cent lower than the first-month payout on a nominal annuity. This reduction in initial benefits is sometimes cited as the reason why some consumers shy away from indexed annuities; later in the paper, we discuss a number of other potential explanations for consumer reluctance to purchase real annuities. The data also indicate differences in the ratio of nominal to real annuity payouts across age groups (real annuities are priced more favorably with rising age) and between men and women (real annuities are priced more favorably for men). These presumably reflect mortality-related differ-

Table 5.1
Summary statistics on nominal and real annuities available in the compulsory annuity market in the United Kingdom, 1998

Annuity buyer characteristics	Average monthly payout for a £100,000 annuity		Coefficient of variation for annuity prices	
	Nominal	Real	Nominal	Real
Man, 60 years old	666.20	476.35	4.26	6.09
Man, 65 years old	754.80	563.20	3.36	6.29
Man, 70 years old	872.94	679.50	2.88	6.31
Woman, 60 years old	602.99	416.81	5.34	5.02
Woman, 65 years old	666.88	482.70	4.27	4.49
Woman, 70 years old	760.50	575.06	3.65	4.48

Source: Authors' calculations based on data provided by U.K. annuity brokers. Reference date is 21 August 1998. Sample consists of fourteen large insurance companies that provide annuities. Data were provided by Annuity Direct, Ltd. All annuity products analyzed in this table offer a five-year guarantee period.

ences in the expected duration of payouts under different annuity contracts.

We also see substantial variation in the annuity benefits paid by the different insurers, as was previously found for the U.S. annuity market by Mitchell, Poterba, Warshawsky, and Brown (hereafter MPWB) (1999). The third and fourth columns of table 5.1 report the coefficient of variation for monthly annuity payouts in both markets; here, we see that the pricing of indexed annuities varies more than that of nominal annuities. For five of the six "products" defined by the age and gender of the buyer, the coefficient of variation is greater for the real than for the nominal annuity. This may be due to the fact that the effective duration of a real annuity is longer than that of a nominal annuity so that the insurer's cost of providing a real annuity is more sensitive to future developments in mortality patterns. Explaining the observed price dispersion in annuity markets is an important task for future research.

1.2   Evaluating the "Money's Worth" of Nominal and Real Annuities

To evaluate the administrative and other costs associated with the individual annuities offered in the U.K. market, we compute the expected present discounted value (EPDV) of payouts for the average nominal and the average index-linked annuity. We compare this EPDV with the premium cost of the annuity to obtain a measure of the "money's worth" of the individual annuity. Warshawsky (1988), Friedman and Warshawsky (1988, 1990), and MPWB (1999) report results of "money's worth" calculations for annuities offered in the United States.

The formula used to calculate the EPDV of a *nominal* annuity with a monthly payout A_n, purchased by an individual of age b, is

$$V_b(A_n) = \sum_{j=1}^{12 \cdot (115-b)} \frac{A_n \cdot P_j}{\prod_{k=1}^{j}(1+i_k)}. \tag{1}$$

We assume that no annuity buyer lives beyond age 115, and we truncate the annuity calculation after $12 \cdot (115 - b)$ months. P_j denotes the probability that an individual of age b years at the time of the annuity purchase survives for at least j months after buying the annuity. The variable i_k denotes the one-month nominal interest rate k months after the annuity purchase.

For a *real* annuity, equation (1) must be modified to recognize that the amount of the payout is time varying in nominal terms but fixed in real terms. The easiest way to handle this is to allow A_r to denote the real monthly payout and to replace the nominal interest rates in the denominator of (1) with corresponding real interest rates. We use r_k to denote the one-month real interest rate k months after the annuity purchase. Such real interest rates can be constructed from the U.K. yield curve for index-linked Treasury securities. The expression that we evaluate to compute the EPDV of a real annuity is

$$V_b(A_r) = \sum_{j=1}^{12 \cdot (115-b)} \frac{A_r \cdot P_j}{\prod_{k=1}^{j}(1+r_k)}. \tag{2}$$

We evaluate (1) and (2) using projected survival probabilities for the U.K. population as a whole. These mortality probabilities are compiled by H. M. Treasury. We use cohort mortality tables for those who reached age sixty, sixty-five, or seventy in 1998. We were not able to obtain mortality tables corresponding to the annuitant population. By using population mortality tables, we are in effect asking what the EPDV of the average annuity would be when viewed from the perspective of an average individual in the population. Of course, the average annuity buyer has a longer life expectancy than the average person in the population. Since a real annuity offers larger payouts near the end of life than a nominal annuity does, using a population rather than an annuitant mortality table overstates the effective cost of purchasing an inflation-indexed annuity relative to a nominal annuity.

Table 5.2 reports EPDV calculations for single-life annuities for men and women of different ages in the compulsory U.K. annuity market. Results for the average annuity payout are given as a simple average across the firms in our sample. We also provide the EPDV using average payouts for the three highest and three lowest annuity payout firms in our sample. The results show that the cost of buying an inflation-protected annuity in the United Kingdom is about 5 per cent of the annuity premium. In addition, we find that the EPDV of a nominal annuity contract purchased in conjunction with a qualified retirement-saving plan is 5 per cent higher than that for a real annuity. While the EPDV for nominal annuities is approximately 90 per cent of the premium cost, the analogous EPDV for real annuities is about 85 per cent. This difference in EPDVs might explain Diamond's (1997) claim that most annuitants in the United Kingdom elect nominal rather than real annuities.

Some of the apparent "cost" of inflation protection may arise from adverse selection across various types of annuities. If annuitants who anticipate that they will live much longer than the average annuitant tend to purchase real annuities because their real payout stream is backloaded, then mortality rates for those who buy real annuities may be lower than those for nominal annuity buyers. We do not know

Table 5.2
Expected present discounted value of annuity payouts for nominal and real annuities available in the compulsory annuity market, United Kingdom, August 1998

Characteristics of annuitant	Nominal annuity			Inflation-indexed annuity		
	Average payout	Highest three	Lowest three	Average payout	Highest three	Lowest three
Male, 60 years old	.921	.953	.873	.867	.916	.808
Male, 65 years old	.908	.936	.868	.854	.898	.797
Male, 70 years old	.889	.917	.853	.836	.881	.783
Female, 60 years old	.928	.966	.861	.876	.924	.832
Female, 65 years old	.907	.942	.857	.857	.892	.812
Female, 70 years old	.886	.920	.841	.836	.869	.790

Source: Authors' calculations as described in the text. Sample consists of fourteen companies with data provided by Annuity Direct, Ltd. See source note to table 5.1 above.

whether such mortality differences actually explain the payout differences between nominal and real annuities.

Our estimates of the EPDV of nominal annuity payouts in the United Kingdom are somewhat higher than analogous estimates for nominal annuity products in the United States at roughly the same date. For example, Poterba and Warshawsky (2000) report that the average EPDV on U.S. nominal annuity contracts available to sixty-five-year-old men in 1998 (using the population mortality table) was 84 per cent for annuities purchased through qualified retirement-saving plans. The lower U.S. payout may reflect differences in the degree of mortality selection, relative to the population as a whole, in the "qualified" (U.S.) and "compulsory" (U.K.) annuity markets.

Table 5.2 also suggests that there are systematic patterns in the money's-worth values across age groups for both nominal and real annuities in the U.K. market. The EPDV declines as a function of the annuitant's age at the time the annuity is purchased. One possible explanation for this pattern may be that those who retire later tend to have lower mortality rates than those who retire earlier. Age at retirement and age at annuity purchase may be linked more closely in the compulsory annuity market than in the noncompulsory market. We suspect that many compulsory annuity buyers purchase their annuities when they retire, even though current U.K. rules do not require such purchases.

The results shown in table 5.2 indicate that, for a retiree of given age/sex characteristics, there is frequently a 10 per cent difference between the average annuity payout from the firms offering the highest payout annuities and those offering the lowest payouts. Such dispersion is consistent with earlier evidence, such as MPWB (1999), suggesting substantial pricing differences in the U.S. market for nominal annuities. This price dispersion raises the question of how potential annuitants choose among the various annuity products. In the U.S. case, MPWB (1999) report little correlation between factors such as the credit rating of the insurance company offering the annuity and the level of the annuity's payout.

In sum, we draw two lessons from the widespread availability of index-linked annuities in the U.K. annuity market. The first is that it is possible for private insurers to develop and offer real annuity products. This is surely easier in a nation with a well-developed market for index-linked bonds. The second lesson is that, on the basis of the current prices of nominal and real annuities, the costs of obtaining inflation insurance are less than 5 per cent of the purchase price of a nominal annuity contract.

2   Real Annuities in the United States: TIAA-CREF and ILONA

The U.S. individual annuity market differs from that in the United Kingdom in that virtually all annuity products are nominal annuities. Individuals can purchase a variety of products with a graded payout structure so that the nominal value of their payouts (and, for low-enough inflation rates, the real value of payouts) is expected to rise over time. Only two annuity products of which we are aware promise some degree of inflation protection. The first is the "Freedom" CPI-indexed income annuity, offered by the Irish Life Company of North America (ILONA), and the second is the inflation-linked bond account annuity, offered by TIAA-CREF. In this section, we describe how these products work, their current prices and payouts, and the degree to which they provide inflation protection for annuity buyers. We also note that, since Treasury inflation-protection securities (TIPS) were introduced to the U.S. market only recently, additional insurers may offer real annuities as familiarity with these new assets grows. Insurance companies can hedge the inflation risk associated with these price-level-indexed annuity products by purchasing TIPS bonds.

2.1   The ILONA Real Annuity

Irish Life PLC, an international insurance firm headquartered in Dublin, offers index-linked annuities in the United States through the Interstate Assurance Company, which is a division of Irish Life of North America. Interstate is a well-regarded company: it had assets of $1.3 billion, and it received a AA rating from Duff and Phelps, an A rating from A. M. Best, and a AA– rating from Standard and Poor's in 1996. The indexed-annuity product from ILONA is the "Freedom CPI-Indexed Income Annuity." The annuity payout rises annually in step with the increase in the prior year's CPI. Annuity benefits from the Freedom CPI-indexed income annuity cannot decline in nominal terms, even if the CPI were to fall from year to year. The minimum purchase requirement for the ILONA annuity product is $10,000, and the maximum purchase is $1 million. The annuity is available to individuals between the ages of sixty-five and eighty-five. There are various payout options, including simple-life annuities, annuities that provide a fixed numbers of years of payouts for certain, and "refund annuities." These annuity products are available both as individual and as joint-and-survivor annuities. Although ILONA offers this real annuity product in the United States, the agent we contacted indicated that thus far no sales of these annuities have been recorded.

Data were obtained on the monthly payouts offered by ILONA's indexed and nominal single-premium immediate annuities for men and women aged sixty-five, seventy, and seventy-five, assuming a premium of $1 million in each case. We also obtained data on joint-and-survivor annuities with 100 per cent survivor benefits. Policies purchased in mid-1998 offered a monthly payout on a real annuity at the start of the annuity contract about 30 per cent smaller than the payout on a nominal annuity issued to the same individual. Table 5.3 shows that, for men at age sixty-five, the ratio of real to nominal payouts is 69 per cent. For women at sixty-five, the ratio is 66 per cent, potentially reflecting the longer life expectancy and therefore greater backloading that occurs with a real rather than a nominal annuity for women rather than for men.

To determine the payouts relative to premium cost for these annuities, we calculate the EPDV of annuity payouts for each of the ILONA policies quoted using a procedure similar to that described above. Interest and mortality rates differ somewhat relative to the U.K. calculations. For discount factors in our EPDV calculations, we use the nominal yield curve for zero-coupon U.S. Treasury bonds. We start from the term structure of yields for zero-coupon Treasury "strips" and

Table 5.3
Monthly annuity payouts on single-premium annuity products offered by ILONA in the U.S. market, 1998

Annuitant age and product	Male, single-life annuity ($)	Female, single-life annuity ($)	Joint-and-survivor annuity with full survivor benefits ($)
Age 65, unindexed	7,452	6,720	6,068
Age 65, indexed	5,149	4,432	3,849
Age 70, unindexed	8,520	7,543	6,663
Age 70, indexed	6,262	5,332	4,549
Age 75, unindexed	10,075	8,825	7,594
Age 75, indexed	7,833	6,643	5,552

Note: All payouts correspond to an initial purchase of $1 million. Data were provided by Irish Life of North America (ILONA). For further details, see the text.

work out the pattern of monthly interest rates implied by these yields under the simple-expectations theory of the term structure. Data on the zero-coupon yield curve are published in the *Wall Street Journal*, and we use information from the beginning of June 1998. Because we do not know the precise date at which ILONA offered the annuities that we are pricing, and in the light of the absence of transactions in this annuity market, we select the term structure for the first week of June 1998 as an approximate guide to discount rates in mid-1998. When evaluating the EPDV of the ILONA real annuity, we use the implied short-term real interest rates that can be derived from the term structure of real interest rates on TIPS in early June 1998.

With regard to survival patterns, we have access to two distinct mortality tables for the United States. The first, developed by the Social Security Administration's Office of the Actuary and reported in Bell, Wade, and Goss (1992), applies to the entire population. We update this mortality table to reflect the prospective mortality rates of a sixty-five-year-old (or seventy- or seventy-five-year-old) purchasing an annuity in 1998. For example, in estimating the money's worth of an annuity for a sixty-five-year-old in 1998, we use the projected mortality experience of the 1933 birth cohort. A second set of projected mortality rates corresponds to that relevant to current annuitants. MPWB (1999) develop an algorithm that combines information from the annuity 2000 mortality table (described in Johansen [1996]), the older 1983 individual annuitant mortality table, and the projected rate of mortality improvement implicit in the difference between the Social Security Administration's cohort and period mortality tables for the population. This algorithm generates projected mortality rates for the set of annuitants purchasing annuity contracts in a given year. It is worth noting that the population and annuitant mortality rates differ. For instance, MPWB (1999) report that the 1995 annual mortality rate for annuitants aged sixty-five to seventy-five was roughly half that for the general population. This mortality differential generates a substantially larger EPDV of annuity payouts with the annuitant rather than the population mortality table.

Table 5.4 reports EPDV calculations for Irish Life real and nominal annuities. (All EPDV calculations use pretax annuity payouts and before-tax interest rates. MPWB [1999] show that pretax and posttax EPDV calculations for U.S. nominal annuities yield similar results.) For nominal annuities valued using the population mortality table, the EPDV of payouts is approximately eighty-five cents per premium

Table 5.4
Expected present discounted value of annuity payouts, freedom inflation-indexed annuities offered by ILONA, 1998

	Male annuitant, Age 65	Male annuitant, Age 75	Female annuitant, Age 65	Female annuitant, Age 75
Calculations using population mortality table				
Nominal annuity	.864	.830	.889	.887
Real annuity	.702	.720	.708	.762
Calculations using annuitant mortality table				
Nominal annuity	.987	.984	.966	.967
Real annuity	.822	.872	.782	.841

Note: Each entry shows the expected present discounted value of annuity payouts using the algorithm described in the text. See note to table 5.3 above.

dollar for men and eighty-nine cents for women. These values are slightly higher than the average EPDV values based on nominal annuities described in A. M. Best's annuity survey of June 1998, as reported in Poterba and Warshawsky (2000). Using the annuitant mortality table for nominal annuities, the EPDV is larger: approximately ninety-eight cents per premium dollar for men and ninety-seven cents for women.

We next turn to EPDV results for the ILONA real annuity, and we see that the value per dollar of premium is much lower than for the nominal annuity. For instance, a sixty-five-year-old man purchasing a real annuity would expect an EPDV of 70 per cent, versus 86 per cent for the nominal annuity. At other ages, a similar pattern applies: the money's worth for real annuity products is typically 15–20 per cent lower than that for nominal annuities. The fact that inflation protection adds more than 15 per cent to the annuity's cost may explain the limited demand for this product in the United States.

2.2 Annuities Linked to the CREF Index-Linked Bond Account (ILBA)

In May 1997, the College Equities Retirement Fund (CREF) launched a new investment account that was intended to appeal to those who are saving for retirement as well as to retirees receiving annuity payouts. This product, called the CREF Inflation-Linked Bond Account (ILBA), followed from the federal government's decision to issue TIPS on 29

January 1997. TIAA-CREF (1997a) indicated that its new inflation-linked account was expected to be useful for providing participants with "another investment option that can enhance portfolio diversification and mitigate the long-term impact of inflation on their retirement accumulations and benefits." The fund's goal was described, in TIAA-CREF (1997b), as seeking "a long-term rate of return that outpaces inflation, through a portfolio of inflation-indexed bonds and other securities."

The CREF inflation-linked bond account has grown slowly since its inception. At the end of September 1998, the account had attracted investments of only $131 million, making it the smallest of all the retirement funds offered by TIAA-CREF. To place this amount in context, on the same date the CREF stock fund held $96.9 billion, the TIAA traditional annuity fund held $94.3 billion, and all other TIAA-CREF retirement funds combined held about $25 billion. Most of the funds held in the ILBA are in the accounts of TIAA-CREF active participants rather than retirees, and as such they are still accumulating rather than drawing down assets.

To describe the inflation protection that an annuity linked to the CREF ILBA provides, we need to provide some background on the structure of this account, on the basic structure of variable-annuity products, and on the specific operation of the CREF variable annuity.

The CREF Index-Linked Bond Account

TIAA-CREF (1998b) explains that the ILBA "invests mainly in inflation-indexed bonds issued or guaranteed by the U.S. government, or its agencies and instrumentalities, and in other inflation-indexed securities" with foreign securities capped at 25 per cent of the assets. At present, the ILBA holds 98 per cent of its assets in U.S. government inflation-linked securities and 2 per cent in short-term investments maturing in less than one year. In principle, the fund's asset allocation could become broader in the future, with corporate inflation-indexed securities and those issued by foreign governments potentially being included as well as money market instruments. Expenses total thirty-one basis points annually. This expense ratio is lower than many mutual and pension fund expense levels, but it is as high as other, more actively managed CREF accounts such as the stock account (thirty-one basis points) and the bond market account (twenty-nine basis points) (see www.tiaa-cref.org).

The ILBA has no sales, surrender, or premium charges. Participants may elect this account as one of several investment vehicles into which new retirement contributions may be made and/or into which existing assets from other TIAA-CREF accounts may be transferred. As with other CREF accounts, the participant is limited to one transfer per business day in or out of the account during the accumulation phase. The ILBA may be used as a vehicle for accumulating retirement assets, or it can be used to back the payment stream for a variable-payout annuity. Most of our interest focuses on the second function.

The ILBA account is marked to market daily, meaning that asset values fluctuate and the account could lose money. For example, if real interest rates rose owing to a decline in expected inflation, bond prices could fall. As the fund prospectus (TIAA-CREF 1998a) points out, in such an event, the inflation-linked bond fund's total return would then not actually track inflation every year. This is a key feature of the ILBA, and it means that the account *does not* effectively offer a real payout stream to annuitants who purchase variable-payout annuities tied to the ILBA.

Real interest rate changes are not the only source of variation in ILBA returns. If the principal value of inflation-linked bonds changes in response to inflation shocks, perhaps because investors infer something about the future of real interest rates from inflation news, this would also affect the returns on the ILBA. Similarly, changes in the definition of the CPI might affect the ILBA return. Both these issues also arise with respect to direct investments in Treasury inflation-protection securities (TIPS). The ILBA return for 1998 was 3.48 per cent. Table 5.5 illustrates

Table 5.5
Total return, 1 January 1998–31 December 1998, by TIAA-CREF account (%)

CREF accounts		TIAA accounts	
Inflation-linked bond account	3.48	Traditional annuity	6.71
Growth account	32.89	Real estate account	8.07
Stock account	22.94	Personal annuity stock index account	23.84
Equity index account	24.12		
Social choice account	18.61		
Global equities account	18.58		
Bond market	8.60		
Money market	5.45		

Source: www.tiaa-cref.org, various pages.

that this made it the lowest-earning fund of all the tax-qualified accounts offered by TIAA-CREF in 1998.

Variable Annuities: General Structure

An annuity with payouts that rise and fall with the value of the CREF ILBA is a special case of a variable-payout annuity. The key distinction between a fixed annuity (including a graded fixed annuity with a pre-specified set of changing nominal payouts over time) and a variable annuity is that the payouts on a variable annuity cannot be specified *for certain* at the beginning of the payout period. Rather, a variable annuity is defined by an initial payout amount, which we denote $A(0)$, and an "updating rule" that relates the annuity payout in future periods to the previous payout and the intervening returns on the portfolio that backs the variable annuity.

To determine the initial nominal payout on a single-life variable annuity per dollar of annuity purchase, the insurance company solves an equation like

$$1 = \sum_{j=1}^{T} \frac{A(0) \cdot P_j}{(1+R)^j},$$ (3)

where R is the variable annuity's "assumed interest rate" (AIR) or the "annuity valuation rate" as in Bodie and Pesando (1983). T is the maximum potential life span of the annuitant. This expression would require modification if the annuity guaranteed a fixed number of payments for certain, regardless of the annuitant's longevity, or if there were other specialized features in the annuity contract. This expression ignores expenses and other administrative costs associated with the sales of annuities or the operation of insurance companies.

The annuity-updating rule depends on the return on the assets that back the annuity, which we denote by z_t, according to

$$A(t+1) = A(t) \cdot (1+z_t)/(1+R).$$ (4)

The frequency with which payouts are updated varies across annuity products, and there is no requirement that the payout be updated every time it is paid. One could, for example, have an annuity with monthly payouts but quarterly updating.

In designing a variable annuity, the assumed interest rate (R) is a key parameter. Assuming a high value of R will enable the insurance company to offer a large initial premium, but, for any underlying portfolio, the stream of future payouts will be more likely to decline as the assumed value of R rises. Equation (4) clearly indicates that an individual who purchases a variable annuity will receive payouts that fluctuate with the nominal value of the underlying portfolio.

Specific Provisions of the CREF ILBA-Backed Annuity
When a TIAA-CREF participant terminates employment, he or she can begin receiving retirement benefits. The participant then decides how to manage the payouts from accumulated retirement accounts. This includes deciding whether to annuitize the retirement assets, how much to annuitize, and whether to use an inflation-linked annuity. (Some employers may restrict their retirees' options.) Benefits are payable monthly, although recipients may elect quarterly, semiannual, and annual payouts as an alternative (TIAA-CREF [1998d] provides more detail on these options). In addition, the participant can choose the form and duration of the payout pattern, subject to minimum-distribution rules set by the IRS. If the participant chooses to annuitize part of his or her accumulation, there are a variety of potential annuity structures, including life annuities, ten- and twenty-year certain-payout annuities, and joint-and-survivor as well as single-life products.

Under TIAA-CREF rules, a CREF participant electing an annuity cannot be more than ninety years of age when he or she initially applies for the annuity. TIAA-CREF (1998b) explains that the applicant must select at least one of the annuity accounts initially for the drawdown phase; thereafter, he or she may switch from one annuity account to another as often as once per quarter. There are restrictions on shifting funds from TIAA to CREF: this must take place over a longer horizon. The choice of annuity fund can be altered, but the form of benefit payout cannot be changed once the annuity has been issued.

In order to understand how CREF annuity payments are determined, it is necessary to define the *basic* annuity unit value. This is an amount set each 31 March by dividing an account's total funds in payment status by the actuarial present value of the future annuity benefits to be paid out, assuming a 4 per cent nominal interest rate and mortality patterns characteristic of existing CREF annuitants. A unisex version of the mortality table for individual annuitants is used when the applicant first files for an annuity "set back for each complete year elapsed since 1986" (see TIAA-CREF 1998d). The same mortality table is applied to all TIAA-CREF annuity accounts, on the basis of participant mortality experience. Mortality experience is adjusted every quarter.

A newly retired participant seeking to annuitize his retirement sum must have his own accumulation amount translated into an *initial annuity amount* (*A*(0)), determined by dividing his accumulation by the product of an annuity factor and the basic annuity unit value just described. The annuity factor reflects assumed survival probabilities based on the annuitant's age and an effective annual assumed interest rate (AIR) of 4 per cent nominal, explained in TIAA-CREF (1998c).

The participant's initial annuity amount is then adjusted over the life of the annuity contract on either a monthly or an annual basis, depending on the participant's election. The adjustment will reflect the actual fund earnings on a "total return" basis, relative to the 4 per cent AIR. Actual investment performance is used to update the annuity values as of 1 May for those electing to have their income change annually or monthly for those electing monthly income changes. Because the investment returns on the underlying accounts affect annuity payouts, these TIAA-CREF annuities are variable-payout annuities.

The Extent of Inflation Protection
It is evident that a variable-payout annuity linked to the CREF ILBA does not provide a guaranteed stream of real payouts since it is marked to market daily. Thus, if the price drops, or if the unit value fails to rise with inflation, the participant's unit value would not be constant in real terms. More important, the CREF annuity may fail to keep up with inflation because of the way in which it is designed. When the first-year annuity payout is set, it assumes the 4 per cent AIR mentioned above, which is the same rate used for other CREF annuities. In subsequent years, if the unit value of the account were to rise less than 4 per cent, payouts would be reduced to reflect this lower valuation. Consider the experience of 1998, when the total return (after expenses) on the ILBA account was 3.48 per cent. Since the AIR for the CREF annuity is 4 per cent, an annuity in its second- or later-year payout phase would experience a decline in payout of 0.52 per cent. Since the price level rose in 1998, it is clear that the annuity payouts are not constant in real terms. A necessary condition for the payouts on this variable annuity not to decline in real terms would be for the real return on the account, that is, on Treasury inflation-protection securities, to exceed 4 per cent. At present, it does not.

The precise extent to which payouts on ILBA-backed variable annuities will vary in real terms in the future is an open question. If the prices of inflation-linked bonds are bid up during high-inflation periods and real interest rates decline at such times, this will partly protect the ILBA account value. One relevant comparison for potential annuitants, however, may be between holding a CREF ILBA-backed variable annuity and purchasing TIPS bonds directly. Two considerations are relevant to such a comparison. First, the TIPS bonds offer a more direct form of inflation protection, although they do not provide any risk sharing with respect to mortality risk. Second, there are tax differences between the two investment strategies. TIPS would be taxable if they were not held in a qualified pension account, while the income from bonds held in the CREF ILBA-backed account is not taxed until the proceeds are withdrawn.

The CREF variable-payout annuity linked to the ILBA would be more likely to deliver a future real payout stream if the AIR on this annuity were set equal to the real interest rate on long-term TIPS at the time when the annuity is purchased. In this case, the return on the bond portfolio would typically equal the AIR plus the annual inflation rate, leaving aside some of the risks of holding indexed bonds, such as changes in the way the CPI is constructed. This would provide a mechanism for delivering something closer to a real annuity payout stream. One difficulty with this approach is that it would make it more difficult for annuitants to take advantage of some of the investment flexibility currently provided by CREF. At present, all CREF annuities assume the same AIR, regardless of the assets that back them. This facilitates conversions from one annuity type to another.

To date, there has been very limited demand for CREF's ILBA-backed variable-payout annuities. This lack of demand raises the perennial question of why retirees are not more concerned about inflation protection. One reason often given is "inflation illusion"; that is, people simply do not understand how inflation erodes purchasing power. Another reason may be that inflation-proof assets are new and that investors have not yet learned how to think about such assets. Hammond (personal communication to O. Mitchell, 10 November 1998) notes that inflation-linked bonds in other countries took some time to become popular after they were introduced: "After a flurry of initial interest, inflation bonds in those countries went through a period of quiescence—low liquidity and little interest. Then, with some sort of trigger—renewed inflation or a strong commitment on the part of central government—the market picked up and people began to figure out what the bonds were good for. In the U.K. this process took about ten years." (cf. Hammond 1999.) The United States today may be in the early stages of this process.

2.3 Conclusions about Real Annuities in the United States

Our analysis of the ILONA and TIAA-CREF experience suggests that there is currently no market for genuine real annuities in the United States. While ILONA offers a product that guarantees a real stream of payouts, no one has yet purchased this annuity. This may reflect the fact that the instrument's pricing requires relatively high rates of inflation to generate benefits with EPDVs similar to those of nominal annuities offered by ILONA and other insurers. The inflation-linked bond account offered by CREF has attracted investment funds since it became available in 1997, but the CREF variable annuity with payouts linked to returns on inflation-indexed bonds does not guarantee its buyers a constant real payout stream. Although in practice it may come close to delivering a constant real payout, its performance will depend on the as yet uncertain movements in the prices of Treasury inflation-protection securities (TIPS).

3 Asset Returns and Inflation: Another Route to Inflation Insurance

We now shift from our focus on insurance contracts that explicitly provide a constant real income stream for retirees, to consider the possibility of using variable-payout annuities linked to assets other than indexed bonds as an alternative means of avoiding inflation risk. Such variable-payout annuities may reduce the effect of inflation in two ways. First, they may offer higher average returns than the assets that are used in pricing real and nominal annuities. These returns may, of course, come at the price of greater payout variability. Second, the prices of the assets that underline the variable-payout annuities may move in tandem with the price level. In this case, a variable-payout annuity could provide a form of inflation insurance.

To examine these arguments, we begin by summarizing the well-known historical real-return performance of U.S. stocks, bonds, and Treasury-bill investments. We consider an individual who invests $1 in cash or in a portfolio of Treasury bills, long-term bonds, or corporate stock. We calculate the real value of an initial $1 investment after five, ten, twenty, and thirty years. We first perform this calculation in 1926 so that the thirty-year-return interval concludes in 1955. We then repeat the calculation in 1927, 1928, and all subsequent years for which we have enough data to calculate long-term returns. The last year for which we have return information is 1997, so we finish our five-year calculations in 1993, our ten-year calculations in 1988, and so on.

To summarize the results on the real value of each investment, we calculate both the average real value of each investment, averaged across all the years with sufficient data, and the standard deviation of this real return. The results of these calculations appear in table 5.6. The underlying calculations have been done using actual returns on stocks, bills, and bonds over the period 1926–97. For the return after five (thirty) years, there are sixty-six (forty-one) overlapping return intervals. The results presented in table 5.6 show that holding cash worth $1 initially would have a real value of only forty-nine cents after twenty years on average. In contrast, a $1 initial investment in bills or bonds would have increased in real value. For bills, the cumulative real return over twenty years was 1.3 per cent, while for bonds it was 16.1 per cent.

The last column of table 5.6 shows comparable calculations for corporate stock. Here, the real value of the investment after twenty years would have increased by a factor of 4.5. This implies that an investor who purchased an income stream tied to the total return on the U.S.

Table 5.6
Real value of a one-dollar investment after various periods, 1926–97 average

		Investment portfolio		
Value after N years	Cash (no investment return)	Treasury bills	Treasury bonds	Corporate stock
5 years	0.864	1.036	1.128	1.477
	(0.150)	(0.163)	(0.315)	(0.517)
10 years	0.729	1.047	1.233	2.214
	(0.205)	(0.245)	(0.561)	(1.071)
20 years	0.490	1.013	1.161	4.569
	(0.160)	(0.285)	(0.560)	(2.941)
30 years	0.356	1.033	1.112	8.679
	(0.129)	(0.324)	(0.478)	(4.728)

Note: Each entry shows the mean value of a one-dollar initial investment, in real terms, and the standard error (in parentheses) of this value. Calculations are based on authors' computations using actual realizations of inflation, bill, bond, and stock returns over the period 1926–97, as reported in Ibbotson Associates (1998).

stock market, such as an equity-linked variable annuity, would have the potential to receive a real income stream that is higher late in retirement than at the beginning of retirement. This stands in stark contrast to the declining real value of the payouts on a fixed nominal annuity contract.

The substantial real return on U.S. equities suggests that one method of obtaining partial long-term protection against inflationary erosion of annuity payouts might be to purchase a portfolio of equities and then to link annuity payouts to equity returns. Such a strategy exposes the annuitant to the substantial intrinsic volatility of the equity market and does not guarantee a fixed real return. The higher average return on equities than on bonds nevertheless reduces the probability of a declining real payout stream from the annuity policy.

In practice, however, variable-annuity policies that offer payouts linked to equity returns do not guarantee real payouts that rise as steeply as table 5.6 suggests. This is because the payouts on a variable annuity depend on the performance of the underlying assets relative to the annuity product's assumed interest rate (AIR) (R in eq. [3]). Therefore, the variable-annuity payout for an equity-linked variable annuity can rise over time only if the equity portfolio returns more than the assumed value of R used in designing the annuity. Bodie and Pesando (1983) assume that R equals the historical average return on the assets that back the annuity in their hypothetical evaluation of variable-payout annuities. In practice, we have found that nominal R values of 3 or 4 per cent per year are common, even for equity-linked variable-payout annuities, in the current annuity market. One should note that, if a variable-payout annuity assumed $R = 0$, then the real payouts in table 5.6 would in fact describe the experience of an annuitant since the nominal payout recursion would become $A(t + 1) = A(t) \cdot (1 + z_t)$.

The high average real return on equities implies that an investor holding U.S. stocks over the last seven decades would have experienced a rising real-wealth profile. But to study whether this is because equities provide a good inflation hedge, we must explore the way U.S. equity returns covary with shocks to the inflation rate. If stocks generate positive returns when the inflation rate rises unexpectedly, then equities operate as an inflation hedge. The fact that U.S. equities have generated substantial positive returns over the period since 1926 does not provide any information on the correlation between inflation and stock returns.

We investigate the historical covariances between real U.S. stock returns, bond returns, bill returns, and unexpected inflation shocks over two sample periods: 1926–97 and 1947–97. If the real return on a particular asset category is not affected by unexpected inflation, then that asset can serve as a valuable inflation hedge. If the real return on the asset declines when inflation rises unexpectedly, however, then that asset does not provide an inflation hedge.

The first step in our analysis involves estimating a time series process for "unexpected inflation." We do this by estimating fourth-order autoregressive models relating annual inflation (π_t) to its own lagged values or to its own lagged values as well as those of nominal Treasury-bill rates (i_t). The basic regression specification is either

$$\pi_t = \rho_0 + \rho_1 \cdot \pi_{t-1} + \rho_2 \cdot \pi_{t-2} + \rho_3 \cdot \pi_{t-3} + \rho_4 \cdot \pi_{t-4}$$
$$+ \phi_1 \cdot i_{t-1} + \phi_2 \cdot i_{t-2} + \phi_3 \cdot i_{t-3} + \phi_4 \cdot i_{t-4} + \varepsilon_{it} \tag{5a}$$

or

$$\pi_t = \rho_0 + \rho_1 \cdot \pi_{t-1} + \rho_2 \cdot \pi_{t-2} + \rho_3 \cdot \pi_{t-3} + \rho_4 \cdot \pi_{t-4} + \varepsilon_{it}. \tag{5b}$$

Table 5.7 presents the findings from estimating (5a) and (5b) for the two sample periods. Two broad conclusions emerge from the table. First, there is a great deal of persistence in inflation. The sum of the four coefficients on lagged inflation for the period 1926–97 is .773, while for the period 1947–97 it is .732. There is somewhat greater inflation persistence in the early years of the sample than in the postwar period. We experimented with extending the length of the lag polynomials in (5a) and (5b). While the fourth-order inflation lag in both equations shows a coefficient that is statistically significantly different from zero, higher lagged values were never statistically significant.

Second, the incremental explanatory power of lagged Treasury-bill yields is relatively small after we have controlled for lagged inflation. Bill rates have somewhat greater explanatory power in the postwar period than in the full sample period. Because most of the estimated coefficients on bill rates for both sample periods are statistically insignificant, however, the unexpected inflation series calculated from specifications (5a) and (5b) are likely to yield similar estimates of the correlation between unexpected inflation and asset returns.

We estimate unexpected inflation ($\pi_{u,t}$) by computing the residuals from either (5a) or (5b). These unexpected inflation series incorporate some future information in each case because the coefficients are

Table 5.7
Estimates of the inflation process for the United States, 1930–97

Explanatory variable	Lagged inflation only, 1930–97	Lagged inflation and bills, 1930–97	Lagged inflation only, 1947–97	Lagged inflation and bills, 1947–97
Constant	.008	.010	.009	.005
	(.005)	(.006)	(.006)	(.006)
Inflation ($t - 1$)	.706	.666	.647	.566
	(.113)	(.124)	(.100)	(.106)
Inflation ($t - 2$)	−.146	−.086	−.161	−.127
	(.142)	(.148)	(.119)	(.120)
Inflation ($t - 3$)	−.223	−.208	−.056	−.066
	(.142)	(.146)	(.118)	(.119)
Inflation ($t - 4$)	.436	.447	.302	.280
	(.112)	(.119)	(.099)	(.103)
Bill yield ($t - 1$)		.370		.549
		(.340)		(.241)
Bill yield ($t - 2$)		−.694		−.677
		(.470)		(.328)
Bill yield ($t - 3$)		−.129		.218
		(.483)		(.338)
Bill yield ($t - 4$)		.108		.053
		(.338)		(.234)
Adjusted R^2	.507	.500	.544	.571

Source: Authors' calculations using data from Ibbotson Associates (1998).

estimated over the full sample period. We then use these time series as the explanatory variables in regression models in which real stock, bond, or bill returns are the dependent variables:

$$R_{it} = \alpha + \lambda_i \cdot \pi_{u,t} + \varepsilon_{it}. \tag{6}$$

Table 5.8 shows the coefficient estimates for λ_i from regression models estimated for the two sample periods.

The results provide no evidence to suggest that stocks or bonds have been inflation hedges during the last seventy years. For both these asset categories, a 1 percentage point increase in the rate of unexpected inflation is associated with a decline of more than 1 per cent in bond and in stock values. The estimated negative effects are larger, although somewhat less precisely estimated, for the period 1947–97 than for the longer sample. As noted above, the two unexpected inflation series, one corresponding to a lagged-inflation-only predicting equation, the other

Table 5.8
Unexpected inflation and real asset returns, United States, 1926–97

Inflation process	1930–97 sample			1947–97 sample		
	Bills	Bonds	Stocks	Bills	Bonds	Stocks
Bills and inflation	−0.827	−1.702	−1.582	−0.580	−3.442	−4.326
	(0.137)	(0.389)	(0.804)	(0.174)	(0.650)	(1.077)
Inflation only	−0.864	−1.672	−1.560	−0.387	−2.515	−4.271
	(0.128)	(0.378)	(0.783)	(0.170)	(0.664)	(0.975)
5-year nonoverlapping	0.191	−1.522	−1.969			
returns, inflation only	(0.437)	(0.657)	(0.670)			

Note: Each entry corresponds to the coefficient λ_i in the regression equation

$$R_{it} = \alpha + \lambda_i \cdot \pi_{u,t} + \varepsilon_{it},$$

where R_{it} denotes the real return on asset i in period t, and $\pi_{u,t}$ denotes the unexpected inflation rate. Estimates are based on authors' analysis of data in Ibbotson Associates (1998), as described in the text.

corresponding to the augmented specification with lagged Treasury-bill returns as well, produce very similar results when they are included on the right-hand side of equation (6).

We also find evidence that unexpected inflation reduces real Treasury-bill returns. The effect on these returns is more muted than that on bond and stock returns, and, for both sample periods, we find that a 1 percentage point increase in unexpected inflation reduces the real return on Treasury bills by less than 1 percentage point. Nevertheless, for both sample periods, we reject the null hypothesis that real Treasury-bill returns are unaffected by inflation surprises.

The finding that unexpected inflation is negatively correlated with real asset returns is broadly consistent with previous research. For example, Barr and Campbell (1996) show that the real interest rate on U.K. indexed bonds appears to covary negatively with inflation. Evans (1998) surveys a number of other empirical papers, using data from several nations and various methodologies, all of which reach similar conclusions. Our findings for equities are consistent with Bodie (1976), who suggested that using equities to hedge inflation risk requires a short position in equities.

One question that some might raise about the results presented in table 5.8 concerns the focus on one-year return horizons. It is possible that the high-frequency correlation between unexpected inflation and asset returns differs from the lower-frequency correlation. Boudoukh and Richardson (1993) present some evidence for both the United States and the United Kingdom suggesting that the nominal return on corporate equities moves together with inflation at long horizons. To explore this issue, we repeated our analysis using real returns and unexpected inflation over five-year intervals. We confined our analysis to the sample period 1926–97 and used an AR(2) model to construct an estimate of unexpected inflation. We focused on nonoverlapping five-year intervals, which provided twelve observations for estimating equation (6). The last row of table 5.8 presents the results. They continue to show a negative correlation between real stock and bond returns and unexpected inflation. The only change relative to the previous findings is that unexpected inflation no longer has a negative effect on real Treasury-bill returns.

Our empirical results therefore suggest that the inflation-hedging properties of equities and long-term bonds are limited. Nevertheless, as Siegel (1998) and others have noted, over long horizons, equities have typically generated very substantial positive real returns. This appears to be the result of a high average real return on equities rather than a positive correlation between equity returns and unexpected inflation. A substantial body of research has tried to explain the high average return on equities in the United States during the last century as a function of the correlation between equity returns and various risk factors. This has proved difficult and has become known as the "equity-premium puzzle."

The weak high-frequency correlation between equity returns and inflation is a challenge to many traditional models of asset pricing since equities represent a claim on real assets that hold their value in real terms. Prior studies have suggested a number of potential explanations for the absence of a positive correlation between inflation and equity returns. Feldstein (1980) focused on the interaction of inflation and corporate tax rules, while Modigliani and Cohn (1979) emphasized inflation illusion among equity investors. We are not aware of any empirical evidence that provides clear guidance for choosing among these explanations.

4   Evaluating the Utility Gains from Access to Real Annuities

We have not yet considered how valuable inflation protection might be for a retiree seeking to annuitize his retirement resources. We now address this issue by estimating a potential annuitant's "annuity equivalent wealth" from access to real, nominal, and equity-linked variable-payout annuities. We focus on equity-linked variable annuities because equities have historically earned higher expected returns than other assets and because the findings presented above showed that, while bills offer some inflation protection, their expected return has historically been very small. Bonds offer limited inflation protection and substantially lower average returns, at least historically, than stocks.

The annuity-valuation framework employed is closely related to that developed in Kotlikoff and Spivak (1981) and MPWB (1999). These two studies examine the utility gain that a representative individual receives from access to actuarially fair annuity markets. Brown (1999) provides empirical evidence suggesting that this framework has predictive value for explaining whether individuals plan to annuitize the balance that they accumulate in a defined-contribution plan. In this section, we compare the utility gains associated with access to different types of annuities. Our findings provide some guidance on the value to retirees of real versus nominal annuities.

4.1   Analytic Framework for Evaluating Alternative Annuities

Our basic algorithm estimates the utility gains accruing to someone with no annuity who is offered a fixed, nominal annuity on actuarially fair terms, a real annuity on fair terms, and an equity-linked variable annuity. To illustrate our procedure, we explain how we calculate an individual's "annuity equivalent wealth" when this individual is offered access to a fixed nominal annuity. We assume that this individual purchases such an annuity at age sixty-five, which we normalize to be "year 0." This individual receives an annuity payment in each year that he remains alive, and his optimal consumption path will be related to this payout. The annuity payout at age a (A_a) depends on wealth at the beginning of retirement (W_{ret}), potentially on the value of the assets underlying the annuity when the annuitant is age a, and on the annual annuity payout per dollar of premium payment (θ). In the case of a fixed nominal annuity, the nominal value of A_a is independent of age: $A_a = \theta \cdot W_{ret}$. For simplicity, we do not consider the taxes paid on annuity payouts or the taxes on the returns to nonannuity assets. MPWB (1999) find that the relative utilities of different annuity products are not sensitive to the inclusion of tax rules.

To find the actuarially fair ratio of nominal annuity payouts to premium cost, θ, for a sixty-five-year-old male in 1995, we use the

Social Security Administration's cohort life table for men born in 1930. We define *actuarial fairness* as equality of the premium cost and the EPDV of annuity payouts. This definition ignores the potentially important role of administrative expenses that are incurred by the insurance company offering the annuity, so it is likely to overstate the payouts that would be available in actual annuity markets. We find θ from the following equation:

$$1 = \sum_{j=1}^{50} \frac{\theta \cdot P_j}{[(1+r)(1+\pi)]^j}. \tag{7}$$

In this expression, P_j denotes the probability of a sixty-five-year-old retiree remaining alive j years after retirement, r denotes the annual real interest rate, and π is the annual inflation rate. For computational simplicity, we use years rather than months in our annuity valuation and continue to assume that no one survives beyond age 115, so $P_{50} = 0$.

After finding the actuarially fair payout value, we compute the expected discounted value of lifetime utility that would be associated with the consumption stream generated by this nominal annuity. To do this, we assume that individuals have additively separable utility functions of the following form:

$$U = \sum_{j=1}^{50} P_j \cdot \frac{\left[\left(\frac{C_j}{(1+\pi)^j} \right)^{1-\beta} - 1 \right]}{(1-\beta) \cdot (1+\rho)^j}. \tag{8}$$

For this functional form, the parameter β is the individual's coefficient of relative risk aversion. This parameter also determines the degree of intertemporal substitution in consumption. The nominal consumption flow (C_j) is deflated by the price index $(1 + \pi)^j$.

We consider a first case in which our sixty-five-year-old uses all his resources to purchase an annuity contract and a second case in which he purchases an annuity with half his resources. In the second case, we assume that the other half of the individual's resources is invested in a real annuity. This case can be thought of as describing the retiree's choice problem when he has both an individual account balance that can be annuitized and a substantial real retirement annuity like that offered by the current social security system. As explained by Hurd (1987) and MPWB (1999), the marginal value of an increase in annuitization is greater when fewer resources are already annuitized.

We assume that the retiree has wealth at age sixty-five of W_{ret}, and, for illustrative purposes, we focus on the case in which the retiree has no preexisting annuity wealth. We find the optimal consumption path for someone who receives a nominal annuity of θW_{ret} per period. For such an individual, the budget constraint at each age a is given by

$$W_{a+1} = (W_a + \theta W_{ret} - C_a) \cdot [(1 + r)(1 + \pi)].$$ (9)

This specification makes the standard assumption that nominal interest rates rise point for point with inflation even though our previous results call this assumption into question. The retiree with budget constraint (9) also faces an initial condition on wealth after purchasing the annuity: $W_0 = 0$. It is possible that the retiree will save some of the payouts from the annuity contract, and thereby accumulate wealth, in the early years of retirement.

Equation (9) assumes that the investment opportunity set for the retiree consists of a nominal bond that offers a fixed real return r. The utility gains from purchasing an annuity are likely to depend on the set of portfolio options that investors have *outside* their annuity contract. Campbell and Viceira (1998) present some evidence on the optimal structure of portfolios at different points in the life cycle for investors who have access to nominal and real bonds. Extending our framework to allow for more realistic portfolio structure is a natural direction for further work.

We compute the retiree's lifetime expected utility by solving for his optimal consumption path $\{C_a\}$ using stochastic dynamic programming, where the stochastic component of the problem arises from uncertainty regarding date of death. The result is lifetime expected utility as a function of wealth at retirement, $U^* = U^*(W_{ret})$, for the case in which the retiree has access to a nominal annuity contract.

When the retiree does not have access to an annuity market, his problem is to maximize the utility function (8) subject to the budget constraint and initial condition:

$$W_{a+1} = (W_a - C_a) \cdot [(1 + r)(1 + \pi)]$$ (10a)

and

$$W_0 = W_{ret}.$$ (10b)

The optimal consumption path in this case yields a value of lifetime expected utility, again as a function of wealth at retirement, $U^{**} = U^{**}(W_{ret})$, for a retiree with no access to an annuity market.

The *annuity-equivalent wealth* is the amount of wealth that a retiree needs—if he does not have access to an annuity market—to achieve the lifetime utility level that he can attain with access to an annuity market. We assume full annuitization when the annuity market is available. We note in passing that, in some cases, full annuitization does not yield the highest possible level of lifetime expected utility. Hurd (1987, 1989) shows that some individuals can be overannuitized when their optimal consumption path is constrained by the annuity-income flow. This could happen to individuals with high discount rates relative to the interest rate. Nevertheless, our calculations compare full annuitization with no annuitization.

Formally, annuity-equivalent wealth W_{aew} satisfies the equation

$$U^{**}(W_{aew}) = U^{*}(W_{ret}).\tag{11}$$

We use a numerical search algorithm to find the value of W_{aew} that satisfies this equation. Since the longevity insurance associated with an annuity makes the individual better off, $W_{aew} > W_{ret}$. The retiree requires more wealth to achieve a given retirement utility level when he does not have access to a nominal annuity market than when he does.

When we report the annuity-equivalent wealth in our results below, we normalize W_{aew} by W_{ret}, and we report W_{aew}/W_{ret}. This makes our calculations directly comparable to those in Kotlikoff and Spivak (1981). Our annuity-equivalent-wealth calculations differ, however, from MPWB's (1999) estimates of the amount of wealth that individuals would be prepared to *give up* in order to invest their remaining wealth in actuarially fair annuities. In MPWB (1999), the central focus is on the divergence between the EPDV of annuity payouts and the purchase price of annuity contracts. Because the EPDV is less than the purchase price, the natural question to ask is what fraction of their wealth individuals would rationally forgo in order to obtain an annuity.

In the present paper, we follow Kotlikoff and Spivak (1981) in asking how much *additional* wealth an individual would need to be as well off without access to an annuity market as with it. Our choice of this approach, rather than the wealth-equivalent approach of MPWB (1999), was largely motivated by computational concerns. In the present setting, we search for W_{aew} in a relatively simple problem, where the only source of uncertainty is mortality risk. Real interest rates are certain in our benchmark case with the budget constraint in (10a). If we used either the nominal or the variable-annuity cases as our benchmark, we would need to search for W_{aew} in a problem that includes both mortality risk and inflation risk. This substantially slowed our numerical solution algorithm.

In simple environments without any preexisting annuities, the annuity-equivalent wealth (AEW) that we report is simply a transformation of the wealth-equivalent (WE) measure in MPWB (1999): WE = 1/AEW. Thus, if we find that a retiree requires 1.5 times as much wealth to achieve a given utility level without access to nominal annuities as with them, we could also interpret this as implying that the retiree would be prepared to give up 33 per cent of his wealth (.50/1.5) if he did not have a nominal annuity in order to obtain access to one. When the retiree has some preexisting annuity wealth, however, the relation becomes more complex, and this relation holds approximately but not exactly.

Our analysis of the annuity-equivalent wealth for a nominal annuity generalizes immediately to the case of a real annuity or a variable-payout annuity. For an actuarially fair real annuity, we determine the annual payout per dollar of premium, θ', from the expression

$$1 = \sum_{j=1}^{50} \frac{\theta' \cdot P_j}{(1+r)^j}. \tag{12}$$

This expression is analogous to (7), but the discount factor involves only real interest rates, and the numerator involves only real payouts. As in the discussion above, we find the optimal consumption profile for a consumer who purchases such an annuity, and we then find the annuity-equivalent wealth associated with access to a real annuity.

We also consider the utility consequences of being able to purchase variable-payout annuity products, in particular the case in which annuity payouts are indexed to an underlying portfolio of common stocks. To compute the actuarially fair payout on such variable annuities, we assume that a risk-neutral insurance company offers a variable annuity with an *initial* payout θ'' determined by

$$1 = \sum_{j=1}^{50} \frac{\theta'' \cdot P_j}{(1+R)^j}. \tag{13}$$

In this expression, R is the AIR for the variable-annuity product. The payout in the first period of the annuity purchase is therefore

$$A_v(0) = \theta'' \cdot W_{\text{ret}}. \tag{14}$$

The nominal payout on the variable annuity is determined in subsequent periods by the recursion

$$A_v(t+1) = A_v(t) \cdot (1+z)/(1+R),$$ (15)

where z denotes the nominal return on the equity portfolio.

In considering the equity-linked variable annuity, it is essential to recognize that the initial payout on the annuity policy is increasing in the AIR. The appeal of the equity-linked variable annuity arises from this higher initial payout stream and from the higher average returns earned on the assets invested in the variable annuity.

4.2   Calibration of Annuity-Equivalent Wealth

To carry out the annuity-equivalent-wealth calculations described in the previous subsection, we must calibrate the lifetime-utility function, the survival probability distribution, and the distributions for inflation and real returns on the assets that might be held in portfolios backing variable-payout annuities. All results will assume that the utility discount rate ρ is equal to the riskless interest rate r.

Risk Aversion

The parameter β in equation (8) represents the household's degree of risk aversion and its willingness to engage in intertemporal substitution in consumption. This risk-aversion parameter is an important determinant of the gains from annuitization when the real value of annuity payouts in future periods is uncertain because of stochastic asset returns or stochastic inflation.

Most empirical studies that attempt to estimate a value of relative risk aversion from household consumption patterns find values close to unity, which corresponds to log utility. Laibson, Repetto, and Tobacman (1998) summarize this literature. Mehra and Prescott (1985), however, note that much higher levels of risk aversion are required to rationalize the presence of the large premium of corporate equity returns over riskless-bond returns in historical U.S. data. It is difficult to reconcile the empirical evidence of low risk aversion and the existence of the large historical equity premium. Recent work based on survey questions about household tolerance of risk, reported in Barsky et al. (1997), also suggests values higher than unity. In the light of this dispersion of findings, we present calculations using risk-aversion coefficients of 1, 2, 5, and 10. In their related study of the utility gains from annuitization, Baxter and King (2001) consider an even wider range of risk-aversion values, ranging from 2 to 25. We are inclined to place the most emphasis on our findings with risk-aversion coefficients between 1 and 5, but we present findings using $\beta = 10$ to provide evidence on the robustness of our findings.

Survival Probabilities

The mortality process that we use in our analysis corresponds to the population mortality table supplied by the Social Security Administration. We use a cohort life table with projected future mortality rates since we are interested in an annuity purchased by someone who is currently of retirement age. We use a 1930 birth cohort table to study a sixty-five-year-old male, so our calculations effectively describe someone who was considering purchasing an annuity in 1995.

The Inflation Process

We use historical data from the period 1926–97 to calibrate the stochastic process for inflation. The average value of inflation over this period is 3.2 per cent per year. We assume that the inflation rate in each "year" takes one of six values: −10.2, −1.44, 1.75, 3.82, 9.06, or 18.2 per cent. The respective probabilities of these inflation outcomes are assumed to be .01, .19, .3, .3, .19, and .01. These inflation values correspond approximately to the first, tenth, thirty-fifth, sixty-fifth, ninetieth, and ninety-ninth percentiles of the annual inflation distribution for the years 1926–97, and they imply an average annual inflation rate of 3.2 per cent. We have devoted special attention to the extreme tails of the inflation distribution to make sure that our analysis captures the possibility of a very high inflation period since we might otherwise overstate the value of an annuity that is fixed in nominal terms.

We consider two cases for the inflation process, corresponding to different assumptions about the degree of inflation persistence over time. The first case treats each annual inflation rate as an independent draw from our six-point distribution. This approach to modeling inflation tends to understate the long-run variance of the real value of fixed nominal payments and thus serves as a lower bound on the effect of inflation. Our empirical findings in the last section demonstrate clearly that inflation is a highly persistent process.

In the second case, we incorporate persistence by allowing inflation to follow a stylized AR(1) process. In the first period, inflation is drawn from the same six-point distribution as in the i.i.d. scenario. In later periods, however, there is a probability γ that π_{t+1} will be equal to π_t and a probability $1 - \gamma$ of taking a new draw from the six-point distribution. An attractive feature of this approach is that γ is equal to the AR(1) coefficient in a regression of inflation on its one-period lagged value, and thus γ can be parameterized using historical inflation data. Using U.S. historical data from the period 1926–97, the AR(1) coefficient for inflation is equal to 0.64, and this is the value of γ that we use in modeling a persistent inflation process.

The benefit of avoiding the inflation risk is shown by comparisons between our annuity-equivalent-wealth values when retirees have access to actuarially fair nominal annuity markets and actuarially fair real annuity markets. Our measure is related to, but not equivalent to, Bodie's (1990) analysis of the value of inflation insurance as the cost of purchasing a call option on the consumer price index. His approach generates the cost of *producing* an inflation-indexed income stream, while our approach focuses on the *consumer valuation* of such an income stream.

Risky Asset Returns

Our analysis assumes that investors have access to riskless real returns of 3 per cent per year ($r = .03$). While this return is higher than the average return on "riskless" Treasury bills over the period 1926–97, it is lower than the current return on long-term TIPS. We think of TIPS as the riskless asset with respect to retirement saving and therefore use a higher return than the historical real return on Treasury bills. We further assume that inflation raises the nominal return on this riskless asset so that the real return is unaffected by inflation. This is tantamount to assuming that the investor is holding an indexed real bond.

When we consider variable annuity products backed by portfolios of risky securities, we must specify both the mean return associated with these securities and the variability of returns around this mean. Higher mean returns on the portfolios that back variable-payout annuities will make these products more attractive to potential annuitants, while greater risk will reduce their attractiveness.

We consider a variable-payout annuity backed by a broad portfolio of common stocks. Table 5.9 presents historical information on real returns and the standard deviation of real returns for U.S. stocks, bills, and bonds over the period 1926–97. This table is another way of presenting the information in table 5.6 above on real returns over different horizons. We assume throughout that the standard deviation of real returns on equities equals its historical average value of 20.9 per cent per year.

Table 5.9
Mean real returns and standard deviations of real returns, 1926–97 (%)

	1926–97		1947–97	
	Mean real return	Standard deviation	Mean real return	Standard deviation
Treasury bills	0.73	4.17	0.87	2.64
Long-term Treasury bonds	2.57	10.53	2.01	11.13
Equities	9.66	20.46	9.93	16.95

Source: Authors' tabulations using data from Ibbotson Associates (1998).

In computing the annuity-equivalent wealth for an equity-backed variable annuity, we consider two different assumptions with regard to the mean real return on equities. First, we assume a 6 per cent real return (i.e., a 3 per cent premium over the indexed-bond return). This assumption about the equity premium is substantially smaller than the historical average differential between stock and bond returns, but it is designed to be conservative. Second, we consider a case with a 9 per cent real return on equities, which translates to a 6 per cent premium above the real bond. This is still a smaller equity premium than historical returns suggest, but it yields a real return on equities close to the historical average. The extent to which historical real returns on corporate stock provide guidance on prospective returns is an open issue (for divergent views, see Campbell and Shiller [1998] and Siegel [1998]). In both cases, we assume an AIR on the variable annuity equal to the expected return on the underlying portfolio, following the approach of Bodie and Pesando (1983).

In order to account for the variability in returns, we again use a discrete six-point approximation to capture the distribution of real equity returns. Specifically, we constructed a distribution of the equity excess return over the period 1926–97. By subtracting off the mean excess return and then adding in our assumed 6 or 9 per cent mean return, we constructed our distribution of equity returns. This approach allows us to alter our assumption about the mean equity premium over the riskless rate while holding the variance of equity returns at historical levels. We pick points from the first, tenth, thirty-fifth, sixty-fifth, ninetieth, and ninety-ninth percentiles of the distribution and use the probabilities .01, .19, .3, .3, .19, and .01 for these draws. For the case of a 6 per cent mean real return, the corresponding points in the return distribution are −.475, −.182, −.036, .156, .306, and .506. For the case of a 9 per cent mean real return, the entire distribution of returns is shifted up by .03. Real equity returns are modeled as independent across time. This does not allow for any possible variance compression at long horizons.

4.3   Results on the Valuation of Real versus Nominal Annuities

Table 5.10 reports our estimates of the annuity-equivalent wealth for real and nominal annuities. The first three columns report results for the case with no preannuitized wealth, when the potential annuitant places all his wealth in an annuity. Columns 4–6 explore the case in which the potential annuitant already holds half his net worth in a real annuity such as social security. To interpret the results, first consider the case in which the potential annuitant has a logarithmic utility function (CRRA = 1). In this case, the annuity-equivalent wealth is 1.502 for a fixed real annuity. This implies that an individual would be indifferent between having $1 in a real annuity or $1.50 in nonannuitized wealth. Note that the annuity-equivalent wealth for this individual is 1.451 in the case of i.i.d. inflation and 1.424 in the case of persistent inflation. These results suggest that a real annuity is more valuable than a nominal annuity and more so when the inflation process is more persistent.

Table 5.10
Annuity-equivalent wealth for real and nominal annuities

Coefficient of relative risk aversion	Individual with no preexisting annuity wealth			Individual with half of initial wealth in preexisting real annuity		
	Real annuity	Nominal annuity: i.i.d. inflation	Nominal annuity: persistent inflation	Real annuity	Nominal annuity: i.i.d. inflation	Nominal annuity: persistent inflation
1	1.502	1.451	1.424	1.330	1.304	1.286
2	1.650	1.553	1.501	1.441	1.403	1.366
5	1.855	1.616	1.487	1.623	1.515	1.450
10	2.004	1.592	1.346	1.815	1.577	1.451

Source: Authors' calculations. The annuity-equivalent wealth for the nominal annuity is calculated under the assumption that inflation takes one of six possible values, roughly capturing the distribution of inflation outcomes over the period 1926–97. Inflation shocks are independent across periods in the i.i.d. case and follow a stylized AR(1) process in the persistent-inflation case. For further discussion, see the text.

For a real annuity, the annuity-equivalent wealth is monotonically increasing with the level of risk aversion. When the CRRA coefficient is 10, for example, the annuity-equivalent wealth rises to 2.004, meaning that an individual is indifferent between $2 of nonannuitized wealth and $1 in wealth that can be invested in a real annuity. For fixed nominal annuities in the presence of uncertain inflation, this monotonic relation between the annuity-equivalent wealth and the level of risk aversion does not hold. This is because there are two effects of risk aversion that work in opposite directions in the case of inflation uncertainty. The first is that higher risk aversion leads one to value an annuitized payout more highly because the annuity eliminates the risk of outliving one's resources. This is the only effect present when examining real annuity products. The second factor, which works in the opposite direction, is that more risk-averse individuals have a greater dislike for the uncertainty introduced into the real annuity stream by stochastic inflation. Increased variability in the real value of the annuity flows reduces utility, and this effect is largest for those with the highest degree of risk aversion.

At low levels of risk aversion, the first effect dominates, and the annuity-equivalent wealth for fixed nominal annuities is rising with risk aversion. For example, moving from CRRA = 1 to CRRA = 2, the annuity-equivalent wealth increases from 1.451 to 1.553 in the i.i.d.-inflation case and from 1.424 to 1.501 in the persistent-inflation case. However, as risk aversion increases further, the second effect becomes stronger, and the annuity-equivalent wealth begins to decrease with risk aversion.

The annuity-equivalent wealth values described above provide information on the amount of incremental wealth that individuals would require to be made as well off as if they had access to annuities, assuming that they have no preexisting annuity coverage. The difference between the annuity-equivalent-wealth values for real and nominal annuities provides information on how valuable a real annuity is relative to a nominal annuity. For example, to achieve a given utility target in a world with i.i.d. inflation, a nominal annuity is worth 5.1 per cent of wealth less than a real annuity (1.502 − 1.451). At higher risk-aversion levels, the differential between real and nominal annuities rises even further. When CRRA = 5 and inflation is i.i.d., the nominal annuity is worth 23.9 per cent of wealth less than the real annuity. In the case that is most unfavorable to nominal annuities, that of persistent inflation and a risk-aversion coefficient of 10, access to a real annuity is equivalent to doubling one's initial wealth, while access to a nominal annuity is equivalent to only a one-third increase in wealth.

The results are attenuated when we consider the annuitization decision of an individual who already holds a substantial amount of his wealth in a preexisting real annuity. Such a potential annuitant would require a smaller increment to wealth to achieve the same utility level—without access to a private annuity market—that he could obtain with such access. For example, a consumer with a risk-aversion coefficient of unity would require only a 33 per cent increment to his wealth to be made as well off as if he had a real annuity, compared to 50 per cent in the case when no wealth was previously annuitized. The presence of a preexisting real annuity offers the potential annuitant some insurance against very low consumption values. This accounts for the diminished value of an additional privately purchased annuity.

When the annuity option is a nominal rather than a real annuity, the effect of having a preexisting real annuity is more complex. When inflation draws are independent across years, the results are similar to those for real annuities: the annuity-equivalent wealth from annuitization declines when there is a preexisting real annuity. When we allow for a persistent-inflation process, however, along with very high values of risk aversion, the results change. For example, when CRRA = 10, the annuity-equivalent wealth is *higher* when the potential annuitant has preannuitized wealth than when he does not. This is because we have assumed that the preexisting annuity is a fixed real annuity, which provides insurance against the annuitant ever experiencing very low values of real income and therefore consumption. Thus, the utility cost of having high and persistent inflation erode the value of a nominal annuity is reduced, and the potential annuitant's willingness to purchase a nominal annuity rises.

4.4 Results on the Valuation of Variable Annuities

Table 5.11 reports our findings for the case of equity-linked variable-payout annuities. We assume that the AIR for such annuities corresponds to the average real equity return that is built into our calculations. Once again, we report two panels, corresponding to different degrees of preexisting annuitization. The first column reports results when the average return on equities exceeds that on bonds by 3 per cent, so the real return on equities averages 6 per cent. For an

Table 5.11
Annuity-equivalent wealth for equity-linked variable-annuity products

Coefficient of relative risk aversion	No preexisting annuities		Preexisting real annuity equal to half of initial wealth	
	Real stock return 6%	Real stock return 9%	Real stock return 6%	Real stock return 9%
Annuity-equivalent wealth				
1	1.623	2.024	1.567	1.953
2	1.499	1.901	1.570	1.957
5	0.921	1.355	1.443	1.789
10	0.331	0.622	1.261	1.563
Annuity-equivalent wealth ratio, variable annuity/real annuity				
1	1.081	1.348	1.178	1.468
2	0.908	1.152	1.090	1.358
5	0.496	0.730	0.889	1.102
10	0.165	0.310	0.695	0.861

Source: Authors' calculations, as described in the text. The calculations in the bottom panel show the ratio of the annuity-equivalent wealth from the upper panel to the analogous annuity-equivalent wealth from holding a real annuity with an assumed real return of 3 per cent. The underlying annuity-equivalent wealth values for the real annuity case are shown in table 9.10, cols. 1 and 4, above. A ratio greater that one indicates that the variable annuity is more valuable than a real annuity. Ratios less than one indicate that the real annuity is more valuable.

individual with logarithmic utility in this return environment, an equity-linked variable-payout annuity generates a higher utility level than a real annuity does. In the case of no preexisting annuities, the annuity-equivalent wealth for the variable annuity, 1.623, is higher than that for the real annuity in table 9.10 above (1.502). For higher levels of risk aversion, however, a variable annuity with a mean return of 6 per cent is worth less than a real annuity. In fact, an individual placing 100 per cent of his wealth in a variable annuity can actually be made worse off than he would be if not annuitizing at all when his degree of risk aversion is high enough and the equity distribution is highly uncertain. This is indicated by annuity-equivalent wealth values below unity.

The lower panel of table 5.11 reports the ratio of the annuity-equivalent wealth with an equity-linked variable annuity to that with a real annuity. When these entries are greater than one, a potential annuitant would prefer a variable annuity to a fixed real annuity. When the entry is less than one, the individual would be better off in a real annuity. In the case of log utility, the individual always prefers an equity-linked variable-annuity product. At higher risk-aversion levels, however, the fixed real annuity usually dominates. The same pattern is evident when we allow a higher real return on equities. For three of the eight combinations of risk aversion and real equity returns that we considered, a potential annuitant who was preparing to annuitize all his wealth would prefer the variable to the real annuity. For five of the eight combinations, this outcome also emerges in the case with a pre-existing real annuity. Variable annuities are relatively more attractive with preexisting real annuities than without. This is again because the preexisting real annuity provides a minimum consumption floor below which the annuitant will not fall. Therefore, the risk of a very low consumption state resulting from a series of negative equity returns is reduced.

These findings suggest that, for rates of risk aversion commonly cited in the consumption literature, and for plausible rate-of-return assumptions, potential annuitants would often prefer to purchase variable annuities with payouts linked to equity returns rather than real annuities offering constant purchasing power throughout the annuity period. Even when the expected real return on stocks is only 3 per cent, the extra return afforded by the variable annuity more than compensates potential annuitants for the inflation risk that they bear. This is particularly evident when the annuitant is already endowed with a real annuity that represents a substantial share of net wealth because, in that case, the risk of very low consumption as a result of adverse variable-annuity returns is mitigated.

Our results on variable annuities are probably sensitive to our restriction of the menu of assets that investors can hold *outside* the variable annuity: we do not allow investments in corporate stock except through the variable-annuity channel. Exploring the robustness of our findings to relaxation of this constraint is an important topic for future work.

5 Conclusions and Further Directions

We have provided new evidence on the functioning of existing real annuity markets and on the potential role of nominal, real, and variable-payout annuities in providing income security to retirees. Three conclusions emerge from the analysis.

First, private insurers can and do offer real annuities to potential annuitants. Although at present there is virtually no U.S. market for real annuity products, in the United Kingdom indexed government bonds have been available for nearly two decades, and, there, indexed annuities are widely available. From the standpoint of an annuity purchaser, the cost of purchasing a real rather than a nominal annuity in the United Kingdom is at most 5 per cent of the annuity principal.

Second, real returns on a broad-based portfolio of U.S. stocks have historically outpaced inflation by a substantial margin. While extrapolating from historical returns must be done with caution, the past returns suggest that there may be benefits for retirees from investing part of their annuity wealth in a variable-annuity product with returns linked to the returns on corporate stock. Nevertheless, our analysis of the correlation between unexpected inflation and equity returns suggests that the appeal of an equity-linked variable annuity is primarily the result of the equity premium rather than a strong positive correlation between inflation shocks and equity returns. At least at high frequencies, U.S. equities do not appear to offer an inflation hedge.

Third, consumers place a modest value on access to real rather than nominal annuities. We consider our results for retirees with a coefficient of relative risk aversion of two as a "benchmark" case. We find that, if a potential annuitant could not purchase a nominal annuity, he would need roughly 1.5 times as much wealth to achieve the same lifetime utility level that he could obtain with his given wealth and access to a nominal annuity. He would need 1.65 times as much wealth to achieve the utility level that he could obtain if he had access to a real annuity market. These two findings can be combined to suggest that a retiree with access to a real annuity who loses such access would be made worse off by approximately the same amount as he would be if he lost 10 per cent of his wealth. Consumers also value access to variable-payout equity-linked annuities, although their demand for such products is quite sensitive to their degree of risk aversion. For moderately risk-averse consumers, with coefficients of relative risk aversion of 2 or less, the annuity-equivalent wealth for an equity-linked variable annuity may be greater than that for a real annuity. This finding obtains even when we assume that the average annual real return on equities is only three hundred basis points higher than the real return on riskless bonds.

These findings bear on two concerns that are raised in connection with social security reform plans that include individual accounts. One is that insurers might not be able to bring to market products providing inflation and longevity protection. Our evidence suggests that this is, in fact, not a concern in the two countries that we have examined. Both have government-issued inflation-indexed bonds that can be used to back private inflation-indexed annuities.

A second concern is that, given a choice, retirees might use their individual account funds to purchase nominal rather than inflation-indexed annuities. This is perceived as a problem to the extent that it exposes retirees to the risk of consumption losses in old age. Our model suggests that the expected utility losses associated with the purchase of a nominal rather than a real annuity are modest. It also implies that consumer demand for inflation-linked annuities in an individual accounts system would be positive, although the extent to which our stylized model describes actual consumer behavior is an open issue. The demand for real annuities is greatest among the most risk-averse consumers. It is also increasing in the degree of persistence of inflation shocks. When inflation is serially independent, the annuity-equivalent wealth for a nominal annuity is higher than when inflation is highly persistent. This is because, conditional on the average inflation rate, the risk of experiencing high and persistent inflation poses a greater threat to real retirement consumption than the risk of a shorter-lived period of high inflation.

The demand for real annuities also tends to be lower for households with a substantial endowment of annuitized wealth. This would include any remaining real defined-benefit promises offered to retirees under a restructured social security system. We estimate that the annuity equivalent wealth of a real annuity is about 5–8 per cent less for a consumer holding half his wealth in social security than for one having no real annuity at all. Moore and Mitchell (2000) show that older Americans currently hold close to half their retirement wealth in real social security annuities. This may explain the limited current demand for real annuity products in the United States. If the social security system were changed in a way that reduced the importance of CPI-indexed real annuity payouts, the demand for privately provided annuity products might increase substantially.

Our examination of the interplay between annuity choice, inflation protection, and portfolio risks raises a number of issues that could productively be explored in future work. One pertains to the use of more complex annuity products than the ones considered here. We have not investigated "graded nominal payout products," discussed by Biggs (1969) and King (1995). While graded policies do not offer inflation protection per se, they do provide annuitants with an opportunity to backload their real annuity payouts. Annuity-equivalent wealth values from annuitization in graded policies, relative to that for fixed nominal or real annuities, would be straightforward to calculate in our framework.

A more difficult issue for future research concerns the set of portfolio options available to the individuals considering annuitization and the extent to which such households have access to assets other than riskless bonds. One reason for our result that investors find equity-linked annuities valuable is that our models assume that investors can access the equity market only by using variable annuities. It may be realistic to assume that some low-income and low-net-worth households accumulating retirement resources in an individual accounts system do not hold stock in any other way. For higher net-worth households with greater financial sophistication, this assumption is less appropriate. Extending the current analysis to allow for a richer portfolio structure on the part of potential annuitants is an important direction for further work.

References

Barr, David G., and John Y. Campbell. 1996. Inflation, real interest rates, and the bond market: A study of U.K. nominal and index-linked government bond prices. NBER Working Paper no. 5821. Cambridge, Mass.: National Bureau of Economic Research.

Barsky, Robert B., F. Thomas Juster, Miles S. Kimball, and Matthew D. Shapiro. 1997. Preference parameters and behavioral heterogeneity: An experimental approach in the Health and Retirement Survey. *Quarterly Journal of Economics* 107 (May): 537–80.

Baxter, Marianne, and Robert G. King. 2001. The Role of International Investment in a Privatized Social Security System. In *Risk Aspects of Investment-Based Social Security Reform*, ed. John Y. Campbell and Martin Feldstein. Chicago: University of Chicago Press.

Bell, Felicitie, A. Wade, and S. Goss. 1992. Life tables for the United States Social Security Area 1900–2080. Actuarial Study no. 107. Washington, D.C.: Social Security Administration, Office of the Actuary.

Biggs, John H. 1969. Alternatives in variable annuity benefit design. *Transactions of the Society of Actuaries* 21 (November): 495–528.

Blake, David. 1999. Annuity markets: Problem and solutions. Discussion Paper no. PI-9907. Pension Institute, Birkbeck College, London.

Bodie, Zvi. 1976. Common stocks as a hedge against inflation. *Journal of Finance* 31 (May): 459–70.

———. 1990. Inflation insurance. *Journal of Risk and Insurance* 57, no. 4: 634–45.

Bodie, Zvi, and James Pesando. 1983. Retirement annuity design in an inflationary climate. In *Financial aspects of the U.S. pension system*, ed. Zvi Bodie and John Shoven. Chicago: University of Chicago Press.

Boudoukh, Jacob, and Matthew Richardson. 1993. Stock returns and inflation: A long-horizon perspective. *American Economic Review* 83 (December): 1346–55.

Brown, Jeffrey R. 1999. Private pensions, mortality risk, and the decision to annuitize. NBER Working Paper no. 7191. Cambridge, Mass.: National Bureau of Economic Research.

Budd, Alan, and Nigel Campbell. 1998. The roles of the public and private sectors in the U.K. pension system. In *Privatizing social security*, ed. Martin Feldstein. Chicago: University of Chicago Press.

Campbell, John Y., and Robert J. Shiller. 1998. Valuation ratios and the long run stock market outlook. *Journal of Portfolio Management* 24 (winter): 11–26.

Campbell, John Y., and Luis Viceira. 1998. Who should buy long term bonds? NBER Working Paper no. 6801. Cambridge, Mass.: National Bureau of Economic Research.

Diamond, Peter A. 1997. Macroeconomic aspects of social security reform. *Brookings Papers on Economic Activity*, no. 2: 1–87.

Evans, Martin D. 1998. Real rates, expected inflation, and inflation risk premia. *Journal of Finance* 53 (February): 187–218.

Feldstein, Martin S. 1980. Inflation, tax rules, and the stock market. *Journal of Monetary Economics* 6 (July): 309–31.

Finkelstein, Amy, and James Poterba. 1999. The market for annuity products in the United Kingdom. NBER Working Paper no. 7168. Cambridge, Mass.: National Bureau of Economic Research.

Friedman, Benjamin, and Mark Warshawsky. 1988. Annuity prices and saving behavior in the United States. In *Pensions in the U.S. economy*, ed. Z. Bodie, J. Shoven, and D. Wise. Chicago: University of Chicago Press.

———. 1990. The cost of annuities: Implications for saving behavior and bequests. *Quarterly Journal of Economics* 105, no. 1 (February): 135–54.

Gramlich, Edward M. 1996. Different approaches for dealing with social security. *Journal of Economic Perspectives* 10 (summer): 55–66.

Hammond, P. Brett. 1999. Using inflation-indexed securities for retirement savings and income: The TIAA-CREF experience. In *Handbook of inflation-indexed bonds*, ed. John Brynjolfsson and Frank J. Fabozzi. New Hope, Pa.: Frank Fabozzi Associates.

Hurd, Michael D. 1987. The marginal value of social security. NBER Working Paper no. 2411. Cambridge, Mass.: National Bureau of Economic Research.

———. 1989. The annuity value of social security. In *The political economy of social security* (Contributions of Economic Analysis, no. 179), ed. B. A. Gustafsson and A. N. Klevmarken. Amsterdam: Elsevier Science.

Ibbotson Associates. 1998. *Stocks, bonds, bills, and inflation: 1998 yearbook.* Chicago.

Johansen, R. 1996. Review of adequacy of 1983 individual annuity mortality table. *Transactions of the Society of Actuaries* 47:101–23.

King, Francis. 1995. *The TIAA graded payment method and the CPI.* TIAA-CREF Research Dialogues, no. 46. New York, December.

Kotlikoff, Laurence, J., and Avia Spivak. 1981. The family as an incomplete annuities market. *Journal of Political Economy* 89:372–91.

Laibson, David, Andrea Repetto, and Jeremy Tobacman. 1998. Self control and saving for retirement. *Brookings Papers on Economic Activity*, no. 1:91–196.

Mehra, Rajnish, and Edward Prescott. 1985. The equity premium: A puzzle. *Journal of Monetary Economics* 15:145–61.

Mitchell, Olivia S., Robert Myers, and Howard Young. 1999. *Prospects for social security reform.* Philadelphia: University of Pennsylvania Press.

Mitchell, Olivia S., James M. Poterba, Mark Warshawsky, and Jeffrey R. Brown. 1999. New evidence on the money's worth of individual annuities. *American Economic Review* 89 (December): 1299–1318.

Modigliani, Franco, and Richard Cohn. 1979. Inflation, rational valuation, and the market. *Financial Analysts Journal* 35 (March): 3–23.

Moore, James, and Olivia S. Mitchell. 2000. Projected retirement wealth and saving adequacy. In *Forecasting retirement needs and retirement wealth*, ed. O. S. Mitchell, B. Hammond, and A. Rappaport. Philadelphia: University of Pennsylvania Press.

National Academy of Social Insurance (NASI). 1998. *Evaluating issues in privatizing social security.* Washington, D.C.

Poterba, James, M., and Mark Warshawsky. 2000. The costs of annuitizing retirement payouts from individual accounts. In *Administrative aspects of investment-based social security reform*, ed. J. Shoven. Chicago: University of Chicago Press.

Siegel, Jeremy. 1998. *Stocks for the long run.* 2d ed. Burr Ridge, Ill.: Irwin Prof.

TIAA-CREF. 1997a. CREF scheduled to launch inflation-linked bond account on May 1, investment forum. New York, spring.

———. 1997b. Introducing the CREF inflation-linked bond account. New York.

———. 1998a. *Choosing income options.* New York.

———. 1998b. The inflation linked bond account: Supplement of June 1998 to the prospectus of May 1998 for the College Retirement Equities Fund. New York.

———. 1998c. Statement of additional information, May 1998. New York.

———. 1998d. Supplement of June 1998 to the prospectus of May 1998. New York.

Warshawsky, Mark. 1988. Private annuity markets in the United States. *Journal of Risk and Insurance* 55, no. 3 (September): 518–28.

6

The Costs of Annuitizing Retirement Payouts from Individual Accounts

James M. Poterba and
Mark J. Warshawsky

One of the crucial questions about the operation of "individual accounts" systems of retirement saving is how participants will draw down their account balances when they reach retirement. Most defined-contribution plans do not specify how accumulated assets will be drawn down. By contrast, most defined-benefit plans sponsored by private companies or by the government provide retirees with mandatory life annuities. Private pension plans purchase these annuities as part of a group annuity contract with an insurance company or underwrite the annuities themselves. In public pension plans such as social security, the government underwrites the annuities.

Some, but not all, current participants in defined-contribution plans wish to obtain life annuities. Roughly one-third of 401(k) plans and most 403(b) plans currently offer participants a voluntary life annuity payout. The annuities purchased with funds from accounts in these pension plans are individual annuities purchased through the group plans. If an individual participates in a pension plan that does not offer life annuities and nevertheless desires such a distribution method, it is necessary to purchase an individual life annuity through an agent or a broker representing a commercial insurance company. The costs of such annuities, including both administrative and sales costs, the "adverse-selection" costs associated with voluntary purchase behavior, and return on capital for the insurance company offering the annuity policy, affect the retirement income that the participant receives for a given level of wealth accumulation.

Questions about the cost of annuitization also arise in discussions of individual account social security reform proposals. Under the present

From *Administrative Aspects of Investment-Based Social Security Reform*, ed. John B. Shoven (Chicago: University of Chicago Press, 2000). © 2000 by the National Bureau of Economic Research. Reprinted by permission of the University of Chicago Press.

social security system, the federal government provides life annuities to all retirees. Because these are compulsory annuities, the adverse-selection problems that may arise in private, voluntary annuity markets are not a concern. In addition, the existing social security arrangement involves none of the sales or marketing costs that might be charged by insurance companies that sell individual annuities, although there are some administrative costs associated with the current social security system.

Most proposals that suggest the use of individual accounts as a supplement to, or partial substitute for, the existing social security system would mandate some type of annuitization when the accountholder retires. This is true, for example, of the proposals advanced by the Committee on Economic Development, the CSIS (Center for Strategic and International Studies), and a subset of participants on the 1994–96 Social Security Advisory Council ("the IA proposal"). While the mandatory annuitization aspects of these proposals reduce concern about adverse selection, structuring annuity options to achieve equitable payouts, at low cost, is nevertheless an important issue.

Previous research on annuity markets provides only limited guidance on the potential operation of an annuity mechanism involving the purchase of individual annuity contracts within a defined-contribution "group" system. Most existing research has focused on the very limited agent-dominated individual annuity market in the United States. Previous studies, including Warshawsky (1988), Friedman and Warshawsky (1990), and Mitchell et al. (1999), have calculated the expected present discounted value of annuity payouts, relative to policy premiums, for individual annuity policies. Because the sales and administrative costs of current individual annuity policies are likely to be substantially greater than those of individual annuities provided in a group plan or a reformed social security system, existing calculations probably provide a lower bound on potential payouts in a system of "private accounts."

The PSA (personal security account) proposal put forward by a subset of the Social Security Advisory Council (see Gramlich 1996) would not mandate annuitization from individual social security accounts or create any group mechanism for providing life annuities. Rather, individuals who desired to convert their account accumulations to a life annuity would have to purchase an annuity from an insurance agent. Calculations of the expected discounted present value of payouts from private annuities therefore provide information that is likely to bear on an evaluation of the PSA proposal. It is possible, however, that administrative costs per policy and the degree of adverse selection in the market would change if wealth accumulation in individual accounts became universal.

In this chapter, we present new findings on the costs of individual annuities, both in the individual annuity market and in two large defined-contribution pension systems, the federal government's Thrift Savings Plan (TSP) and TIAA-CREF. While we do not assess directly the cost of annuitization for any particular individual accounts social security system, we report background information that should be helpful in evaluating such costs. We provide a detailed summary of the structures employed by the TSP and by TIAA-CREF to offer individual annuities to their participants. Our goal is to inform discussion of potential options and structures for providing annuities under individual account systems that might be considered as part of a social security reform plan.

The chapter is divided into four sections. Section 1 presents updated information on the expected present discounted value of annuity payouts in the market for individual single-premium-immediate annuities. These calculations draw on data for annuity premiums and payouts in June 1998 and extend the analysis in Mitchell et al. (1999) to consider individual annuities purchased through agents and brokers as part of qualified retirement-saving plans (like IRAs) as well as in nonqualified accounts. The results in this section indicate that the present value of annuity payouts, relative to premium costs, has increased in recent years.

Section 2 examines the annuity options that are available to individuals who participate in the federal government's TSP. This is a large, voluntary, 401(k) plan that is available to federal employees. We present information on the structure of the "request for proposals" that the TSP issues when it solicits bids from private insurance companies that may wish to provide life annuities to TSP participants. We also present information on the payouts associated with individual annuities purchased through this plan.

Section 3 describes the annuities offered by TIAA-CREF, which provides basic and supplementary pension plans to the employees of universities and other nonprofit educational and research institutions. TIAA annuities, which include a nonguaranteed element, offer payouts that are among the highest in the individual annuity market owing to their superior investment returns and low expenses. TIAA-CREF variable annuities offer payouts that reflect, on at least an annual basis, the investment experience of various underlying equity, fixed-income, and real estate investment portfolios.

The conclusion provides a summary and suggests several topics related to the cost of annuitization that require further investigation and analysis.

1   Individual Annuities Offered through Agents by Commercial Insurance Companies

With individual nonparticipating, single-premium-immediate life annuities offered by commercial life insurance companies, individuals make an initial premium payment and typically begin receiving annuity payouts in the month after their purchase. We focus on non-participating annuities, which provide a fixed and guaranteed benefit payment.

Premiums for life annuities are reported each year in A. M. Best's publication *Best's Review: Life and Health*. We analyze data from the August 1998 issue, which presents the results of an annuity market survey carried out at the beginning of June 1998. The *Best's* data correspond to single-premium annuities with a $100,000 premium. Ninety-nine companies responded to the survey, reporting information on the current monthly payouts on individual annuities sold to men and women at ages fifty-five, sixty, sixty-five, seventy, seventy-five, and eighty. Companies also reported their payouts for similar annuities purchased with funds in qualified retirement-saving plans. Qualified annuities must begin payouts by age seventy, so there are no data for qualified annuities that start at ages seventy-five or eighty. Roughly two-thirds of the companies reported the same payout value for both the qualified and the nonqualified annuity, while one-third reported different values. Virtually all companies reporting differences between qualified and nonqualified annuities at a given age reported the same qualified annuity payouts for men and women of the same age, reflecting their use of a "unisex" mortality table in pricing the qualified annuities, in contrast to gender-distinct pricing of nonquali-fied annuities.

Table 6.1 provides summary information on the monthly annuity payouts associated with a representative set of annuity products. Each entry in the table shows the monthly payout per $100,000 of annuity premium. Because earlier research has documented wide dispersion in

Table 6.1
Monthly payments ($) per $100,000 premium for annuities available from commercial insurers in June 1998

Buyer	All-policy average		Average for ten policies with highest payouts	
	Qualified	Nonqualified	Qualified	Nonqualified
Male, age 55	596.22	606.44	671.60	675.70
Male, age 65	719.91	732.73	809.30	806.58
Male, age 75	N.A.	988.84	N.A.	1,084.69
Female, age 55	568.46	563.04	639.70	630.62
Female, age 65	671.47	661.62	748.77	728.35
Female, age 75	N.A.	857.69	N.A.	948.58

Sources: Data are drawn from *Best's Review: Life and Health* (August 1998) and authors' tabulations.
Note: N.A. = not available.

the annuity payouts offered by different companies, we report both the average payout across companies and the average payout for the ten firms that offered the highest payout products. A sixty-five-year-old man purchasing a $100,000 single-premium annuity would receive, on average, a monthly payment of $733, or $8,793 per year, for life. Because women live longer than men on average, a sixty-five-year-old woman paying the same $100,00 premium would receive about 10 per cent less, $662 per month or $7,939 per year. These average payouts are roughly 8 per cent lower than the payouts in the 1995 *Best's* survey, which provided the basis for the analysis in Mitchell et al. (1999). This presumably reflects the decline in interest rates since 1995.

One important feature of annuity prices, which is present in the June 1998 data as well as in those for earlier dates, is the substantial variation in the payouts offered by different insurance companies. The average monthly payout for the ten companies with the highest payout for a sixty-five-year-old man, for example, is $807, which is 10 per cent higher than the average payout for all firms. There are similar differences in the prices offered to annuitants at other ages. In Mitchell et al. (1999), a variety of possible explanations for these payout differences were explored, such as apparent differential riskiness of different insurance companies, but no systematic pattern in the payouts was found. (The companies offering the "ten highest-payout" annuities in table 6.1 generally are small and medium-size life insurers.) Payout differences across firms may reflect different assumptions about mortality rates, different rate-of-return assumptions in pricing policies, and differences in administrative costs and expense ratios. The heterogeneity in annuity prices suggests that, if individuals were allowed to purchase their own annuity contracts in a system of "individual accounts," different individuals might receive substantially different annuity benefits.

Unfortunately, we do not have data on the volume of annuities sold by different firms in the *Best's* database, which would help judge the actual extent of payout dispersion in the annuitant population. In addition, such information would help determine whether the surveyed rates represent active lines of business or are just used to bolster illustrations in sales materials for deferred annuities. The calculations presented below focus on cases in which individuals purchase annuities that offer the average payout.

Table 6.1 presents information on nonqualified as well as qualified annuities. For men, the average monthly payout on qualified annuities is below that on nonqualified annuities, as a result of the use of "unisex" mortality tables in pricing the qualified annuities offered by some insurance companies, as mentioned above. For a sixty-five-year-old man, a qualified annuity offers payouts that average about 1.8 per cent less than payouts on nonqualified annuities. For women, the pattern is reversed. The average payout from qualified annuities is greater than that from nonqualified annuities. For a sixty-five-year-old woman, qualified annuities offer an average payout that is roughly 1.5 per cent greater, each month, than the average payout for nonqualified annuities.

To provide insight on the administrative and other costs associated with individual annuity products, we compute the expected present discounted value (EPDV) of payouts for the average annuity product. We compare this EPDV with the premium cost of the annuity. This yields a measure of the "money's worth" of the individual annuity, as in Warshawsky (1988), Friedman and Warshawsky (1988, 1990), and Mitchell et al. (1999).

The formula that we use to calculate the EPDV of a nominal annuity with monthly payout A, purchased by an individual of age b, is

$$V_b(A) = \sum_{j=1}^{12 \times (115-b)} \frac{A \times P_j}{\prod_{k=1}^{j} (1 + i_k)}. \tag{1}$$

The upper limit of the summation, $12 \times (115 - b)$, is the number of months that a person of age b would live if he or she reached age 115. We assume that no one survives beyond this age. P_j denotes the probability that an individual of age b years at the time of the annuity purchase survives for at least j months beyond this purchase.

The term i_k denotes the one-month interest rate k months after the annuity purchase. In our baseline calculations, we measure these interest rates using the term structure of yields for zero-coupon Treasury "strips." We estimate the pattern of monthly interest rates that is implied by these yields. The data on the zero-coupon yield curve are published each Thursday in the *Wall Street Journal*, and we use the data from the first Thursday in June 1998 to coincide with the timing of *Best's* annuity-price data. This approach to measuring discount rates differs from that in previous studies of the EPDV of nominal annuities. Friedman and Warshawsky (1990) assumed a constant nominal discount rate for all periods. Mitchell et al. (1999) used a term structure of riskless government bond yields, but they did not use the yields on zero-coupon bonds to construct this yield curve. We used the zero-coupon yields because they seem the best available information on the discount rates for the present-value calculations.

We also consider a second set of discount rates that correspond to a risky corporate bond. To construct these discount rates, we measure the difference between the yield on a BAA corporate bond and that on a ten-year Treasury bond in early June 1998. This yield spread was 137 basis points. We then add this "risk premium" to the entire term structure of riskless interest rates that we estimate from the Treasury yield curve.

We evaluate equation (1) using two sets of projected survival probabilities. Projections are needed because P_j describes the *prospective* survival experience of today's annuity buyers. The first set of survival probabilities corresponds to the population at large. We use cohort-mortality-rate projections developed by Bell, Wade, and Goss (1992) at the Office of the Actuary of the Social Security Administration (SSA). One of the key difficulties in evaluating the effective cost of purchasing an annuity, however, is that the pool of actual annuity purchasers has different mortality experience than the population at large. There is "adverse selection" in this market; annuitants tend to have longer life expectancies than individuals in the broader population. From the standpoint of an insurance company writing annuities, the annuitant mortality table must be used to determine the relation between premium income and the EPDV of payouts. Adverse selection is a "cost" of annuitization from the perspective of an individual in the population at large.

One important question about the potential effect of expanding individual account retirement-saving vehicles is how this expansion would affect the degree of adverse selection in the annuity market. A universal system of individual accounts, coupled with mandatory annuitization, would reduce adverse selection, although it would not eliminate it entirely because individuals would still presumably be allowed choices among annuity options and the age of settlement. The account-balance-weighted mortality table might also differ from the population mortality table because of income-related differences in mortality rates.

The second set of projected mortality rates that we use corresponds to that for current annuitants. Mitchell et al. (1999) develop an algorithm that combines information from the new Annuity 2000 mortality table (Johansen 1996), the older 1983 individual annuitant mortality table, and the projected rate of mortality improvement in the SSA's population mortality tables. The algorithm generates projected mortality rates for the set of annuitants who purchase annuity contracts in a given year. There are substantial differences between the population and the annuitant mortality rates. Mitchell et al. (1999) show that, in 1995, the annual mortality rate for annuitants between the ages of sixty-five and seventy-five was roughly half the mortality rate for those in the general population. This translates into a substantially larger EPDV of annuity payouts when we use the annuitant mortality table, rather than the population mortality table, for valuation.

We focus exclusively on valuing annuities in a pretax environment. While this follows in the tradition of most previous studies, Mitchell et al. (1999) also report information on the after-tax value of annuity payouts, recognizing that payouts from nonqualified annuities are partially taxable, and using an after-tax nominal interest rate for discounting. The EPDV of annuity payouts relative to premium costs was very similar in the pretax and posttax cases, however, so we focus on the simpler pretax case in this analysis.

Table 6.2 reports our estimates of the expected discounted value of annuity payouts using the all-company average payout rates from table 6.1 above. The first column shows calculations based on our estimate of the 1998 cohort mortality table for the general population, while the

Table 6.2
EPDV of annuity payouts, per dollar of premium payment, individual annuity policies
offered by commercial insurers, June 1998

Age and gender of annuity buyer	EPDV/premium using population mortality table		EPDV/premium using annuitant mortality table	
	Qualified	Nonqualified	Qualified	Nonqualified
Treasury discount rates				
Male, age 55	.873	.888	.953	.970
Male, age 65	.835	.850	.953	.970
Male, age 75	N.A.	.815	N.A.	.966
Female, age 55	.902	.893	.959	.950
Female, age 65	.888	.875	.966	.952
Female, age 75	N.A.	.815	N.A.	.940
BAA discount rate				
Male, age 55	.773	.786	.835	.849
Male, age 65	.759	.772	.856	.871
Male, age 75	N.A.	.794	N.A.	.891
Female, age 55	.790	.782	.833	.825
Female, age 65	.797	.785	.860	.847
Female, age 75	N.A.	.794	N.A.	.861

Source: Authors' tabulations based on data in table 6.1 above and information described
in the text.
Note: N.A. = not available.

second column presents calculations based on the 1998 cohort mortality table for annuitants. The first panel presents results using riskless
Treasury bond discount rates, while the second panel corresponds to
our "risky interest-rate" discount factor. We report the EPDV of annuity
payments per premium dollar. Using the general population mortality
tables for a sixty-five-year-old man and the Treasury yield curve, the
value per premium dollar for a life annuity is 0.849 for a nonqualified
annuity. For a woman of the same age, the average value is 0.875. When
we value the same annuities using the annuitant mortality table, the
EPDV of payouts rises to 0.970 for men and 0.952 for women. These
values are closer to unity than the estimates in previous studies that
have used the riskless yield curve to discount annuity payouts.

The lower panel of table 6.2 reports our findings using riskier interest rates. In this case, the expected discounted value of payouts is lower
than in the first panel. The calculations using the population mortality
table suggest that the EPDV of payouts is between seventy-five and

eighty cents per premium dollar. Using the mortality table for annuitants raises this estimate to between eighty-two and eighty-seven cents per dollar. Whether it makes more sense to use the riskless or the risky discount rate is open to some question. The historical default risk on annuity payouts has been extremely low, so annuity purchasers probably view their annuity income stream as riskless. Yet the portfolio held by insurance companies that offer annuity products is not restricted to riskless Treasury securities. It is clear from the results in table 6.2 that assumptions about the risk premium that should be included in the discount factor have an important effect on the estimated level of annuity payouts relative to premium costs.

In table 6.2, payout values per premium dollar that are less than unity imply that an annuity purchaser would effectively face a "transaction cost" when purchasing an annuity from a commercial insurance carrier. This is equivalent to purchasing an actuarially fair annuity, defined as one for which the EPDV of payouts equals the policy's premium cost but one that involves having to give up a fraction of one's wealth before investing the remainder in this annuity product. An annuity with payouts that have an EPDV equal to the premium cost is likely to be unattainable since this does not allow for any administrative costs, premium taxes, corporate taxes, commissions, advertising, overhead, assumption of risks, or other costs on the part of the insurance company selling the policy.

The difference between the EPDV calculations based on the population mortality table and those based on the annuitant mortality table provides some insight into the costs of adverse selection in the individual annuity market. For example, for an annuity sold to a sixty-five-year-old man, the cost of adverse selection is 12.1 per cent of the annuity premium (97.0 − 84.9). This is roughly the same magnitude as the estimated cost of adverse selection in several previous studies of the annuity market. When we use the "risky term structure" to reform the annuity valuation exercise, the resulting estimates suggest that adverse selection accounts for a smaller fraction of the differential between the EPDV of payouts and the premium cost for a randomly selected individual in the population.

The findings in table 6.2 suggest that the insurance companies offering annuities are currently charging annuitants less for the administrative, sales, and other charges associated with individual annuity products than previous studies have suggested. This move toward more aggressive pricing may alternatively reflect declining investment risks to insurance companies, rising competition in the annuity market, or the slow adaptation of the assumed mortality tables to improvements in life expectancy. An important issue for further analysis is the source of time-series variation in the EPDV, relative to premium costs, for individual annuities.

Calculations like those in table 6.2 have been interpreted as suggesting that annuities are "expensive" because a sixty-five-year-old buyer with the average mortality in the population gives up at least fifteen cents per dollar of premium in order to buy an annuity. Although it is true that the EPDV of annuity payouts is less than the cost of the annuity, it does not follow that annuities are unattractive to those in the population at large. Results on the utility gains associated with annuitization for representative individuals, with plausible risk tolerance and facing the population mortality risk, suggest that the gains from avoiding uncertainty about length of life are sufficient to warrant purchasing an annuity, even if the EPDV is substantially below the premium amount. Mitchell et al. (1999) report simulation results that support this conclusion. They also suggest that these results are sensitive to several features of the economic environment. In particular, individuals who already have a substantial share of their retirement wealth in an annuitized form, such as social security or a defined-benefit pension plan, will be willing to pay less for an annuity. Married individuals also tend to value annuities less than single individuals. Brown and Poterba (1998) show that this is because of the partial "mortality-risk pooling" that takes place within the household. Finally, there may be a perception among investors of better value from life annuities when interest rates are low.

2   Individual Annuities Available to Participants in the TSP

The last section described individual annuity policies that are universally available in the private annuity market. In this section and the next, we describe policies that are available only to participants in two large group retirement-saving plans. The experience with these plans may provide some insight into the potential operation of annuitization options under various government individual accounts saving programs.

The Thrift Savings Plan (TSP) is a 401(k) defined-contribution retirement plan for federal employees. Congress established the TSP in the Federal Employees' Retirement System (FERS) Act of 1986. For federal employees hired after 31 December 1983, the TSP is an integral part of the retirement-income package, which also includes social security and the FERS basic annuity, a standard defined-benefit pension plan. For federal employees hired before 1984 who did not elect to switch to FERS, the TSP is a voluntary supplement to the Civil Service Retirement System (CSRS) annuity, a generous back-loaded defined-benefit plan.

Employees in FERS can contribute up to 10 per cent of pay to the TSP. The federal government contributes 1 per cent of pay automatically, matches the first 3 per cent of pay contributed by the employee dollar for dollar, and matches the next 2 per cent at fifty cents on the dollar. Employees in CSRS can contribute up to 5 per cent of pay to the TSP but receive no federal government contributions. For all employees, contributions to the TSP are capped at $10,000 per year. There are no nondiscrimination requirements limiting contributions, as occurs in the private sector, although the same dollar limits on contributions apply. There is full and immediate vesting for employee and government matching contributions and earnings, while the service requirement to vest in the automatic government contribution and earnings is generally three years. The service requirement for TSP eligibility is as long as one year.

Contributions can be directed to three investment funds: a short-term government securities (G) fund, a common stock index (S&P500) (C) fund, and a fixed-income index (Lehman Brothers Aggregate) (F) fund. There are plans to add two more investment choices: a small-capitalization stock index fund and an international stock index fund. All investment funds use only a passive indexation strategy. Valuation occurs on a monthly basis; interfund transfers occur at the end of the month. Redirection of future contributions among the various investment funds as well as enrollment can be done only during semiannual open seasons in the winter and summer months. Account-balance statements are sent out semiannually. Loans are allowed from employee contributions and earnings while the participant is in federal service. Limited in-service withdrawals for financial hardship or after reaching age fifty-nine and a half are also allowed.

After a federal employee leaves government service, there are three ways to withdraw assets from the TSP: a life annuity, a lump sum, or a series of monthly payments; these methods may be used in any combination. The lump-sum or monthly payments can be rolled over to another qualified retirement plan, such as an IRA. Like other retirement plans, balances in a TSP account are subject to the federal minimum distribution requirements, mandating distributions after age seventy and a half according to IRS life-expectancy tables. Warshawsky (1998) provides a detailed description and analysis of these requirements.

The Federal Retirement Thrift Investment Board (FRTIB), an independent federal agency, administers the TSP. Governance of the agency is carried out by a five-person, part-time board of presidential appointees and by a full-time executive director selected by the appointees. The board members and the executive director are fiduciaries for the TSP, and they are required to act solely in the interest of participants. Administrative and most investment expenses are paid out of investment earnings and forfeitures of the automatic 1 per cent-of-pay contributions, not through any annual congressional appropriation. In 1997, these expenses were 0.09 per cent of assets, or nine basis points. This gross expense ratio has declined rapidly from sixty-seven basis points in 1988 as average TSP account size has grown. The FRTIB controls a single record-keeping system, coordinating among 130 different federal agency payroll systems. Administrative personnel throughout the federal government also assist with administration for, and the education of, participants.

The latest available data show that participation in the TSP by FERS employees is 86.1 per cent and by CSRS employees about 61 per cent. As of October 1998, the TSP had 2.4 million individual accounts, $71.5 billion in investment assets ($28.3 billion in the G fund, $39.2 billion in the C fund, and $4.0 billion in the F fund), and loans totaling more than $2.4 billion outstanding. During 1997, the TSP received $7 billion in contributions and disbursed almost $1.4 billion in benefits. In dollar terms, most payments are disbursed as transfers to IRAs and other qualified plans; the second- and third-largest disbursement categories are lump sums and death benefits. Net investment income, which equals the net change in market value plus investment earnings, was over $8.6 billion.

2.1 TSP Life-Annuity-Payment Options

Federal law requires the FRTIB to make available to participants who have left federal service five types of life annuities: a single-life annuity with level payments, a single-life annuity with increasing payments, a joint-life annuity (with spouse) with level payments, a joint-life annuity (with spouse) with increasing payments, and a joint-life annuity (with someone other than a spouse who has an insurable interest in the participant) with level payments. Monthly payouts begin thirty days after a TSP annuity is purchased. Joint-life annuities are available either as 50 per cent or as 100 per cent survivor annuities. In an increasing-payment annuity, the amount of the monthly payment can change each year on the anniversary date. The amount of the change is based on the change in the consumer price index (CPI-W). Increases cannot exceed 3 per cent per year, but monthly payments cannot decrease even if the CPI declines. The fact that the TSP offers a kind of inflation-indexed annuity is of some note. One concern sometimes raised about the private annuity market in the United States has been that most annuities are specified in nominal rather than real terms and that, as such, they expose annuitants to inflation risk. It is noteworthy that partially indexed TSP annuities were offered by a private insurance carrier prior to the introduction of inflation-linked Treasury bonds in the United States.

The FRTIB offers two additional annuity features: cash refund and ten-year certain. Under these features, minimum amounts will be paid to a named beneficiary if the participant (and his or her joint annuitant if applicable) dies before the minimum amounts have been paid out. In particular, under a cash refund, if the participant dies before an amount equal to the balance used to purchase the annuity has been paid out, the difference between the purchase balance and the sum of monthly payments already made will be paid to the beneficiary in a lump sum. Under a ten-year certain annuity, if the participant dies before receiving annuity payments for a ten-year period, payments will continue to the beneficiary for the rest of the ten-year period. This latter feature, however, cannot be combined with a joint-life annuity in the TSP. Of course, utilization of these features reduces the monthly annuity payments that can be made. The TSP does not offer any variable annuities with payouts linked to the investment performance of an underlying fund or asset class.

2.2   The Most Recent Request for a Private Insurance Carrier to Supply TSP Annuities

TSP annuities are purchased from a commercial annuity vendor. They are not guaranteed by the federal government but depend on the annuity issuer's claims-paying ability. These tax-qualified, single-premium-immediate annuities are currently provided through a master annuity contract between the FRTIB and the Metropolitan Life Insurance Company (MetLife), a company chosen by the FRTIB. The competitive bidding process is handled through a request for proposal (RFP) inviting submissions to provide annuity services. The following is a summary of the RFP issued in July 1995 by the FRTIB inviting submissions to provide annuity services. The prior RFP was issued in 1990 and was also awarded to MetLife for three years and a two-year extension. With some exceptions noted below, the 1990 RFP was identical to the 1995 RFP.

The RFP stated that the annuity program had to conform to certain requirements. In particular, the amount of the monthly payment from a life annuity provided by the insurance company (the contractor) per $1,000 of single premium had to be an "interest-adjusted tabular monthly annuity payment for the specified annuity option times the Contractor annuity payment rate." The higher the annuity-payout rate, the more attractive the annuity contracts are from the standpoint of the annuitant. The specified annuity options have been described above. The interest adjustment and tabular monthly annuity-payment methods, described explicitly in the RFP, were based generally on actuarial formulas and will be summarized below. The contractor annuity-payment rate is the single number indicating the relative value of the entire bid; it has to be guaranteed for the term of the contract. In the 1990 RFP, there were two contract rates, one for the first three years of the contract, another for the last two years if the TSP decided to extend the contract. Our calculations suggest that MetLife's winning 1995 bid had a contractor rate of 1.039. This is not a statistic supplied by the FRTIB; it is based on our estimates, which have not been validated by the FRTIB.

The tabular monthly annuity-payment approach was chosen as a mechanism to readily adjust payment levels from newly purchased individual annuities to reflect changes in market interest rates over the course of the contract with the insurance company. This approach tends to reduce the interest-rate risk of the contractor, and it was hoped that it would lead to a more competitive contractor annuity-payment rate. Tabular monthly annuity payments were specified in the RFP on the basis of two assumptions: (1) an interest-rate index and (2) a mortality table. No explicit provision for expenses was allowed. The mortality table selected was the 1983 individual annuity mortality table (1983 IAM) on a unisex basis, assuming 50 per cent females and 50 per cent males would be using the annuity program. Selection of the 1983 IAM was based on very limited mortality experience with TSP annuities since the start of the TSP in 1987. As of December 1994, the gender distribution for the TSP population was 42 per cent female and 58 per cent male, although, in older groups, the male share was higher, 63 per cent. In the 1990 RFP, the indicated mortality table was the 1971 IAM table based on 80 per cent males and 20 per cent females. In joint-life situations, the second life was assumed to be 20 per cent male and 80 per cent female. According to the 1990 RFP, the 1971 IAM was selected because its rates were similar to 90 per cent of the mortality experienced between 1983 and 1987 under the CSRS; the 10 per cent reduction of CSRS experience factors was to recognize as of 1990 projected future mortality improvement and adverse selection.

The interest-rate index, calculated monthly, is a three-month moving average of the ten-year Treasury note constant maturity series. The monthly calculation of the interest-rate index applies to new annuity purchases only; payments under previously issued annuities are not affected.

The table of monthly annuity payments presented in the RFP was based on the mortality table described above and a 7 per cent interest rate. Table 6.3, copied from the RFP, shows the worksheet that describes the interest-adjustment calculations. The interest-adjustment factors were also presented in the RFP in tables for given age ranges and annuity-option combinations. The factors were calculated as a simple linear interest-rate adjustment by taking the ratio of the monthly payment at an 8 per cent interest rate to the monthly payment at a 7 per cent interest rate and subtracting one; that is, the factors are just a linear interpolation. The adjustment factors are to be multiplied by the difference in the current interest-rate index and 7 per cent; this product, in turn, is to be multiplied by the tabular monthly annuity payment to produce the change in the monthly annuity payment, finally resulting in the interest-adjusted monthly annuity payment.

The RFP states that the interest-adjustment factors are highly accurate at market interest rates between 7 and 8 per cent. It also noted, however, that accurate adjustment would not be achieved if market rates were to differ greatly from the base 7 per cent interest-rate assumption. Therefore, if annuitants were to become disadvantaged, the FRTIB retained the right to recalculate the tabular monthly

Table 6.3
Annuity calculation worksheet from RFP for annuities provided to TSP participants

Participant information	
1. Annuity option	J&S-50%, level, no cash refund
2. Participant age	62
3. Joint annuitant age (if a joint-life annuity)	59
4. Age difference (if a joint-life annuity). Joint annuitant is	3 years younger
5. TSP account balance	$30,000.00
Calculation of monthly annuity payment (before interest adjustment)	
6. Amount available for annuity in thousands of dollars: line 5 ÷ $1,000	$30.00000
7. Monthly annuity factor per $1,000 account balance: For single-life annuity, use table J.2.1.a For joint-life annuity, use table J.2.1b	7.64 (see B.3., step 1)
8. Preliminary estimate of monthly annuity payment	$226.20 (see B.3., step 2)
Interest-adjusted monthly annuity payment	
9. Current interest-rate index	6.625
10. Interest-rate index used in monthly annuity factor tables	7.000
11. Index increase (decrease): line 9 − line 10	(0.375)
12. Interest-adjustment factor: For single-life annuity, use table J.2.2.a For joint-life annuity, use table J.2.2b	0.086
13. Adjustment multiplier: line 11 × line 12	(0.032)
14. Increase (decrease) to estimate: line 8 × line 13	($7.24)
Interest-adjusted monthly annuity payment line 8 + line 14	$218.96 (see B.3., step 3)

Source: RFP-TIB-95-02 (a request for proposal dated 21 July 1995 from the Federal Retirement Thrift Investment Board), p. J-14.

payments on the basis of a revised interest-rate index assumption reflecting significant long-term changes in market conditions. The November 1998 interest-rate index was 5.25 per cent; for a single-life level-payment annuity of $1,000 issued to a participant age sixty-five, the difference between a precisely calculated monthly annuity payment of $7.02 and an interest-adjusted monthly annuity payment of $7.40 was $0.38, to the advantage of the annuitant. This outcome, of course, results in a loss for the insurance company, relative to an exact calculation.

As noted above, the contractor also had to offer an increasing life annuity tied to year-over-year CPI changes (calculated as an average over July, August, and September), capped at 3 per cent. The actuarial formula used in the RFP to produce the tabular monthly annuity payment assumes that the annual increases will always be 3 per cent; if, however, inflation runs below 3 per cent, as in recent quarters, the insurance company issuing these annuities will reap a profit. Furthermore, newly purchased increasing-level annuities are priced to the disadvantage of the TSP annuitant in the current economic environment, in which inflation rates are below 2 per cent.

The contract was to run for three years; the contract that we study expired at the end of December 1998. The FRTIB, however, had the option to extend the contract for two more years. Administration and reporting for annuities purchased under the terms of the contract are the responsibility of the insurance company through the termination of the last annuity purchased. There are numerous reporting requirements placed on the contractor, pertaining to the types and amounts of annuities purchased, mortality experience, and significant corporate events of the contractor. If the FRTIB views any corporate events, such as loss of customers or change in agency rating, as particularly harmful, it has the right to terminate the contract at any time or to demand corrective action.

In picking a winning bid, the RFP indicated that technical quality was more important than cost. Technical quality factors included the contractor's rating by Standard and Poor's, Moody's, or Duff and Phelps (required to be AA or higher), ability to do business nationally, a balance sheet indicating financial strength, demonstrated continuing profitability, diversification in lines of business, experience with large master annuity contracts, a sound business plan, and the quality of past performance. Cost factors were evaluated by sole reference to the contractor annuity-payment-rate bid.

2.3 Current Annuity-Payout Rates and Utilization Rates

The amount of the monthly payment coming from a TSP life annuity depends on the annuity options chosen, the age of the participant when the annuity is purchased (and the age of the joint annuitant if applicable), the balance in the TSP account used to purchase the annuity, the market interest levels when the annuity is purchased, and the contractor annuity-payment rate. Table 6.4 shows initial monthly payments per $100,000 premium for various issue ages and options for life annuities purchased in June 1998. For example, a level-payment single-life annuity purchased by a sixty-five-year-old will provide $763 monthly per $100,000 premium. This is 4.2 per cent greater than the average payout on a nonqualified annuity offered to men by commercial insurance firms (table 6.1 above) and 6 per cent greater than their average payout on qualified annuities. As a point of comparison, a qualified SPIA (single premium individual annuity) issued by MetLife through an agent to a sixty-five-year-old in June 1998 will provide $664 monthly per $100,000 premium. The TSP interest-rate index in June 1998 was 5.625 per cent.

Table 6.4 demonstrates that initial monthly payments are an increasing function of the age at which the annuity is issued, that they are higher for single as opposed to joint-and-survivor annuities, and that they are higher for level- as opposed to increasing-payment annuities. For example, for an individual age sixty-five, the level payment is 31

Table 6.4
Initial monthly payments ($) per $100,000 accumulation from TSP annuities purchased in June 1998

Age	Single-life annuity		Joint-and-survivor annuity	
	Level payment	Increasing payment	Level payment	Increasing payment
55	635	446	568	382
60	688	504	601	422
65	763	581	650	477
70	858	676	709	540
75	996	813	796	628

Note: Increasing-payment annuity is based on the year-over-year change in the CPI, up to 3 per cent. The joint-and-survivor annuity rates quoted here are for benefits of 100 per cent to a survivor the same age as the annuitant. All annuity rates are unisex. There are no guaranteed periods or cash-refund features chosen.

per cent higher than the initial payment from an increasing annuity. For those age sixty-five, the level monthly single-life annuity payment is 25 per cent higher compared to a level-payment joint-and-survivor annuity.

Almost 12 per cent of the TSP participant population is age fifty-five or older. Hence, each year, there should be a considerable number of retiring participants settling their TSP accounts potentially interested in purchasing a life annuity. At the same time, because most of the retiring federal workers are still CSRS as opposed to FERS participants, the TSP system currently represents a relatively unimportant component of the retirement resources of the average retiring worker settling his or her TSP account. The significance of the TSP system for federal workers' retirement incomes will grow over time as the average size of the account balance increases and as FERS participants begin to retire.

Table 6.5 shows the basic type, number, and amount of TSP annuities purchased between the inception of the program and September 1998. Over one thousand annuities worth over $30 million were purchased in 1995, the high point thus far for TSP annuity activity. Since then, annual activity has fallen to about seven hundred purchased. It is possible that the absence from the option menu of a variable annuity whose payout is tied to the performance of the equity market, which boomed in 1996 and 1997, led to reduced interest in TSP annuities. The average size of a TSP annuity purchased has increased significantly, however, in line with the increase in the average size of a TSP account balance as the overall TSP program begins to mature. In 1990, the average annuity purchased was worth only $8,500; by 1998, the average was over $42,000.

Table 6.5 indicates that the majority of annuities purchased contain the joint-and-survivor option, most providing a 100 per cent benefit to the survivor. A large minority of annuities purchased, however, are for single lives. FRTIB statistics through March 1995 indicate that most annuities purchased, whether single or joint and survivor, are level payment with no cash refund or ten-year certain features chosen. The increasing-payment annuity was chosen by fewer than 12 per cent of annuity purchasers. Female participants are more likely than male participants to choose a single-life annuity than a joint-and-survivor annuity.

These statistics provide important information on the operation of the TSP annuitization program. The most important finding is that annuity payouts within the TSP annuity contract are approximately 5

Table 6.5
Basic type, number, and amount of TSP annuities purchased, 1988–September 1998

Year	Single life	Joint life—50%	Joint life—100%	Insurable interest	Total
	Number of annuities purchased				
1988	3	4	10	0	17
1989	56	33	51	1	141
1990	126	57	103	1	287
1991	248	114	221	2	585
1992	246	111	188	0	545
1993	394	173	226	4	797
1994	366	177	285	7	835
1995	483	220	338	4	1,045
1996	340	137	249	3	729
1997	326	135	240	6	707
1998[a]	241	108	180	7	536
	Amount of annuities purchased ($millions)				
1988	0.015	0.026	0.049	0.000	0.090
1989	0.359	0.240	0.39	0.005	0.914
1990	1.050	0.498	0.892	0.005	2.445
1991	2.664	1.516	2.599	0.018	6.797
1992	3.409	1.847	3.044	0.000	8.300
1993	6.544	3.201	4.322	0.037	14.105
1994	7.080	4.565	6.927	0.117	18.691
1995	12.187	7.392	10.524	0.133	30.236
1996	9.751	5.370	8.815	0.123	24.060
1997	11.475	5.916	9.875	0.209	27.476
1998[a]	9.287	5.749	7.399	0.149	22.585

Source: FRTIB.
a. Through September.

per cent greater than those in the private annuity market. This may reflect cost reductions associated with selling a large volume of annuities of a specified type or a weakened competitive position of the annuity provider when negotiating with the federal government. If we use the TSP annuity payouts for a sixty-five-year-old man in our EPDV algorithm, because these payouts are 4.2 per cent greater than the average payout for commercial single-premium nonqualified annuity policies at the same time, the EPDV of payouts will also be 4.2 per cent greater than the value reported in table 6.2 above. In this case, we conclude that the EPDV is 0.886 (or 1.042×0.850, where 0.850 is the entry in table 5.2, col. 2, row 2) times the premium payment.

3   Individual Annuities Offered by TIAA-CREF for Pension-Plan Participants

The Teachers Insurance and Annuity Association (TIAA) is a nonprofit stock life insurance company, organized under the laws of New York State. It was founded on 4 March 1918 by the Carnegie Foundation for the Advancement of Teaching to aid education and research institutions by providing low-cost retirement products and counseling about lifelong financial security to their employees. TIAA is the companion organization of the College Retirement Equities Fund (CREF), the first company in the United States to issue a variable annuity. CREF was established in 1952 by a special act of the New York State Legislature and, since 1988, has been registered with the SEC as an open-end investment company. Together, TIAA and CREF form the principal retirement system for the nation's education and research communities. In addition to funding vehicles for employer-sponsored pension plans, TIAA-CREF also offers a variety of other financial services, including IRAs, individual and group insurance products, mutual funds, trust services, and tuition saving plans.

The basic principles of the TIAA-CREF pension system in higher education, established as a result of a 1917 study by a group of educators and actuaries, still generally hold: (1) institutions provide immediately vested defined-contribution plans sponsored by the employer (obviating the need for insurance agents selling individual annuity policies); (2) plans are funded by contributions from employers and employees adequate to provide acceptable incomes in retirement under reasonable assumptions; and (3) retirement accounts are owned by employees through individual TIAA and CREF retirement-annuity contracts (creating portability as employees, particularly faculty and administrators, move from institution to institution). In this system, TIAA-CREF acts as a kind of multiemployer pension plan, achieving economies of scale and scope in investment management, plan design, and account administration, pooling risks, and acting in the best interests of plan sponsors and participants.

The "classic" TIAA-CREF basic pension plan consists of an immediately vested individual contract arrangement with a 7.5 per cent-of-pay contribution from the employer and a 5 per cent-of-pay contribution from the employee. Because each TIAA-CREF pension plan is sponsored by a separate institution, however, the contribution rates and other plan rules will differ across institutions. TIAA-CREF assists each institution in the establishment and administration of its pension plans, but the final decision on plan features is made by the sponsoring institution. If an employee wishes to make additional tax-favored contributions, he or she may do so through salary reductions paid to the basic pension plan or to a supplemental retirement annuity (SRA) plan sponsored by the institution. Most pension plans established by educational institutions are governed by the requirements of section 403(b) of the tax code.

As of 1998, participants in TIAA-CREF pension plans may allocate their contributions and accumulations among ten different investment accounts, which can be categorized into four asset classes. There is some institutional control at each participating institution with respect to the accounts offered, and some institutions do not offer all the accounts.

Table 6.6 shows these accounts and classes, with their inception dates, and asset amounts as of 31 October 1998. Ameriks, King, and Warshawsky (1997) trace the choices that TIAA-CREF participants have been making in recent years in their allocation of contributions and of accumulations under basic employer-sponsored pension plans. Although each of the investment accounts has unique risk and return characteristics, we will describe only the two largest and oldest accounts—the TIAA traditional annuity and the CREF stock account.

For the traditional annuity—a stable-value account—TIAA guarantees principal and a 3 per cent interest rate for accumulations. All major ratings agencies currently give TIAA the highest possible ratings for its claims-paying ability. In addition, there are dividends declared by the TIAA Board of Trustees that remain in effect through the end of the

Table 6.6
TIAA-CREF investment accounts and asset classes

Asset class and investment account	Inception date	Asset amounts as of 31 October 1998 ($millions)
Guaranteed		
TIAA traditional annuity (general account)[a]	23 April 1918	99,008
Equity		
CREF stock	1 July 1952	104,069
CREF social choice[b]	1 March 1990	2,987
CREF global equities	1 May 1992	5,405
CREF growth	29 April 1994	6,108
CREF equity index	29 April 1994	2,889
Fixed income		
CREF money market	1 April 1988	5,976
CREF bond market	1 March 1990	2,939
CREF inflation-linked bond	1 May 1997	138
Real estate		
TIAA real estate	2 October 1995	1,082
Total		229,973

a. Also includes investments held for after-tax (nonpension) fixed annuities and various reserves and liabilities.
b. The CREF social choice account is a balanced account composed of bonds and, mainly equities.

"dividend year" and are added to the guaranteed interest rate. Dividends have been paid every year since 1948. The dividend schedules are somewhat complex, tied to the timing of past contributions and intended to assure equity across groups of participants who contributed to TIAA at varied interest-rate levels. Dividend levels are set at the discretion of the TIAA board and reflect TIAA's investment experience.

To back its guarantees, and to maximize dividends, TIAA invests in publicly traded bonds, direct loans to business and industry, commercial mortgages, and real estate. Many of the loans and mortgages (both domestic and foreign) entail long-term commitments, are relatively illiquid, and hence offer higher returns than publicly traded securities. TIAA's investment returns are consistently among the highest of general accounts in the life insurance industry. Because of the illiquidity of many of its loans, TIAA restricts payouts from the traditional annuity to life annuities or over a ten-year period. (Investment in the traditional annuity through SRAs, however, does not entail these restrictions, although the dividends paid on these accumulations are fifty basis points less than those on accumulations in the basic pension plans. Beginning in 1999, restrictions on converting from a TIAA lifetime-annuity income to an equity-based variable annuity were relaxed, with transfers of up to 20 per cent of income in each year permitted.) This restriction on payouts also encompasses the transfer of TIAA traditional annuity accumulations to the other TIAA and CREF investment accounts. All other accounts are variable, marked to the market daily, and generally have no restrictions on transfers or withdrawals. Individual institutions may impose restrictions on withdrawals by participants in their basic pension plans from the TIAA traditional annuity and from the variable accounts.

The CREF stock account is an omnibus growth and income equity account, investing in U.S. and foreign stocks, using a blend of investment styles. The domestic portion of the account, currently over 80 per cent of the portfolio, is invested according to an "enhanced" index strategy. The index is the Russell 3000, and the enhancement refers to various quantitative trading techniques intended to take advantage of arbitrage opportunities. The remainder of the portfolio employs active management for domestic and foreign stocks. There are no guarantees of principal or investment return for CREF stock or the other variable accounts. For the variable accounts, valuation occurs on a daily basis; interfund transfers occur at the end of each trading day.

Transfers of accumulated assets and the redirection of future contributions among the various investment accounts can be done at any time through an automated telephone service and via the Internet. Account-balance statements are sent out quarterly; balances are also available daily through phone-service centers and the Internet. An annuity benefit report is sent out annually, projecting for the individual, under reasonable assumptions, future retirement-income flows under certain life annuity options and investment returns. Consultants offer individual and group counseling at regional offices or participating institutions.

Administrative and investment expenses for the TIAA-CREF pension system are paid from investment earnings. At the current level of about thirty to thirty-five basis points, these expenses are among the lowest in the insurance and mutual fund industries. The responsibility for oversight of TIAA-CREF management lies with its boards of trustees. Because TIAA and CREF, the main components of the parent organization, are incorporated under different laws and are regulated by different government agencies, there is one board for TIAA and another for CREF. A board of overseers ensures that TIAA-CREF is meeting its charter purposes; this board also elects trustees to the TIAA Board. CREF participants directly elect CREF trustees, in the same manner as mutual fund shareholders who have votes in proportion to the shares they own. Members of the boards are a diverse group of men and women, representing academic (faculty and administration), business, and philanthropic institutions, with a wide range of expertise and interests, including education, management, government, economics, finance, law, and corporate governance. Most board members are themselves longtime TIAA-CREF participants; only two are TIAA-CREF executives.

Warshawsky and Ameriks (1996) report that pension coverage (at over 95 per cent) and participation (at 80 per cent) are significantly greater in the higher education sector than in the rest of the full-time labor force (71 per cent and 59 per cent, respectively). As of 31 October 1998, there were 1,792,942 participants in the accumulation phase, 290,616 participants receiving annuity-income payments in the TIAA-CREF pension system, and 8,711 institutions of all sizes sponsoring TIAA-CREF pension plans.

3.1 Life-Annuity-Payment Options

At one time, all TIAA-CREF basic pension plans allowed for distributions only through a life annuity or death benefit (supplemental plans have always been "cashable"). In 1988, this systemwide restriction was removed for basic plans, although a small number of sponsoring institutions chose to retain it. Hence, with the exception of accumulations in the TIAA traditional annuity, for most TIAA-CREF pension plans, when an employee leaves the service of his or her employer, accumulations can be withdrawn as a life annuity, in a lump sum, in a systematic series of payments, or in any combination of lump sum, systematic withdrawals, and life annuities. In addition, for all plans, participants over age seventy and a half can, since 1991, withdraw funds through a minimum-distribution option (MDO), and participants age fifty-five and over can, since 1989, receive payments of current interest credited to TIAA accumulations through an interest-only payment retirement option (IPRO). A retirement-transition benefit is also available from TIAA and CREF, whereby 10 per cent of accumulations are available as a lump sum on retirement.

Despite the flexibilities available, most TIAA-CREF participants still choose a life annuity when they retire. TIAA-CREF offers both single- and two-life annuities, with or without guaranteed periods of ten, fifteen, or twenty years. The options available for two-life annuities are two-thirds benefit to survivor, full benefit to survivor, and half benefit to second annuity partner. Payout levels reflect the option chosen. Payments can be made on a monthly, quarterly, semiannual, or annual basis.

Life annuities can be drawn from any of the investment accounts. The TIAA traditional annuity guarantees the interest rate ($2\frac{1}{2}$ per cent) and mortality assumptions for payouts through life annuities. These payout guarantees actually begin in the accumulation phase and hence can be in effect for several decades. In addition, the TIAA board declares annual dividends to annuitants.

There are two different life-annuity-payment methods available from TIAA—standard and graded. For both methods, payment is based on assumed mortality, guaranteed interest, and dividends. Under the standard payment method, the initial income level is maintained until there is a change in dividends; year-over-year dividend changes in the payout phase historically have been small. Under the graded payment method, initial income is based on a 4 per cent payout. Any remaining dividends are reinvested and used to buy additional future income. This method was first proposed by Biggs (1969) and put in place by TIAA in 1982 to help protect annuitants from inflation. King (1995) calculated hypothetical payments under the graded method for various periods beginning in the 1970s and found that purchasing power was preserved, indeed enhanced, through 1995, although, in the years of high inflation in the late 1970s and early 1980s, purchasing power lagged somewhat. Annuitants who initially choose the graded method can later switch to the standard method, but not vice versa.

Life annuities can also be drawn from any of the variable accounts. Payouts are entirely variable, reflecting the investment performance and expenses of the account and the mortality experience of annuitants using the account. Initial payments are calculated using the accumulation, the income option chosen, an assumed effective interest rate of 4 per cent, and mortality assumptions, currently the unisex version of the 1983 IAM table set back two months for each complete year that has elapsed since 31 March 1986 to account for ongoing gains in longevity. After the initial payment, payment amounts change to reflect mainly the performance of the investment portfolio either annually or monthly, at the option of the participant.

Although income from the variable accounts is generally more volatile than that from the TIAA traditional annuity, participants with variable annuities are able to devise a retirement-income portfolio more aligned with their risk tolerances. For the equity accounts, over long time periods, variable annuitants participate in general economic performance, which has been significantly positive in the United States and other countries over most recent historical periods. Annuitants may switch among the variable accounts or to the TIAA traditional annuity on any business day, as often as once per calendar quarter. Income options, annuitant(s), and guaranteed period, however, must be maintained on the switch.

3.2 Current Annuity Payout Rates and Annuity Utilization

Table 6.7 shows initial monthly payments per $100,000 accumulation in a basic pension plan for various issue ages and options for life annuities issued by TIAA-CREF on 1 June 1998. For TIAA, the annuity payout reflects current dividend levels assuming that the participant has made contributions from salary, increasing at 5 per cent annually, to TIAA since 1 June 1968; various TIAA vintages are represented in

Table 6.7
Initial monthly payments ($) per $100,000 accumulation from TIAA and CREF annuities issued in June 1998

	Single-life annuity		Joint-and-survivor annuity	
Age	TIAA standard	CREF	TIAA standard	CREF
55	665	489	612	435
60	704	534	636	465
65	759	597	670	507
70	838	683	719	566
75	953	807	792	648

Note: Issuance of annuity on 1 June 1998. The joint-and-survivor annuity rates quoted here are for benefits to a survivor the same age as the annuitant. TIAA rates reflect 30 years of participation (1 June 1968–1 June 1998) in TIAA and past salary growth of 5 per cent per year; TIAA vintages are recognized. All annuity rates are unisex. There are no guaranteed periods chosen.

this example and produce a blended investment return of 6.9 per cent. For CREF, the assumed interest rate is 4 per cent. Future payouts on a CREF annuity will reflect investment performance in an underlying variable-investment account, and, if returns exceed 4 per cent, payouts will increase.

For a single-life annuity issued to a sixty-five-year-old, TIAA is paying, as of 1 June 1998, an initial monthly payout of $759 per $100,000 accumulation under the standard payment method. This value is higher than the average commercial market payout for men ($732 in nonqualified accounts) and even more dramatically greater than that for women ($662). For a joint-and-survivor annuity issued to a couple, both of whom are sixty-five years old, TIAA is paying $670 monthly per $100,000, higher than the payout rate for TSP annuities. With a 4 per cent assumed interest rate, CREF is initially paying on any of its accounts $597 monthly for the single-life annuity and $507 monthly for the joint-life annuity.

Comparing the TSP (table 6.4 above) and TIAA (table 6.7), we note that TIAA offers superior rates on joint-and-survivor annuities at all ages except the oldest and higher rates on single-life annuities at the younger ages. These generally higher rates result from TIAA's superior investment performance. Comparisons between the TSP and TIAA should be made cautiously as payouts from TIAA may fluctuate somewhat, either downward or, as has occurred in the last several years, upward. Moreover, as noted above, with current market interest rates significantly below the 7 per cent assumption of the tabular annuity rates, the TSP offers higher rates than it would if its annuity rates were set precisely like TIAA's. In addition, where mortality is a more important consideration, for example, in single-life annuities issued at older ages, the mandated use of a liberal, that is, old and outdated, mortality table by the TSP will lead to higher annuity-income rates. It is impossible to compare the increasing-payment TSP annuity with a CREF annuity because the assumed interest rate is fixed at 4 per cent for CREF while it is (implicitly) constantly changing for the TSP. In June 1998, the (implicit) TSP assumed interest rate for its increasing-payment annuity was 2.625 per cent (= 5.625 per cent − 3 per cent).

About 16,300 TIAA-CREF participants converted some or all of their accumulations into streams of periodic income in 1997. Of these, 11,700 chose a life annuity, 2,200 the MDO, 1,500 the IPRO, and 900 systematic withdrawals. The MDO is particularly popular among participants age seventy and a half and older; nearly three-quarters of this age group chose this form of income stream in 1997. This opting for flexibility represents an expected movement away from life annuities since 1988, when a life annuity was the only distribution form available. Settlements into life annuities are occurring at older ages, and partial settlements into life annuities are becoming more common, as participants choose to keep their options open longer. The graded-benefit payment method for TIAA traditional annuity accumulations has also grown more popular: Almost a quarter of new TIAA annuitants now select this method, compared to 2 per cent when it was first introduced in 1982.

King (1996) looked at the choices in 1994 of TIAA-CREF participants among the life-annuity payout options. About three-quarters of male primary annuitants chose the two-life annuity, while about two-thirds of female primary annuitants chose the single-life annuity. About a third of the male and female annuitants choosing the single-life annuity selected no guaranteed period; the rest chose fairly evenly among ten-, fifteen-, and twenty-year guaranteed periods. Nearly all annuitants choosing a two-life annuity selected a guaranteed period. Male annuitants among the two-life annuity group predominantly selected the full-benefit-to-survivor form. Female annuitants in this group also favored the full benefit to survivor but were more likely than men to select the half-benefit-to-second-annuitant form. Among payout sources, the majority of annuity payouts in 1994 came from TIAA, but a sizable minority of payouts were from a CREF variable annuity. More recently, there has been a trend toward payouts from the variable accounts. This may provide some guidance for the design of annuitization systems within other individual account structures. In particular, it suggests a substantial demand for variable as opposed to fixed annuities.

4 Conclusions and Future Directions

The results in this chapter provide information on the costs of obtaining an individual annuity in three different market environments. The first environment, the current market for single-premium individual annuities, is one in which each annuity buyer has full discretion in choosing among different insurance carriers and no economies of scale occur through participation in a group retirement-saving program. The costs in this environment are higher than those in the other two settings that we consider, namely, the federal government's TSP and the TIAA-CREF retirement system that is available to college and university employees. This is reflected in the higher average annuity payouts offered in these systems, for a given premium, than in the market at large. We show that the annuity payouts available to TSP participants in June 1998 were roughly 4 per cent greater than those available (on average) in the private market. It is difficult to make a precise comparison between the annuity payouts of TIAA-CREF, the private market, and the TSP because of differences between nonguaranteed-element, variable, and nonparticipating annuity products. However, the TIAA-CREF payouts appear to be greater than those of the TSP or (on average) the private market.

Our results provide some potential guidance on the costs of annuitization but also raise questions. One concerns the time-series pattern of annuity payouts relative to the premiums for single-premium annuity policies. Comparing the calculations in Friedman and Warshawsky (1990), Mitchell et al. (1999), and the present paper suggests that the EPDV of annuity payouts has been rising, relative to premiums, for the last decade. Explaining this trend is an important issue for further investigation. It may result from declining risk perceived by the insurance companies that offer these products, particularly with respect to interest-rate fluctuations. It could also reflect a failure to take into account ongoing improvements in mortality. For example, consider what would happen if annuity providers were to use information from a given past year (say, 1983, the date of the last major release of annuitant mortality rates by the Society of Actuaries) on the mortality rates of annuitants. If actual mortality rates are declining, then the EPDV of payouts will be rising. While this explanation is consistent with what we observe in the annuity market, we are not aware of any way to distinguish this possibility from alternative explanations.

A second question concerns the design of a menu of annuity options that might be available for potential annuitants. Experience with TIAA-CREF suggests that a substantial number of participants are interested in variable as opposed to fixed annuities. While TSP participants can choose annuities that are partially inflation indexed, relatively few do; the TSP experience, however, does not provide any evidence on whether annuitants would choose real (fully indexed), partially indexed, or nominal annuities if they could make such a decision. Further work should investigate the behavior of individual annuitants in settings in which they can choose among different potential annuity options.

References

Ameriks, John, Francis King, and Mark Warshawsky. 1997. Premium allocations and accumulations in TIAA-CREF—trends in participant choices among asset classes and investment accounts. *TIAA-CREF Research Dialogues*, no. 51 (July).

Bell, Felicitie, A. Wade, and S. Goss. 1992. Life tables for the United States social security area, 1900–2080. Actuarial Study no. 107. Washington, D.C.: Social Security Administration, Office of the Actuary.

A. M. Best. Various issues. *Best's Review: Life and Health*. Oldwick, N.J.

Biggs, John H. 1969. Alternatives in variable annuity benefit design. *Transactions of the Society of Actuaries* 21 (November): 495–528.

Brown, Jeffrey R., and James M. Poterba. 1998. Joint and survivor annuities and the demand for annuities by married couples. NBER Working Paper no. 7199. Cambridge, Mass.: National Bureau of Economic Research.

Friedman, Benjamin, and Mark Warshawsky. 1988. Annuity prices and saving behavior in the United States. In *Pensions in the U.S. economy*, ed. Z. Bodie, J. Shoven, and D. Wise. Chicago: University of Chicago Press.

———. 1990. The cost of annuities: Implications for saving behavior and bequests. *Quarterly Journal of Economics* 105, no. 1 (February): 135–54.

Gramlich, Edward M. 1996. Different approaches for dealing with social security. *Journal of Economic Perspectives* 10 (summer): 55–66.

Johansen, R. 1996. Review of adequacy of 1983 individual annuity mortality table. *Transactions of the Society of Actuaries* 47:101–23.

King, Francis. 1995. The TIAA graded payment method and the CPI. *TIAA-CREF Research Dialogues*, no. 46 (December).

———. 1996. Trends in the selection of TIAA-CREF life-annuity income options, 1978–1994. *TIAA-CREF Research Dialogues*, no. 48 (July).

Mitchell, Olivia, James M. Poterba, Mark Warshawsky, and Jeffrey R. Brown. 1999. New evidence on the money's worth of individual annuities. *American Economic Review* 89 (December): 1299–1318.

Warshawsky, Mark. 1988. Private annuity markets in the United States. *Journal of Risk and Insurance* 55, no. 3 (September): 518–28.

———. 1998. Distributions from retirement plans: Minimum requirements, current options, and future directions. *TIAA-CREF Research Dialogues*, no. 57 (September).

Warshawsky, Mark, and John Ameriks. 1996. Pensions and health benefits for workers in higher education. *TIAA-CREF Research Dialogues*, no. 49 (December).

7

Taxing Retirement Income: Nonqualified Annuities and Distributions from Qualified Accounts

Jeffrey R. Brown,
Olivia S. Mitchell,
James M. Poterba, and
Mark J. Warshawsky

Die early and avoid the fate.
Or, if predestined to die late,
Make up your mind to die in state.

Robert Frost in "Provide, Provide"

The taxation of retirement saving is an important and growing policy issue. Income tax exclusions for contributions to qualified retirement plans and for the income that accrues on the assets held in such plans have an important impact on the structure of retirement saving for many households. A substantial fraction of those reaching retirement age in recent years have accumulated very few financial assets outside retirement saving plans. Moore and Mitchell (2000) and Poterba, Venti, and Wise (1998a) show that Social Security wealth, employer-provided pensions, and owner-occupied housing equity were the most substantial components of household net worth for all but the wealthiest one-fifth of retirees in the 1990s.

For households that do accumulate substantial assets during their working lives—both inside and outside qualified retirement plans—reaching retirement raises questions about how to draw down these assets. Someone who has no interest in leaving a bequest, and who does not know how long he will live, faces the problem of choosing a level of consumption that will take advantage of his accumulated assets, without incurring too great a risk of outliving his resources. One way to avoid this risk is to purchase an immediate life annuity contract. Annuities, which are sold by life insurance companies, typically

From *National Tax Journal* 52 (September 1999): 563–586. Reprinted by permission of the *National Tax Journal*.

promise a fixed stream of nominal payouts for as long as the policy-holder is alive.

Payouts from retirement assets can be stratified along two dimensions: whether the payouts are structured as a life annuity and whether the accumulation took place in a qualified retirement plan.[1] This typology gives rise to four types of withdrawals from retirement asset stocks. The first category, income from nonannuitized nonqualified asset accumulation, is simply taxable saving. We do not consider this type of retirement saving in the present analysis, because it is the subject of essentially all textbook analyses of how taxation affects saving behavior. The second category is annuitized payouts resulting from nonqualified asset accumulation. The tax treatment of annuities purchased with after-tax dollars is complex. The fraction of annuity payouts that is included in the recipient's taxable income depends on how long the annuity has been paying benefits. Annuitants who have been lucky enough to live a long time and to receive annuity benefits for a long period are taxed on a higher fraction of their annuity income than are those who have recently purchased their annuity. This complexity arises from the fact that part of each payout on an annuity policy is treated as a return of the policyholder's principal and part is treated as a payment from the capital income that has accrued on the policyholder's initial premium.

The third payout option consists of annuities purchased with assets in qualified retirement accounts. The tax treatment in this case hinges on the presence or absence of after-tax contributions to the qualified account. For annuities purchased with funds in qualified accounts that were partially funded with after-tax dollars, the tax treatment is more complex than for annuities purchased from accounts that were funded only with pretax contributions.

Finally, there is a fourth category of payouts: nonannuitized payouts from qualified retirement plans. These payouts are subject to a complex set of tax rules, in particular, minimum distribution requirements that affect the permissable time path of nonannuitized distributions. These rules have the potential to affect the time path along which many elderly households draw down their assets.

This chapter focuses on two of the four types of withdrawals from retirement savings: annuities purchased using assets that are held in nonqualified accounts and nonannuitized withdrawals from qualified accounts. It is divided into seven sections. The first summarizes the current federal income tax rules that apply to nonqualified immediate annuities. Our analysis focuses on the *payout* phase of annuity products, and we do not consider the important issues concerning asset accumulation that are raised by the rapid recent growth of variable annuity products. The second section describes our framework for calculating the expected present discounted value of pretax and after-tax payouts on annuity policies. It also explains how we can apply a standard model of consumer behavior to estimate the utility consequences of various tax rules for annuity products. The third section presents our basic findings on how the current income tax system affects the after-tax value of annuity purchases. We find that the current income tax rules do not substantially affect the incentives to purchase annuities rather than taxable bonds. We nevertheless find some differences across categories of individuals in the effective tax burden on annuity contracts.

The fourth section develops an alternative tax scheme for nonqualified annuities that would include a constant fraction of annuity payouts in taxable income, regardless of how long the annuity had been paying benefits. We calibrate this tax scheme by finding the inclusion rate at which it would raise the same expected present discounted value of revenues as the current tax system, and we also ask how such a tax system would affect the incentives for annuity purchase.

The fifth section moves beyond the discussion of nonqualified annuity products to an overview of tax issues that arise in connection with qualified accounts. First, we consider annuitized payouts funded with after-tax contributions. We describe the minimum distribution requirements associated with nonannuitized payouts from qualified retirement accounts. Our discussion focuses on how these requirements constrain the feasible time path of payouts. We examine detailed provisions such as assumptions about mortality tables and allowable distribution methods.

The sixth section presents evidence on the amount of retirement assets and the fraction of retiree households that are potentially affected by minimum distribution rules. We report the value of assets in qualified pension plans that are held by individuals who are approaching the age at which minimum distributions must begin. The conclusion raises several issues that warrant further research attention, and an Appendix presents estimates of the revenue consequences of changing the current minimum distribution rules.

1 The Current Tax Treatment of Nonqualified Annuities

The current U.S. federal income tax system taxes both the income from annuity contracts and the capital income that a potential annuitant might earn on his alternative investment options. Throughout this paper, we consider an investment in a taxable bond as the alternative to purchasing an annuity contract. The U.S. General Accounting Office (1990) provides an introduction to the tax rules that govern non-qualified annuities. First, the Internal Revenue Service (IRS) specifies the time period over which the annuitant can expect to receive bene-fits. We denote this expected payout period T'. The IRS regulations refer to it as the "Expected Return Multiple," and it is currently based on the unisex IRS annuitant mortality table as well as the annuitant's age at the time when the annuity begins paying benefits. The current tax rules apply the same mortality rates, and hence expected payout periods, to annuity payouts received by men and by women, even though the actual mortality rates facing men and women are substantially different.

Second, the tax law prescribes an *inclusion ratio* (λ), which determines the share of each annuity payment that must be included in the recip-ient's taxable income. The inclusion ratio is related to the fraction of each annuity payout that results from capital income on the accumu-lating value of the annuity premium rather than from a return of the annuitant's principal. This method of taxing annuity payments, known as the "General Rule," is required for all nonqualified annuity pay-ments starting after July 1, 1986. A second approach, known as the "Simplified Method," applies to certain qualified annuities purchased after November 19, 1996. It specifies different values of the inclusion ratio than the general rule, but otherwise operates in a similar fashion.

For an annuity policy with a purchase price of Q and an annual payout of A, the inclusion ratio during the first T' years of payouts is defined by

$$\lambda = 1 - \frac{Q}{A * T'}. \tag{1}$$

After T' years, all payouts from the annuity policy are included in taxable income (thus $\lambda = 1$ after T' years).[2] If the annuitant faces a com-bined federal and state marginal income tax rate of τ, then the after-tax annuity payment in each year is $(1 - \lambda\tau)A$. If an equivalently risky taxable bond yields a pretax nominal return of i, its after-tax return is

$(1 - \tau)i$. The expected return multiple, T', is equal to the annuitant's life expectancy as of the starting date of the annuity, calculated using the IRS's unisex annuitant mortality table.

2 Comparing Annuities with Alternative Assets

We use two approaches to analyze the current tax treatment of annuities versus taxable bonds. The first emphasizes the expected present discounted value of after-tax annuity payments and the comparison between this value and the purchase cost of the annuity. The second, which uses an explicit utility function, asks how much wealth a stylized consumer would need if he could not buy an annuity in order to be as well off as if he could invest his actual current wealth in a nominal annuity contract. We now describe each of these approaches in turn.

2.1 The Expected Discounted Present Value of Annuity Payouts

The expected present discounted value (EPDV) of the payouts from an immediate annuity depends on the amount of the annuity payout (A), the discount rate that applies to future annuity payouts, and the mortality rates that determine the annuitant's chances of surviving to receive the promised future payouts. We denote the probability of surviving for j months after purchasing the annuity as P_j. We focus on months as the basic time unit because annuities typically pay monthly benefits. If there were no taxes, the expected present discounted value of annuity payouts ($EPDV_{notax}$) for someone at age 65, and who was certain to die before age 115 (600 months into the future), would be

$$EPDV_{notax} = \sum_{j=1}^{600} \frac{A * P_j}{\prod_{k=1}^{j}(1 + i_k)} \tag{2}$$

where i_k denotes the nominal one-period interest rate k periods into the future. Expressions such as $EPDV_{notax}$ have been used in a number of earlier studies, including Warshawsky (1988), Friedman and Warshawsky (1988, 1990), and Mitchell, Poterba, Warshawsky, and Brown (hereafter, MPWB) (1999).

In the current income tax environment, this expression must be modified to recognize both the income tax treatment of annuity payments and the taxation of the returns on the alternative asset that determines the discount rate for the annuity cash flows. The modified expression in an income tax world. $EPDV_{tax'}$ is

$$EPDV_{tax} = \sum_{j=1}^{12*T'} \frac{(1 - \lambda * \tau) * A * P_j}{\prod_{k=1}^{j}(1 + (1 - \tau) * i_k)} + \sum_{j=12*T'+1}^{600} \frac{(1 - \tau) * A * P_j}{\prod_{k=1}^{j}(1 + (1 - \tau) * i_k)} \tag{3}$$

with T' and λ defined as above. The difference between $EPDV_{notax}$ and $EPDV_{tax}$ provides a direct measure of the extent to which the current income tax structure affects the attractiveness of annuities rather than taxable bonds, relative to a world in which capital income is untaxed. If the two EPDV values are similar, then the current income tax code does not substantially affect the incentive to purchase annuities rather than taxable bonds. It is the *relative* tax treatment of annuities and bonds that determines the effective tax burden on annuities.

2.2   Data Inputs to EPDV Calculations

We apply this framework to evaluate the expected discounted value of annuity payouts for annuity products that were available in the U.S. marketplace in 1998. We focus on individual nonparticipating, single-premium-immediate life annuities offered by commercial life insurance companies. These are annuity policies for which individuals make an initial premium payment and then usually begin receiving fixed annuity payouts in the month after their purchase.

Payments on life annuities (variable A in equations 2 and 3) are reported each year in the August issue of A. M. Best's publication *Best's Review: Life and Health*. We analyze data from the August 1998 issue, which reports the results of an annuity market survey conducted at the beginning of June 1998. The Best's data correspond to single-premium annuities with a $100,000 premium. Ninety-nine companies responded to the survey, reporting information on the current monthly payouts on individual annuities sold to men and women at ages 55, 60, 65, 70, 75, and 80. We restrict our current analysis to annuities available for 65-year-old men and women. Poterba and Warshawsky (1999) summarize the average annuity payouts at different ages. The computations below focus on a hypothetical individual who purchases an annuity that offers the average payout across all companies. We recognize, and document in MPWB (1999), that there is substantial variation in annuity payouts across insurers.

To evaluate the rate of return that potential annuitants might receive on alternative assets, we assume that annuity payouts are riskless. We then use the term structure of yields for zero-coupon Treasury "strips" to estimate the pattern of future monthly short-term interest rates. These data are published in the *Wall Street Journal,* and we use the reports from the first week of June 1998 to coincide with the timing of Best's annuity price survey.

Our EPDV calculations are sensitive to our marginal tax rate assumptions. Because there is very little publicly available information on the household incomes, and even less on the marginal tax rates, of annuity purchasers, we consider two different marginal tax rate assumptions. In the first case, we assume that the annuity buyer faces a 15 per cent federal marginal tax rate; and in the second case, the annuity recipient is assumed to be in the 36 per cent federal tax bracket. The first case, corresponds to a married couple filing jointly with total taxable income of less than $42,350, while the second would correspond, in 1998, to taxable income between $155,950 and $278,450. We also report EPDV calculations for the no-tax case.

We evaluate equations 2 and 3 using projected survival probabilities for people purchasing annuities in 1998. One difficulty in evaluating the effective cost of purchasing an annuity, however, is that the pool of actual annuity purchasers has a lower risk of dying at any given age than the population at large. Insurance companies use an annuitant mortality table to determine the relationship between premium income and the expected present discounted value of payouts. We use the MPWB (1999) approach to projecting future annuitant mortality rates by combining information from the Annuity 2000 Mortality table, the older 1983 Individual Annuitant Mortality (IAM) table, and the projected rate of mortality improvement in the Social Security Administration's population mortality tables from the 1995 Social Security Trustee's Report.

The choice of a mortality table is a key issue in the taxation of annuity payouts. In this respect, the current IRS use of the 1983 IAM table has important consequences. The 1983 IAM table was based on actual annuitants' mortality experience in a large group of companies over the period 1971–6, updated to reflect 1983 conditions. The Society of Actuaries' Individual Annuity Experience Committee (1991–2) studied the annuity experience of a small group of companies over the period 1976–86 and concluded that the 1983 table was adequate of the 1980s.

More recently, however, Johansen (1996)—one of the actuaries involved in the earlier studies—has called for a new individual annuity table, after evaluating population mortality statistics from the Social Security Administration and the National Center for Health Statistics and evolving conditions in the group annuity market. Unfortunately, there are no recent studies of industry-wide annuitant mortality experience. A Society of Actuaries committee therefore suggested using the basic 1983 annuity table projected forward to the year 2000, with mortality improvement factors consistent with the recent experience of the general population as well as that of one company with substantial annuity business. This is the Annuity 2000 table. We construct a 1998 annuitant mortality table by interpolating between the 1983 IAM and the Annuity 2000 tables and then applying forward looking mortality improvement factors to create a 1998 annuitant cohort table. The age and gender-specific mortality rates in the 1998 table are substantially lower than those in the 1983 IAM table due to significant mortality improvements.

Table 7.1 shows selected mortality rates from five sets of mortality tables. The first column corresponds to our estimate of the 1998 annuitant mortality table for men. The second column reports male annuitant mortality rates taken from the 1983 IAM table. These rates are

Table 7.1
Comparison of mortality rates, various mortality tables, and genders

Age	1998 annuitant male mortality	1983 IAM male mortality	IRS unisex life table	1983 IAM female mortality	1998 annuitant female mortality
65	0.01096	0.01425	0.00978	0.00824	0.00706
70	0.01842	0.02381	0.01683	0.01303	0.01138
75	0.03074	0.03899	0.02791	0.02238	0.01898
80	0.04983	0.06313	0.04695	0.04053	0.03285
85	0.07763	0.10126	0.07974	0.07237	0.05777
90	0.11696	0.15010	0.13150	0.12594	0.10142
95	0.16738	0.21229	0.19703	0.19380	0.15626
100	0.22782	0.30072	0.27041	0.26399	0.20762
105	0.33098	0.44071	0.38932	0.37843	0.29490
110	0.51959	0.66342	0.61283	0.60212	0.47429

Source: 1983 IAM from Society of Actuaries, Transactions, Volume XXXIII. 1998 mortality based on authors' calculations as explained in text. IRS unisex mortality table courtesy of Norman Greenberg of the IRS.

substantially greater than those in the 1998 annuitant table. For most ages, the mortality rate for men according to the 1983 IAM table is approximately 30 per cent higher than the mortality rate in the 1998 annuitant table. The third column shows the 1983 Unisex Individual Annuitant Mortality table, which is what the IRS currently uses to determine the inclusion ratio and other tax parameters associated with annuity taxation. The last two columns show the 1998 and 1983 annuitant mortality rates for women.

The 1983 Unisex Mortality table that the IRS uses is a weighted average of the 1983 IAM basic mortality tables for men and women, with different weights on the two tables at different ages. We have "reverse engineered" these weights and have found them to vary with age and to place heavier emphasis on female than male mortality. For example, at age 65, the Unisex table places a weight of 0.74 on the female mortality rate and 0.26 on the male rate. This weight on the female mortality rates decreases to 0.65 at age 70 and then increases every five years until it peaks at 0.825 for age 95 and above. We have been unable to learn the motivation for this particular choice of weights. The U.S. Treasury Department has recently revised the mortality tables that are used to value the benefits of group life insurance and several other insurance products, but there have been no changes since 1986 in the mortality table that is used to compute T' in single-premium annuity markets.

For men, the fact that the IRS Unisex Mortality table overstates mortality rates by using an old mortality table is almost exactly offset by the heavier weighting on the lower female mortality rates. Therefore, the IRS Unisex table does not substantially differ from the 1998 male annuitant mortality table. For women, how-ever, the differences between the two tables are large. Both the weighting scheme and the outdated table result in IRS mortality rates for women that are substantially larger than the mortality rates from the 1998 annuitant table. These differences are especially large at the younger ages. At age 65, for example, a woman's mortality rate is 40 per cent greater in the IRS table than in the 1998 annuitant table.

The use of a unisex mortality table implies that there are differences in the effective tax burdens on annuities for men and women. According to the IRS unisex table, the life expectancy of a 65-year-old indi-vidual is 20 years. This is the value used for T' in the construction of the inclusion ratio. The actual life expectancy of a 65-year-old man, according to the 1998 annuitant table, is 19.8 years, while that for a 65-year-old woman is 22.7 years.

The fact that T' for women is less than their actual life expectancy has two effects on the lifetime tax burden on annuities. First, using the IRS table results in a smaller inclusion ratio (λ) than a woman would face if her actual life expectancy were used. In the early years of an annuity payout, a lower inclusion ratio implies that a smaller fraction of the annuity payment is subject to taxation. This effect therefore reduces the tax burden on annuities.

For example, in 1998, a 65-year-old woman purchasing the average single-premium-immediate annuity offered in the private market could expect to receive approximately $662 per month for a $100,000 policy. Under current IRS rules, the value of T' is 20 years, which implies an inclusion ratio (λ) for this woman of 0.37. This means that $245 of the $662 annuity payment is included in taxable income, while the remainder is considered a return of basis and is tax free. If instead of using the 20-year life expectancy implied by the 1983 unisex table, the IRS used the 1998 female annuitant mortality table, this would increase the value of T' to be equal to her actual life expectancy of 22.7 years. This in turn raises the inclusion ratio to $\lambda = 0.445$, which would result in $295 of the $662 monthly annuity payment being included in taxable income. Therefore, by using the 20-year life expectancy of the 1983 unisex mortality table instead of the life expectancy from the 1998 female annuitant table, the 65-year-old female annuitant's taxable income is reduced by $50 per month, or $600 per year.

The second effect of using a lower value of T, and one that offsets the first effect to a small degree, is the fact that using the IRS unisex table also reduces the number of years for which part of the annuity payment is excluded from taxes. Under current law, after 20 years (when the woman reaches age 85), the after-tax annuity payment falls from $(1 - \lambda\tau)A$ to $(1 - \tau)A$. (Taxes rise from $\lambda\tau A$ to τA.) Using actual life expectancy, this drop would occur after 22.7 years. Therefore, the woman would not have to report the full $662 as taxable income until she was age 87.7.

The net effect of using the 1983 unisex table rather than the current annuitant mortality table is a positive effect on the EPDV of annuity purchase for women. Specifically, a 65-year-old woman with a marginal income tax rate of 28 per cent would have an after-tax EPDV of 0.968 using $T = 20$ from the 1983 Unisex table, versus 0.956 using $T = 22.7$ from the 1998 female annuitant table. The first effect discussed above, the lower inclusion ratio when part of the annuity income can be excluded from taxable income, is quantitatively more important than the second effect, the change in the length of the time period over which some annuity income can be excluded.

2.3   A Utility-Based Approach to Valuing Annuity Products

In addition to our analysis of the expected present discounted value of annuity payouts, we also compare annuities and alternative assets in terms of the expected utility that they would generate for a potential annuitant. Because annuities offer individuals insurance against the risk of outliving their assets, they generate benefits that are not captured in a simple present discounted value framework. Calculating the expected utility of annuitization recognizes these benefits, and it provides an explicit framework for evaluating the welfare effects of age-dependent taxation of annuity payouts.

Our analysis assumes that a hypothetical individual compares investing in a riskless taxable bond and investing in an actuarially fair annuity contract. This is different than our approach in analyzing the EPDV of annuity products, where we use the *actual* annuity payouts available in the marketplace rather than hypothetical actuarially fair annuities. We find the actuarially fair payout per premium dollar, A_f, for a 65 year old by solving the equation

$$1 = \sum_{j=1}^{600} \frac{A_f * P_j}{\prod_{k=1}^{j} (1 + i_k)} \tag{4}$$

This expression assumes that the insurance company providing the annuity is not taxed, because it uses the pretax riskless rate of return to discount annuity payouts. Allowing for insurance company taxes and other administrative costs of providing annuities would reduce the actuarially fair payout, while allowing the hypothetical insurance company to hold riskier, higher return assets would increase the actuarially fair payout.

We consider an individual who purchases a fixed nominal annuity at age 65. To simplify our calculations, we now assume that the annuity pays *annual* benefits. The individual will receive an annuity payment in each year that he remains alive, and his optimal consumption path will be related to this payout. The aftertax annuity payout that the individual receives at age a (A_a) depends on his wealth at the beginning of retirement (W_{ret}), the annual annuity payout per dollar of premium payment (A_f), and the tax rules that govern annuity income:

$$A_a(W_{ret}) = [1 - \lambda * \tau * I_{a<65+T'} - \tau * I_{a>65+T'}] * a_f * W_{ret}. \tag{5}$$

The variable $I_{a<65+T'}$ is an indicator variable set equal to one for ages less than the date at which all annuity income is included in taxable income, and zero otherwise.

We compute the expected discounted utility associated with the consumption stream generated by the annuity contract by assuming that individuals have additively separable utility functions of the form

$$U = \sum_{j=1}^{50} P_j * \frac{C_j^{1-\beta} - 1}{(1-\beta)*(1+\rho)^j}. \tag{6}$$

The parameter β determines the individual's risk aversion and also the degree of intertemporal substitution in consumption. The variable C_j denotes the real consumption that the annuity contract provides j periods after payouts begin. As MPWB (1999) explain, this does not necessarily equal the real value of the annuity payout, because the recipient may decide to follow a consumption profile that differs from the stream of real annuity payments. Saving a fraction of early annuity payouts, for example, permits higher consumption in later life.

Our utility analysis begins by finding the optimal consumption path for someone with assets of W_{ret} at age 65 who uses all of these assets to purchase an actuarially fair nominal annuity. The budget constraint that governs the evolution of consumption at age a (C_a) in this case is

$$W_{a+1} = (W_a + A_a(W_{ret}) - C_a)*[1 + i(1-\tau)] \tag{7}$$

where $A_a(W_{ret})$ is the annuity payout stream that can be purchased with an initial wealth of W_{ret}. Because we assume that all of the retiree's wealth is used to purchase an annuity, at the beginning of the retirement period, nonannuity wealth is zero. This implies that $W_0 = 0$, along with equation 7, describes the household budget constraint. We find the optimal consumption path $\{C_a\}$ using stochastic dynamic programming, where the stochastic component of the problem arises from uncertainty regarding date of death. We normalize the value of individual wealth by setting $W_{ret} = 1$, and we find the resulting value of expected utility U^* that the individual can achieve by purchasing a nominal annuity.

To compare annuitization with the alternative of investing in taxable bonds, we specify the budget constraint for an individual who follows such a portfolio strategy. We search for the amount of "annuity equivalent wealth," W_{aew}, that is required to make an individual as well off without annuities as that individual would be if he were able to purchase actuarially fair annuities with his initial retirement wealth, W_{ret}. In this case, if the individual has retirement wealth of W_{aew}, he maximizes the utility function in equation 6 by choosing a consumption path $\{C_a\}$ subject to the constraint that $W_0 = W_{aew}$ and the budget constraint

$$W_{a+1} = (W_a - C_a)*[1 + i(1 - \tau)]. \tag{8}$$

The resulting value of the expected utility function is $U^{**}(W_{aew})$. We use a numerical search algorithm to find the value of W_{aew} that yields $U^{**}(W_{aew}) = U^*$. Because the longevity insurance provided by the annuity market makes the individual better off, W_{aew} is greater than W_{ret}. Given our earlier normalization of $W_{ret} = 1$, we are able to define the proportionate increase in wealth that an individual would require to compensate him for the absence of an actuarially fair annuity market as $W_{aew}/W_{ret} = W_{aew}$. This is analogous to the calculations for various types of annuity products that we report in Brown, Mitchell, and Poterba (1999).

We compute annuity-equivalent wealth in both the current income tax environment and in a case with no taxes, i.e., $\tau = 0$ in equations 5, 7, and 8. The *difference* between the annuity-equivalent wealth calculations in the cases with and without income taxation provides information on the incentive effects of the current income tax treatment of annuities.

3   Taxation and the Valuation of Annuities

This section reports our basic findings on how current income tax rules affect the valuation of annuity products, using both the EPDV and expected utility framework. Table 7.2 reports the expected present discounted value of annuity payouts. The first row reports the EPDV under the assumption that there are no income taxes, while the second and third rows report the EPDV results for income taxes at 15 and 36 per cent, respectively. The columns in Table 7.2 show results for men and women separately for ages 55, 65, and 75. These calculations use individual survival probabilities from the 1998 annuitant mortality

Table 7.2
EPDV of annuity payouts at various income tax rates

Income tax rate	Age 55 male	Age 55 female	Age 65 male	Age 65 female	Age 75 male	Age 75 female
0	0.970	0.950	0.970	0.952	0.966	0.940
15%	0.977	0.966	0.969	0.962	0.954	0.942
36%	0.980	0.985	0.959	0.970	0.930	0.939

Source: Authors' calculations based on formulas described in the text. Annuity payouts are from Best's Review and reflect prices from June 1998. Term structure of interest rates calculated from Treasury Strips in the *Wall Street Journal* for the first week of June, 1998. Mortality is based on the 1998 annuitant cohort table as described in text. Calculation of the inclusion ratio for income tax purposes is based on the IRS unisex life table.

table, but they use life expectancy from the IRS Unisex table to calculate the inclusion ratio. This approach ensures that these calculations represent current tax treatment for the typical annuity purchaser in 1998. To place these results in perspective, note that if the discount rate that the annuitant is using is equal to the discount rate being used by the insurance company offering the annuity product, and if the annuity is actuarially fair, then the EPDV of the potential annuity will be 1.0.

The results in the first column, for a 55-year-old man, show that varying the marginal tax rate from 0 to 15 per cent to 36 per cent has only a modest effect on the EPDV. The EPDV is actually increased by a percentage point, from 0.970 in the no tax regime to 0.980 in an income tax regime with a 36 per cent marginal rate. At older ages, the effect of an income tax on men is to reduce the EPDV slightly, from 0.970 to 0.959 for a 65 year old and from 0.966 to 0.930 for a 75 year old. Overall, the effects are quite modest, indicating that variations in marginal tax rates have relatively little impact on the relative attractiveness of annuities and taxable bonds.

The tax rules affect men and women differentially. This is because of the choice of T' in equation 1. For men, the value of T' used by the IRS is approximately equal to the actual life expectancy of a male annuitant in 1998. For women, however, the value of T' used by the IRS is lower than actual annuitant life expectancy by several years. As discussed earlier, using a value of T' that is smaller than actual life expectancy can improve the EPDV, as is the case for women in Table 7.2. When the income tax rate is zero, we find that the EPDV for men is higher than that for women at all ages by approximately two percentage points. This is due to differences in the pricing of annuities for men and for women in the private market. As the marginal income tax rate rises, we find that the EPDV rises more quickly for women than for men. In fact, for an income tax rate of 36 per cent, the EPDV for women is actually higher than that for men at any age.

Table 7.3 reports our findings on the expected utility effects of annuity purchases. It shows the annuity equivalent wealth for typical 65-year-old male and female annuitants. Because we want to understand the impact of the tax rules on the population that actually annuitizes, we construct our measure of the annuity equivalent wealth using the 1998 annuitant mortality table. We assume that the individual receives an annuity that is actuarially fair, based on the 1998 gender-specific annuitant mortality table. This stands in contrast to previous studies, such as MPWB (1999) and Brown, Mitchell, and Poterba (1999), in which we investigated how an average individual in the population would benefit from gaining access to an annuity market. In those calculations, we used population mortality tables, rather than annuitant tables, to construct actuarially fair annuities. Because mortality rates

Table 7.3
Annuity equivalent wealth for different income tax regimes

Parameters	Age 65 annuitant	
	Male	Female
Risk aversion = 1		
Tax rate = 0	1.355	1.272
Tax rate = 15%	1.372	1.302
Tax rate = 36%	1.382	1.333
Risk aversion = 2		
Tax rate = 0	1.429	1.328
Tax rate = 15%	1.467	1.375
Tax rate = 36%	1.522	1.444
Risk aversion = 3		
Tax rate = 0	1.458	1.351
Tax rate = 15%	1.508	1.406
Tax rate = 36%	1.569	1.477

Source: Authors' calculations based on formulas described in the text. Mortality is based on the 1998 annuitant cohort table. Calculations assume that the risk-free interest rate and the utility discount rate are both equal to 0.03. Inclusion ratio is based on the IRS unisex mortality table.

are lower for annuitants than for the population as a whole, the actuarially fair annuity payment for an annuitant is less than that for a random individual facing the population life table. This makes the annuity-equivalent wealth measures reported here lower than those in previous studies.

When the marginal income tax rate is zero, we find that the annuity-equivalent wealth for a 65-year-old male annuitant is 1.355. Such an individual would be indifferent between $1 invested in a nominal annuity and $1.35 invested in riskless government bonds. This value rises slightly, to 1.372 with a 15 per cent marginal tax rate and to 1.382 with a 36 per cent marginal tax rate.

It is important to recognize that these results, as well as our EPDV calculations, focus on the relative tax burdens on annuities and taxable bonds. As the tax rate rises, the return to investors holding either annuities or taxable bonds declines. Thus, the individual's utility level, with or without an annuity, declines as the tax rate rises. Our annuity equivalent wealth calculations, however, are driven by the relative declines in utility with and without an annuity.

Holding the income tax rate constant, Table 7.3 shows that a higher level of risk aversion is associated with a higher annuity equivalent wealth. As discussed in MPWB (1999), this is because more risk averse individuals value the insurance aspect of annuities more highly. We also see, however, that the impact of risk aversion is greater in a high income tax regime. For example, increasing risk aversion from 1 to 3 increases the annuity equivalent wealth from 1.355 to 1.458 when the marginal tax rate is zero, an increase of 0.103, while with a 36 per cent marginal tax rate, the annuity-equivalent wealth rises from 1.382 to 1.569, an increase of 0.187.

The second column of Table 7.3 reports the same results for a 65-year-old woman. Overall, a female annuitant's annuity equivalent wealth for an actuarially fair annuity is lower than for a man. This difference arises due to women experiencing lower mortality rates than men. The rate of return on an annuity can be viewed as being the sum of the risk-free interest rate, r, plus a mortality premium that is an increasing function of an individual's mortality rate q. For an infinitely lived individual, the mortality premium is zero, and an annuity is identical to a riskless bond. For a person facing a constant probability q of dying each period, the gross return on an actuarially fair annuity is $(1 + r)/(1 - q)$ each period. For small values of r and q, the net return is approximately equal to $r + q/(1 - q)$. The second term reflects the probability that other annuity buyers in the individual's annuity cohort die during the period, scaled up by a $1/(1 - q)$ factor that reflects the division of the principal of those annuitants who die among the fraction, $1 - q$, who remain alive. Because mortality is higher for men than women, their mortality premium, $q/(1 - q)$, is also higher.

Men find actuarially fair annuities more attractive than women do, provided that annuities are priced in this gender-specific manner. While the annuity equivalent wealth differs, we find that the effect of different tax regimes is quite similar for men and women. Specifically, the annuity equivalent wealth rises with the marginal income tax rate, and this difference is rising with risk aversion for both groups.

Our numerical analysis focuses on the relative tax burden on annuities and taxable bonds, but it does not consider the question of how annuities would be taxed in an ideal income tax setting. This is a difficult question, and one for which our decomposition of the annuity return into interest on the invested principal and a payout based on the invested principal of those annuitants who have already died proves helpful. The fixed nominal annuity payouts offered by the annuity contracts we consider in fact combine these two sources of return with a partial return of principal in each period. In general, the relative importance of each of these components will vary over the annuity's lifetime. Right after the annuitant purchases his annuity, a relatively large fraction of the annuity payout will represent a return *on* principal, while a relatively small share will represent a return *of* principal. (It may be helpful in this context to think of a level payment, self-amortizing mortgage, in which the fraction of each mortgage payment that represents a repayment of principal rises over the life of the contract.) This consideration alone would suggest that the share of each annuity payout treated as taxable income would rise over time under an ideal income tax.

However, there is another potentially offsetting effect, due to variation over time in the share of the annuity payouts, which is due to mortality within the annuity pool. Because mortality rates rise with age, the mortality premium $q/(1 - q)$ described above is also increasing with age. Because most annuity contracts provide a fixed nominal stream of payments, however, this mortality premium is smoothed over the potential life of the annuitant. This complicates the decomposition of the annuity payment into its component parts.

Furthermore, it is not clear how such payouts should be taxed under an ideal income tax. If they were taxed in the same way as other *insurance* products, such as life insurance, they would be excluded from the tax base. Life insurance is currently purchased with after-tax dollars, and the payouts from life insurance policies are usually untaxed. If the return of principal invested by other annuitants is treated instead as a lottery winning, it would be included in the income tax base. Recognizing this important and potentially time-varying source of annuity payouts, and its ambiguous tax treatment, makes it difficult to make any simple yet general statement regarding the fraction of annuity payouts that would be taxed under an ideal income tax.

4 Alternatives to the Current Approach to Taxing Annuities

The use of a time-varying inclusion ratio, with a single step change when the annuitant has received benefits for the expected return multiple (T'), is a key feature of the current income tax treatment of annuity payouts. This tax provision has the effect of raising the tax burden and reducing the after-tax income from an annuity for those individuals who have received the largest total payouts from their annuity contracts. A difficulty with this approach is that it results in a significant drop in the level of benefits at a discrete point in time, after which the after-tax benefit stays at this lower level for the duration of the annuitant's life.

For example, a 65-year-old woman purchasing an average priced annuity in 1998 will, under current tax rules, face an inclusion ratio (λ) of approximately 0.43. If she faces a 36 per cent marginal tax rate (τ), this means that at the start of her annuity contract, for every \$1 of nominal annuity income received on a before-tax basis, she will be able to consume ($1 - \lambda\tau$) dollars, or \$0.845. Twenty years after the annuity payouts begin, at age 85, her tax rate on annuity income rises from $\lambda\tau = 15.5$ per cent to $\tau = 36$ per cent. This reduces her after-tax consumption stream to \$0.64. This discontinuous drop in the after-tax nominal annuity exacerbates the decline in the real value of a fixed nominal annuity that occurs as a result of inflation. If the inflation rate is a fixed 3 per cent per year, over a 20-year period, the real value of the annuity income declines to 55 per cent of its initial value on a before-tax basis. Combining this with the increase in the inclusion ratio means that the after-tax, real income available for consumption at age 85 is only \$0.354 per dollar of real annuity income at the beginning of the annuity contract. This represents nearly a 60 per cent decline in the after-tax real value of the annuity over a 20-year period.

One alternative to the current income tax structure is a system in which the inclusion ratio is fixed for the life of the annuity contract. The modified inclusion ratio λ' that would raise the same expected present discounted value of revenue as the current tax rules would satisfy

$$\sum_{j=1}^{600} \frac{\lambda'*t*A*P_j}{\prod_{k=1}^{j}(1+i_k)} = \sum_{j=1}^{12*T'} \frac{\lambda*t*A*P_j}{\prod_{k=1}^{j}(1+i_k)} + \sum_{j=12*T'+1}^{600} \frac{\tau*A*P_j}{\prod_{k=1}^{j}(1+i_k)} \tag{9}$$

The after-tax annuity payout in this setting would be $(1 - \lambda'*\tau)*A$ regardless of the number of years over which the annuity had been paying benefits. The effect of this rule is to increase the fraction of the annuity income that is taxable in the first T' years while decreasing the amount that is taxable in years T' and beyond. While this alternative exclusion ratio does not address the decline in the real value of the annuity that results from inflation, it does prevent the additional discrete drop in after-tax income that occurs at the end of the IRS life expectancy (20 years for a 65 year old).

To find λ', we assume that future tax flows are discounted using the pretax nominal interest rate on government bonds. This seems like the natural choice when the federal government is the discounting agent. We can repeat both the EPDV and equivalent wealth gain calculations using this modified income tax rule. While we have held the expected discounted value of revenue constant across regimes with different inclusion ratios, the revenue is discounted at the before-tax rather than the after-tax Treasury rate. This means that there can be differences in the EPDV of after-tax annuity payouts in the different inclusion ratio regimes, because the EPDV calculation is done from the perspective of the individual annuitant using after-tax interest rates.

Table 7.4 compares the value of λ and the resulting EPDV of annuity payout streams for the current income tax with a time varying inclusion ratio to the case in which individuals are faced with a constant inclusion ratio. The second row shows the value of the current inclusion ratio (λ) for the first T' periods of the annuity contract and the constant inclusion ratio (λ') that we calculate. In the case of a 65-year-old man, the current inclusion ratio is 0.431. It would rise to 0.477 under our modified tax regime. For 65-year-old women, the change would be from 0.370 to 0.435. The changes would be larger at older ages. For a 75-year-old man purchasing an annuity, the inclusion ratio would rise from 0.326 to 0.417.

Table 7.4
EPDV of annuity payouts for modified income tax with constant inclusion ratio at all ages

	Age 55 male	Age 55 female	Age 65 male	Age 65 female	Age 75 male	Age 75 female
Current inclusion ratio	$\lambda = 0.520$	$\lambda = 0.482$	$\lambda = 0.431$	$\lambda = 0.370$	$\lambda = 0.326$	$\lambda = 0.223$
Modified inclusion ratio	$\lambda' = 0.543$	$\lambda' = 0.516$	$\lambda' = 0.477$	$\lambda' = 0.435$	$\lambda' = 0.417$	$\lambda' = 0.350$
EPDV with modified inclusion ratio						
Income tax rate = 15%	0.977	0.967	0.970	0.963	0.955	0.944
Income tax rate = 36%	0.986	0.993	0.966	0.980	0.938	0.950

Source: Authors' calculations based on formulas described in the text. Annuity payouts are from Best's Review and reflect prices from June 1998. Term structure of interest rates calculated from treasury Strips in the *Wall Street Journal* for the first week of June 1998. Mortality is based on the 1998 annuitant cohort table as described in text. Current IRS exclusion ratio (λ) is based on current rules and correspond to the EPDV's presented in Table 7.2. Modified inclusion ratio (λ') is constant over the life of the annuitant, as explained in the text, and is used in calculating the EPDV's in this table.

Table 4 shows that for the case of a 15 per cent marginal tax rate, the EPDV values under the time-invariant inclusion ratio regime are virtually identical to those under the current tax regime (Table 7.2). At a higher tax rate of 36 per cent, the constant inclusion ratio leads to a slight increase in the EPDV of the annuity from the perspective of the individual. Therefore, the alternative rule has the advantage of increasing the EPDV of payouts to an individual while keeping the present value of government tax receipts fixed. This result arises from the fact that the government discounts using the pretax interest rate, while the individual EPDV calculation makes use of an after-tax rate.

Table 7.5 examines the effect of adopting a constant inclusion ratio on lifetime utility. It shows that utility is higher in this setting than with the current time-varying inclusion ratio. The annuity-equivalent wealth for a 65-year-old male facing a 36 per cent marginal tax rate is 1.400 under the constant inclusion ratio, up from 1.382 in the time-varying case. At higher levels of risk aversion, the differences are even greater. A 65-year-old male facing a 36 per cent tax rate sees his annuity-equivalent wealth rise from 1.569 under the current method to 1.639 under the constant inclusion ratio method. In other words, the change

Table 7.5
Annuity equivalent wealth for modified income tax with constant inclusion ratio at all ages

Parameters	Age 65 annuitant	
	Male current inclusion ratio 0.431, level inclusion ratio 0.477	Female, current inclusion ratio 0.370, level inclusion ratio 0.435
Risk aversion = 1		
Tax rate = 15%	1.377	1.309
Tax rate = 36%	1.400	1.358
Risk aversion = 2		
Tax rate = 15%	1.481	1.390
Tax rate = 36%	1.573	1.497
Risk aversion = 3		
Tax rate = 15%	1.528	1.423
Tax rate = 36%	1.639	1.546

Source: Authors' calculations based on formulas described in the text. Mortality is based on the 1998 annuitant cohort table. Calculations assume that the risk-free interest rate and the utility discount rate are both equal to 0.03. Inclusion ratio is modified to be constant over the life of the annuitant, as explained in the text.

to a constant inclusion ratio for this individual is worth an additional seven per cent of initial non-annuitized retirement wealth.

This increase in utility comes from two sources. First, the change in the inclusion ratio method increases the EPDV of the annuity income, as seen in Table 7.4. Second, risk averse individuals gain utility from the elimination of the discontinuous income change at year T'. This is because the risk aversion coefficient β also controls the willingness to engage in intertemporal substitution in consumption. Higher β individuals are more interested in smoothing their consumption, and this is more difficult when the after-tax income flow changes abruptly at a point in time. Thus, the shift to a constant inclusion ratio increases utility more for more risk averse individuals.

5   Tax Treatment of Payouts from Qualified Accounts

Employee contributions to tax-qualified retirement plans are not subject to income tax and investment earnings within the plans are tax exempt at the time these are earned.[3] But at the point that benefits are paid out, beneficiaries are responsible for income taxes on any outflows generated by previously nontaxed contributions. This follows the general principle that benefits received by plan participants are taxable when received, as long as they have not previously been incorporated in taxable income. This section discusses several issues that arise in the tax treatment of payouts from qualified accounts. It also considers the minimum distribution rules that the tax system specifies for the time path of payouts for qualified plans. In discussing these tax rules, it is helpful to distinguish between annuitized and other forms of payouts.

5.1   Tax Treatment of Annuitized Payouts

Consider first the simple case of a traditional pension plan in which the employer makes all contributions. Under a corporate *defined benefit* pension plan where retirees are provided with old-age benefits from retirement until death, the benefit stream—which may be either a single or joint and survivor annuity—is taxed as ordinary income.[4] In the case of a company-sponsored *defined contribution* pension, the taxation of payouts is also simple when the employer has directly financed the entire contribution or when the plan participant pays into the pension using only pretax income, as is common under 401(k) pension plans. In these situations, retirement benefit streams are again fully taxable at the recipient's marginal tax rate.

The taxation of qualified plans becomes more complicated when employees are required to contribute to their qualified retirement accounts using *after-tax* income. In the private defined benefit arena, this is uncommon, but the practice is widespread among state and local pensions. Mitchell and McCarthy (1999) find that almost three-quarters of all full-time public sector plan participants are required to contribute to their defined benefit pensions, while only five per cent of private sector workers make such contributions. When a worker must contribute after-tax dollars to a plan, the plan participant is generally permitted to recover his contribution—called the "basis"—tax-free. If benefits are then paid out as an annuity, then the income tax treatment is similar to that for nonqualified annuities. The inclusion ratio from equation 1 is again used, although the value of T' differs.

Prior to November 1996, qualified annuities with a starting date after July 1, 1986 were taxed according to the same General Rule, and thus used the same value for T' in equation 1, that currently applies to nonqualified annuities. A new "Simplified Method" for recapturing basis in qualified plans, which results in a different value of T', was implemented in November 1996.[5] Under the General Rule, T' is the age-specific life expectancy as determined by the 1983 IRS unisex mortality table. Under the Simplified Method, T' is constant over various age ranges. Thus, the simplification from the "Simple Rule" comes from a reduction in the number of possible values of T'. The values of T' under the two methods are quite similar for the age in the middle of each age interval, but can differ by several years at the endpoints.

Table 7.6 shows the value of T', in months, for both the General Rule and the Simplified Method. The first column of Table 6 is the age of the annuitant when annuity payouts begin. The second column is the value of T' under the General Rule. The third column is the value of T' for the Simplified Method for those annuities starting after November 18, 1996. This is the column that will apply to most qualified annuities from today forward. The fourth column is the value of T' for the Simplified Method for those annuities subject to the Simplified Method, but with starting dates before November 19, 1996.

As discussed earlier, raising the value of T' has two offsetting effects on the after-tax value of an annuity relative to a taxable bond. We have evaluated the sensitivity of our EPDV findings to changes in T' and, in general, find relatively modest effects. For example, for a 65-year-old

Table 7.6
Comparison of expected return multiples (*T'*), in months, using general rule and simplified methods

Age	General rule	Simplified method for annuity starting date after November 18, 1996	Simplified method for annuity starting date before November 19, 1996
50	397.2	360	300
51	386.4	360	300
52	375.6	360	300
53	364.8	360	300
54	354.0	360	300
55	343.2	360	300
56	332.4	310	360
57	321.6	310	360
58	310.8	310	360
59	300.0	310	360
60	290.4	310	360
61	279.6	260	240
62	270.0	260	240
63	259.2	260	240
64	249.6	260	240
65	240.0	260	240
66	230.4	210	170
67	220.8	210	170
68	211.2	210	170
69	201.6	210	170
70	192.0	210	170
71	183.6	160	120
72	175.2	160	120
73	166.8	160	120
74	158.4	160	120
75	150.0	160	120

Source: Entries represent the value or *T'* used in equation 1 for the calculation of the inclusion ratio. The General Rule figures are from IRS Publication 939, Table V, multiplied by 12 to convert into months. The Simplified Method figures are from IRS Publication 575, Table 1.

male facing a marginal tax rate of 36 per cent, a shift from a T' value of 20 years to a value of 21 years raises the inclusion ratio from 0.431 to 0.458. This change reduces the EPDV of an annuity from 0.959 to 0.953, or by 0.6 cents per dollar of annuity premium.

One potentially significant effect of the Simplified Method, rather than the General Rule, is that it makes the tax treatment of an annuity a function of when the individual begins receiving payouts. Individuals who are near an "endpoint" age under the Simplified Method can, through the choice of their annuity starting date, affect the time path of taxes on their annuity income. If an individual turns 66 on June 15, whether he chooses June 1 or July 1 as his annuity starting date will have important consequences for the tax treatment of the annuity. If he chooses June 1, he will face a T' of 260 months, whereas waiting until July 1 will reduce T' to 210 months. This is over a four-year difference in the period over which basis recapture is spread. The discontinuous changes in T' associated with the Simplified Method therefore may affect the behavior of annuity buyers.

5.2   Taxation of Nonannuitized Payouts

Qualified plans can pay out nonannuitized benefits before or after the plan participant's retirement date. When such benefits are paid *prior to the participant's retirement date*, they are typically either a lump sum distribution or a rollover.[6] If an individual takes his pension in the form of a lump sum, this generally triggers the payment of income tax on the amount distributed. Adney, McKeever, and Seymon Hirsch (1999) note that there is a 10 per cent additional penalty levied if the retiree is under age $59\frac{1}{2}$ and a 25 per cent tax for certain distributions under SIMPLE plans. For tax purposes, the benefit amount is divided into the portion due to employee contributions out of after-tax income and the portion due to contributions from pretax income. Special circumstances permit a retiree taking a lump sum to opt for a one-time option to smooth the sum using a five-year averaging period.

Moving a lump sum to a rollover Individual Retirement Account (IRA) does not trigger immediate tax payments. An employer must withhold 20 per cent of a rollover, however, unless the recipient chooses to have the funds transferred directly to a tax qualified retirement plan. In the case of a successful tax-free rollover, at some point, the retiree would be required to begin receiving the rollover funds in accordance with minimum distribution rules described below.

With respect to nonannuitized benefits paid *to retirees*, it is worth emphasizing that historically, most qualified pension plans offered only annuity benefits and prohibited all other payout alternatives. Today, however, many pension plan participants have some choice about the form of their pension payout. The U.S. Bureau of Labor Statistics (1998) reports that 85 per cent of private defined contribution pensions currently offer lump sums to retirees, and 15 per cent of private defined benefit pensions do so as well. In fact, annuity payouts are apparently available to only 17 per cent of private sector defined contribution pension participants, underscoring the importance of nonannuity payout options.

5.3 *Minimum Distribution Rules*

The expanding set of options for taking distributions from qualified accounts means that a qualified pension plan participant who does not want to take a lump sum or rollover, and who chooses not to purchase an annuity, must, and increasingly does, turn to a nonannuitized payout formula. Tax law holds that these benefits must be paid out under "minimum distribution requirements." Retirement plan payouts must start at least by a specified time and may continue periodically, at least annually, over the relevant lives or life expectancies of the plan participant and his designated beneficiary.[7] These requirements were first adopted in 1962 when there were no limits on contributions to retirement plans and plan assets were not counted in taxable estate. Their goal was mainly to prevent Keogh plans, used frequently by professionals, from becoming vehicles for income and estate tax avoidance. Coverage by the requirements was expanded to all types of retirement plans in 1984 and 1986.

The date at which minimum distributions must begin, relative to life expectancy of those receiving such distributions, has declined significantly since these regulations were introduced. Bell, Wade, and Goss (1992) report that life expectancy for the average 30-year old man in 1960 was 70.45 years. Hence, the age of $70\frac{1}{2}$ might have been deemed a reasonable age by which to expect retirees to begin taking distributions. Today, however, the life expectancy of a 30-year-old man is $74\frac{1}{2}$ years. Life expectancy for a 30-year-old woman is 80.8 years, and the labor force today includes a much higher fraction of women than it did in 1960. Thus, minimum distribution requirements today apply to many more years of retirement, on average, than they did when they were introduced.

Current federal minimum distribution requirements indicate the minimum amount that must be distributed each year to a plan participant and when payments must begin, regardless of whether the payments are made as a lump sum withdrawal, a series of systematic payments over a period of time, or a life annuity. For example, if the retiree turned $70\frac{1}{2}$ on October 1, 1997, he would have to begin receiving minimum distributions from the pension no later than April 1, 1998. If a plan participant fails to receive qualified plan benefits at a rate at least equal to the minimum required amount during the year, he would be liable for an excise tax equal to 50 per cent of the difference between the required payments and the actual payments. If the amount distributed exceeds the minimum required in any calendar year, *no* credit may be recognized in subsequent years for such excess distribution.[8]

A plan participant may elect to receive benefit payouts over his life expectancy. In this event, the minimum required payment is determined every year by dividing the accumulation by the applicable life expectancy factor. One other person's life expectancy can also be included in the factor, and the calculation is then based on the joint life expectancy of the participant and that other person, subject to certain limitations. If such a "designated beneficiary," in the language of the regulations, is not selected, payments are based on the single life expectancy of the participant, calculated using the IRS unisex mortality table that we described above.

A plan participant may choose both primary and contingent beneficiaries. Primary beneficiaries receive the accumulation remaining upon the death of the participant, and contingent beneficiaries receive benefits only if there are no primary beneficiaries remaining alive and a residual accumulation exists. If a plan participant names several primary beneficiaries, only the oldest one can be the calculation beneficiary. If a trust satisfies certain conditions, its oldest beneficiary can serve as a calculation beneficiary. Anyone may be designated as the calculation beneficiary, but if he is not the participant's spouse, the "incidental benefit rule" limits the maximum age difference to 10 years in calculating the joint life expectancy.

If a retiree holds assets in an individual account plan such as a 401(k) plan or IRA, the participant may choose, at the time of the first distribution, between two methods of calculating his life expectancy and that of his designated beneficiary. (The designated beneficiary is also known as the calculation beneficiary.) Under the *recalculation* method, which is available to a participant and to his spouse if the spouse is the calculation beneficiary, the actual age-appropriate life expectancy factor is used each year. For example, for an individual with no calculation beneficiary, the life expectancy factor is 15.3 at age 71, 14.6 at age 72, 13.9 at age 73, and so on. In contrast, under the *one-year-less* method, which is available to a participant and to any type of calculation beneficiary, one year is subtracted from the original life expectancy factor as he ages. For example, for a recipient with no calculation beneficiary, the factor is 15.3 at age 71, 14.3 at age 72, 13.3 at age 73, and so on. The life expectancy factors under either the recalculation or one-year-less method are applied to the account balance as of the last valuation date in the prior calendar year, adjusted for any contributions, allocated forfeitures, and distributions made in the prior year after the last valuation date. Under the one-year-less method, the goal is to distribute the entire retirement asset by the age of (joint) life expectancy, whereas under the recalculation method, payments can continue, albeit in dwindling amounts, until the last age in the IRS mortality table.

Minimum distribution rules can affect many aspects of assets draw-down by retirees. These effects are discussed in detail in Warshawsky (1998), but we summarize them here. First, for the significant minority of elderly individuals who are still working at age 70½, the current rules require them to begin taking distributions from IRA and prior-employer's plans, even though they may still be contributing to their current pension plans.

Second, these rules create awkward situations when a spouse, who survived a plan participant who had not yet received distributions from the plan, must initiate payments no later than the date the participant would have turned 70½, regardless of the surviving spouse's age or labor force status. Spouses in this setting could roll over pension accumulations into an IRA and postpone distributions until they reach age 70½, but it is not clear how many spouses are aware of this option and pursue it.

Third, one consequence of using a unisex life table in the calculation of minimum required distributions is that women, who have longer life expectancies as a group, must receive higher distributions than would be consistent with a female-only life table. For example, at age 71, the life expectancy factor for a woman is 17.2 under the Annuity 2000 table, nearly two years more than under the IRS table.

Finally, minimum distribution rules may affect retirees' patterns of consumption spending in retirement. It is difficult to evaluate such linkages, because we are not aware of any direct evidence on the relationship between payouts from retirement plans and the level of household expenditures for those who are subject to minimum distribution rules. If a couple chooses to consume their minimum distributions as they are paid out, however, there is a nontrivial risk that at least one spouse will outlive their retirement assets. Minimum distribution requirements may also reduce the amount held in tax-deferred accounts faster than an account beneficiary might otherwise desire. If someone wishes to consume more in the later years of retirement than in the early years, he will want to hold a large balance of assets in tax-deferred (and therefore high return) form at the beginning of retirement. The minimum distribution rules may reduce the level of consumption late in retirement for such an individual by lowering his tax-deferred asset balance early in retirement. This effect is particularly powerful in inflationary times when minimum distribution rules are specified in nominal terms, as they are at present.[9]

6   The Quantitative Importance of Minimum Distribution Rules

A number of current legislative proposals call for modifying minimum distribution rules by raising the age of mandatory distribution, updating the mortality table used in the distribution methods to recognize recent mortality improvements, and/or exempting from the requirements individuals with accounts below certain amounts. These proposals would reduce the number of retirees who are affected by the current minimum distribution rules. In the short run, this could lead to a reduction in the amount of distributions from qualified accounts, in turn reducing income tax collections on qualified account distributions. The longer-term effect on revenues is more difficult to evaluate, because some of the assets that are not distributed from qualified plans in the near term will need to be distributed in the future.

To evaluate the economic significance of changing the minimum distribution requirements and to begin the process of estimating the revenue effects of such changes, we need to explore the number of individuals who are affected by these rules and the value of their qualified account balances. Unfortunately, there is no nationally representative database on the extent of forced distributions that are due to the minimum distribution rules. Estimating the potential revenue effects of reforming the minimum distribution requirements therefore requires drawing on data from a variety of different sources to project future retirement assets by age of household, by household marginal tax rate, and by account balance. These data must also be used to predict which individuals will be constrained by the current requirements. The Appendix presents calculations on the revenue consequences of eliminating minimum distribution rules entirely, excluding a threshold amount such as $100,000 or $300,000 per person in retirement plan assets from these rules, or raising the age at which minimum distribution requirements apply.

A starting point for the revenue estimates is information on the distribution of retirement plan assets across households. This information is drawn from the 1995 Survey of Consumer Finances (SCF). The Survey is a nationally representative survey of households, stratified to oversample households with high income and high net worth. It is the premier source of information on asset holdings and wealth accumulation by households in the United States.

Table 7.7 presents one type of data that is relevant for evaluating these revenue effects. This is information from the SCF on retirement plan balances of households in which the head of household or the spouse was over the age of 59. When we expand the set of households

Table 7.7
Assets in qualified accounts that are not in distribution, 1995 SCF

| Summary measure | Age of older of head of household or spouse | | | | | |
	60–5	66–70	71–5	76–80	80+	Total
IRA/Keogh accounts						
Assets ($billion)	190.9	133.4	112.3	31.4	11.7	479.8
Households (million)	2.75	2.34	1.68	0.76	0.34	7.86
Nondistributing pension accounts						
Assets ($billion)	115.7	99.9	2.9	2.3	0.2	221.0
Households (million)	1.45	0.39	0.03	0.01	0.01	1.88
Total						
Assets ($billion)	306.7	233.3	115.2	33.7	11.9	700.8
Households (million)	3.36	2.50	1.68	0.76	0.34	8.64

Source: Authors' tabulations using 1995 Survey of Consumer Finances.

in the SCF to mirror national totals, we find that 8.6 million households with at least one member over age 59 held just over $700 billion in qualified retirement accounts, including pension accounts as well as IRAs and Keogh plans. The information from the SCF unfortunately is not ideal for our purposes, because questions about account balances were not asked for pension accounts if the account was already in distribution. For respondents over the age of 71, this essentially eliminates information on pension accounts, because the minimum distribution rules require payouts from these accounts. The table nevertheless shows that households in which the oldest member was between the ages of 66 and 70 held $233.3 billion in assets in 1995. This is the pool of assets that are most likely to be affected by the minimum distribution requirements.

7 Conclusions and Future Directions

This study has assessed the current tax treatment of payouts from retirement assets, focusing on nonqualified annuity products and qualified retirement plans. We explore the economic effects of current tax rules, and we find that the current system does not substantially alter the relative attractiveness of taxable bonds and annuity products. We also show how a simpler method of taxing annuities would avoid changing the tax rules as an annuitant aged while still raising the same expected present discounted value of revenues as the current tax rules. With respect to qualified plan payouts, we first consider annuitized payouts and then outline the minimum distribution requirements associated with nonannuitized payouts. We note that minimum distribution rules were initially implemented in an economic and demographic environment that was different from the current setting and that such rules may have a number of initially unintended effects on current retirees.

Our current analysis suggests several directions for further work. One is to move beyond the present discussion of income tax issues to consider estate tax issues as well. While Poterba (1997) reports that the estate tax currently applies to less than two per cent of all decedents, estate tax rates are higher than the income tax rates facing most households. The estate tax therefore could have substantial effects on the behavior of those high net worth households who may be subject to it.

A second direction for further work concerns the utility consequences of minimum distribution rules. We have described the operation of these rules, but we have not tried to link these rules to the consumption flow available to retirees. While our analysis of annuities uses an explicit utility function to compare a representative household's lifetime expected utility under various annuity tax regimes, we have not tried to apply such a framework to minimum distribution rules. This extension is not straightforward, because it requires assumptions about the link between required distributions and household consumption. Future work could usefully explore both this link and the corresponding impact of minimum distribution rules on household welfare.

A third limitation of our current analysis is our focus on the choice between taxable bonds and taxable annuities. Households in practice face a much wider menu of investment choices, many of which are taxed less heavily than taxable bonds. The comparison between annuities and corporate stock, which generate part of their return in the form of capital gains, would be particularly interesting. This is especially true for high-income households, facing a marginal tax rate of 36 or 39.6 per cent on interest and annuity income. For these households, the top marginal tax rate of 20 per cent on long-term capital gains could have an important impact on the choice between annuities and capital assets that are expected to appreciate.

A final direction for further analysis concerns potential changes in the mortality tables that the IRS uses for annuity valuation. Changes to these mortality tables affect the after-tax payouts from annuities through changes in the expected return multiple, T'. We noted that such changes have two effects: they change the fraction of annuity payouts that are included in taxable income when the inclusion ratio is not 100 per cent, and they change the number of months or years over which the inclusion ratio is less than 100 per cent. A quantitative framework such as the one we have developed is very helpful in evaluating the net impact of such changes on the relative attractiveness of annuities and other taxable investments.

Notes

1. The most common type of qualified retirement plan is offered to employees by an employer and meets Internal Revenue code criteria permitting the plan to accumulate tax-protected assets. The employer's contributions to such plans are deductible and they are not considered taxable income to the employee. The investment earnings on assets in the account are tax exempt at the time they are earned. IRAs, tax-deferred annuities, and 401(k) and 403(b) plans funded exclusively by employee contributions are also qualified retirement plans.

2. Adney, McKeever, and Seymon-Hirsch (1998) discuss the estate tax treatment of annuity contracts where payments continue after death. These issues are beyond the scope of this paper. It is worth noting, however, that, according to most interpretations of the current law and regulations, payouts from a deferred annuity contract must be taxed either as a lump sum payment or, under the General Rule, as a life annuity. This forces an either/or payout choice on contract holders and thus denies them the possibility of using both payout options in a single contract.

3. Achieving tax-qualified status for a retirement plan requires that the plan be approved by the IRS; for further discussion of these conditions, see McGill et al. (1996).

4. This presumes that the retirement benefit does not exceed ERISA limits spelled out in Section 415 of the Internal Revenue Code and its amendments (McGill et al., 1996). These rules limit the straight life annuity payable under a defined benefit pension to 100 per cent of a worker's average compensation over the highest three years prior to retirement, or $90,000 (indexed) at the Social Security normal retirement age. The cap is reduced for earlier retirement and/or for less than ten of service. Other ceilings apply if an employer offers two or more pension plans. A 15 per cent excise tax was levied on individuals who received defined contribution distributions in excess of the ERISA limits, but this limit was suspended for tax years after 1997; see Adney, McKeever, and Seymon-Hirsch (1998).

5. The Simplified Method *must* be used if either the annuity starting date is after November 18, 1996 and the payments are from a qualified plan, or if the annuitant was at least 75 years old when the annuity payments began, payments were from a qualified plan, and payments were guaranteed for fewer than five years. All other payments, such as those from nonqualified annuities, must continue to use the General Rule.

6. Poterba, Venti, and Wise (1998b) present summary information on the importance of lump sum distributions and on how these distributions are used by their recipients.

7. Federal minimum distribution requirements include basic and incidental benefit rules appearing in Section 401(a)(9) of the Internal Revenue Code as well as the very detailed proposed Treasury Regulations 1.401(a)(9)-1 and 2. The requirements currently apply to all types of tax-advantaged retirement arrangements, including 401(a) plans (defined benefit and money purchase pension plans and profit sharing and stock purchase plans (including 401(k) plans)), 403(b) plans (defined contribution plans available to workers in nonprofit institutions and public schools), 457 plans (nonqualified deferred compensation plans available to workers in governmental bodies), and individual retirement arrangements (Keogh plans and IRAs). The regulations constrain, in variuos ways, plan design for the annuity payout form. In this paper, however, we concentrate on the impact of the minimum distribution requirements on nonannuitized payouts. Warshawsky (1998) describes other issues in some detail.

8. These rules apply when payments were begun prior to the death of the plan participant. If, however, the participant dies before minimum distributions have begun, the entire accumulation must generally be distributed by the end of the fifth year from the date of the participant's death. An exception to this general rule allows for the accumulation to be paid over the life or period of life expectancy of the designated beneficiary if elected by December 31 of the year after the year of death of the plan participant. For spouses, distributions under the exception must commence before the later of (a) the last day of the year following the participant's

death or (b) the last day of the year the participant would have attained age 70½ (regardless of the spouse's age). Either the recalculation or one-year-less method (described below) may be used. Again, rollover to an IRA is allowed. For other beneficiaries, the benefits must commence by the last day of the year following the participant's death. Only the one-year-less method may be used by nonspouse beneficiaries.

9. Defined benefit plans may adjust periodic payments upward to reflect price inflation, and variable annuities are allowed to adjust payments to reflect changes in the asset values underlying the annuity. Warshawsky (1998) argues that optimal consumption rules would produce distributions that dissipated assets at a slower rate than under the current one-year-less method and along a different path than under the current recalculation method.

References

Adney, John T., Joseph F. McKeever, and Barbara N. Seymon-Hirsch. *Annuities Answer Book*. A Panel Publication. New York: Aspen Publishers, Inc., 1999.

Bell, Felicitie, A. Wade, and S. Goss. "Life Tables for the United States Social Security Area 1900–2080." Actuarial Study No. 107. Social Security Administration, Office of the Actuary, 1992.

Brown, Jeffrey, Olivia Mitchell, and James Poterba. "The Role of Real Annuities and Indexed Bonds in an Individual Accounts Retirement Program." In John Campbell and Martin Feldstein, eds., *Risk Aspects of Social Security Reform*. Cambridge, MA: National Bureau of Economic Research, 1999.

Bureau of Labor Statistics. *Employee Benefits in Medium and Large Private Establishments*. 1995. U.S. Department of Labor Bulletin 2496, April, 1998.

Committee to Recommend a New Mortality Basis for Individual Annuity Valuation. "Report (Derivation of the 1983 Table a)." *Transactions of the Society of Actuaries*. 33 (1981): 675–751.

Friedman, Benjamin, and Mark Warshawsky. "Annuity Prices and Saving Behavior in the United States." In *Pensions in the US Economy*, edited by Z. Bodie, J. Shoven, and D. Wise, 53–77. Chicago: University of Chicago Press, 1988.

Friedman, Benjamin, and Mark Warshawsky. "The Cost of Annuities: Implications for Saving Behavior and Bequests." *Quarterly Journal of Economics* 105 No. 1 (February, 1990): 135–54.

Individual Annuity Experience Committee. "Report: Mortality Under Individual Immediate Annuities, Life Income Settlements, & Matured Deferred Annuities Between 1976 & 1986 Anniversaries." *Transactions of the Society of Actuaries: 1991–2 Reports*, 65–116.

Johansen, R. "Review of Adequacy of 1983 Individual Annuity Mortality Table." *Transactions of the Society of Actuaries* 47 (1996): 101–23.

McGill, Dan, John Haley, Kyle Brown, and Sylvester Schieber. *Fundamentals of Private Pensions 7e*. Philadelphia: University of Pennsylvania Press, 1996.

Mitchell, Olivia S., and David McCarthy. "The Structure and Performance of State and Local Pension Plans." Pension Research Council Working Paper. Philadelphia: Wharton School, April 1999.

Mitchell, Olivia S., James Poterba, Mark Warshawsky, and Jeffrey Brown. "New Evidence on the Money's Worth of Individual Annuities." *American Economic Review*. (1999).

Moore, James, and Olivia S. Mitchell. "Projected Retirement Wealth and Saving Adequacy." In *Forecasting Retirement Needs and Retirement Wealth*, edited by O. S. Mitchell, B. Hammond, and A. Rappaport, 2000.

Pension Research Council. Philadelphia, PA: University of Pennsylvania Press, *forthcoming*.

Poterba, James. "The Estate Tax and After-Tax Investment Retures." NBER Working Paper 6337. Cambridge, MA: National Bureau of Economic Research, 1997.

Poterba, James, Steven Venti, and David Wise. "Implications of Rising Personal Retirement Saving." In *Frontiers of the Economics of Aging*, edited by D. Wise, 125–67. Chicago: University of Chicago Press, 1998a.

Poterba, James, Steven Venti, and David Wise. "Lump Sum Distributions from Retirement Saving Plans: Receipt and Utilization." In *Inquiries in the Economics of Aging*, edited by D. Wise, 85–105. Chicago: University of Chicago Press, 1998b.

Poterba, James, and Mark Warshawsky. "The Costs of Annuitizing Retirement Payouts from Individual Accounts." In John Shoven, ed., *Administrative Aspects of Investment-Based Social Security Reform*. Cambridge, MA: National Bureau of Economic Research, 2000.

Sabelhaus, John. "Modeling IRA Accumulation and Withdrawals." Congressional Budget Office Working Paper. Washington, D.C., December, 1998.

U.S. General Accounting Office. *Tax Treatment of Life Insurance and Annuity Accrued Interest*. Washington, D.C.: U.S. General Accounting Office, 1990.

Warshawsky, Mark. "Private Annuity Markets in the United States." *Journal of Risk and Insurance* 55 No. 3 (September, 1988): 518–28.

Warshawsky, Mark. "The Optimal Design of Minimum Distribution Requirements for Retirement Plans." *Benefits Quarterly* 14 No. 4 (Fourth Quarter, 1998): 36–53.

Yakoboski, Paul. "IRAs: Benchmarking for the Post-TRA '97 World." *EBRI Notes* 19 No. 12 (December, 1998).

Appendix: Estimating the Revenue Impact of Changes in Minimum Distribution Rules
by Mark J. Warshawsky

This Appendix presents estimates of the revenue loss from changing the current minimum distribution requirements. The estimates draw on data on the distribution of retirement plan assets as reported in the 1995 SCF, but they also embody a number of assumptions about the share of assets that will be subject to various methods of distribution. The analysis in this appendix is similar in spirit, although different in scope, detail, and application, to that of Sabelhaus (1998).

Appendix Table 7.A1 presents information on age-specific asset patterns in the 1995 SCF. Broad patterns are apparent in the data: for age groups in their early 60s, assets are still being built up, age groups in their middle 60s seem to have the peak asset accumulations, while age groups in their late 60s and beyond (who are also shrinking in numbers) have declining asset balances. As will be explained further below, the key number in the revenue estimate model is retirement assets held by households age 70. Looking at Table 7.7 and Appendix Table 7.A1 together, our rough estimate is $35 billion in 1995 for this single age group. Appendix Table 7.A2 shows retirement account assets by household adjusted gross income (AGI) in 1994. The five income groups shown delineate the federal income tax brackets in 1998 for married couples filing joint tax returns (corresponding marginal tax rates are 15, 28, 31, 36, and 39.6 per cent). Over two-thirds of the older households with retirement accounts are in the lowest income group, holding almost one-third of the retirement assets. The next two groups, representing middle- and upper-middle-class households, number more than a quarter of all older households with retirement accounts and they hold nearly half of all retirement assets. Finally, the upper-income group accounts for about one-twelfth of the population and it holds over one-sixth of the retirement assets.

It is necessary to know how retirement assets are distributed, and how household AGIs and hence effective tax rates vary, in order to estimate potential revenue losses from changes in the minimum distribution requirements. The analysis continues by examining how retirement account assets vary by level and income. Appendix Tables 7.A3 and 7.A4 report this information. Roughly 40 per cent of the relevant older population holds only one-tenth of all retirement assets, totaling under $25,000 per household. By contrast, the top five per cent of the population holds almost half the assets, amounting to over $300,000 per household. When IRA, Keogh, and pension assets are cross-tabulated by household AGI, two findings stand out. First, as expected, higher income groups have larger accounts; and second, even low-income households have some retirement assets.

To estimate federal income taxes collected because of the minimum distribution requirements, it is necessary to forecast the aggregate sum of retirement assets into the future. First, beginning with the age 70 cohort, asset values from the 1995 SCF are projected to 2000 using an annual growth rate of 20 per cent, reflecting actual increases in defined contribution pensions in 1997, 20 per cent for 1998, and 10 per cent for 1999 and 2000. This relies on increases reported in Table L.119.c of the Flow of Funds Accounts and actual increases in IRAs reported by Yakoboski (1998). This produces an estimate of $73 billion for assets held in retirement accounts by households age 71 in the year 2000. Similar forecasts are computed for aggregate retirement assets in the year 2000 for households age 71–76 and older. While SCF retirement assets decline with age, sample sizes are too small to provide a precise estimate of wealth drawdowns by age group. Instead, these drawdowns are estimated by taking the age 70 retirement assets in the year 2000 and assuming that balances will decline by five per cent per year between ages 71 and 75. Retirement assets for households age 76 and older are based on the IRA, Keogh, and pension account assets reported earlier for that age group, then incremented by 66 per cent (the share of pension assets in total retirement assets for the under-70 groups) to reflect unreported pension accounts being distributed. The 66 per cent increment for unreported pension accounts probably is an overcorrection because many plan participants transfer their pension account to an IRA at, or soon after, retirement. Forecasts of the retirement assets of households in the years 2001 and beyond assume that the assets of households initially age 70 and younger will grow from the year 2000 base at an annual rate of $9\frac{1}{2}$ per cent, reflecting a $4\frac{1}{2}$ per cent real investment return, a $1\frac{1}{2}$ inflation rate, $2\frac{1}{4}$ per cent growth of contributions to retirement accounts, and an increase in the number of households with retirement accounts of 1 per cent. Assets of households initially age 71 and older are also assumed to grow from their respective bases at a $9\frac{1}{4}$ per cent annual rate.

A crucial next step is evaluating the level of retirement account distributions produced by the current minimum distribution requirements in order to assess the counterfactuals of interest. There are no nationally representative data on this statistic, so the calculations are based on information from TIAA-CREF showing that about 20 per cent of the retirement accumulations are subject to minimum distribution requirements each year; the other 80 per cent are distributed as life annuities, lump sum withdrawals, and systematic withdrawals. It seems reasonable to assume that a quarter of the accounts currently being distributed according to the minimum rules will not be held until the death of the plan participant and spouse, but instead will be distributed in some fashion over the retirement years. Furthermore, some proportion of the assets in the accounts will be distributed upon the death of the couples holding the accounts. Lacking better empirical information, the calculations assume that 15 per cent of IRA, Keogh, and pension accumulations are forced distributions that are due to the federal requirements. Also, we make a reasonable assumption in the revenue estimation procedure that forced distributions are more likely as income increases; in particular, we assume that 10, 12.5, 15, 20, and 30 per cent of retirement account assets are distributed currently because of the minimum distribution requirements currently in effect. Applying these percentages to the proportion of retirement assets held by each income group shown in Table 7.7 yields a share of about 15 per cent of assets that would be inferred to be distributed as a result of the federal requirements. These forced distributions are then multiplied by effective tax rates assumed for each of the five income groups identified above, assumed to be 10, 20, 25, 30, and 35 per cent, respectively. Finally, potential tax revenue generated by the current minimum distribution rules is estimated by summing across the projected populations by age and income. This is also summed over the ten-year period beginning in 2000.

If the minimum distribution rules were repealed, the estimated revenue loss would be estimated to be approximately $21 billion over ten years. Because retirement assets are assumed to grow over time, the annual foregone revenue also grows. Lost revenues are estimated at about $13 billion over ten years if the minimum distribution rules are changed to exclude the first $300,000 in peoples' retirement plans. This proposal is similar in spirit to a pension reform bill previously proposed by Representatives Portman and Cardin (H.R. 3788); such a rule change would protect nearly 8 million older households from having to comply with the minimum distribution regulations. Households holding over $300,000 in their accounts would still pay tax on about 58 per cent of retirement assets $[=(321.7 - (448*0.3))/321.7$ of retirement assets for the households in the category labeled "$300,000+" mainly including the top four income groups]. These estimates assume that the exclusion amounts are indexed to expected returns.

Revenue losses would be about $8 billion over ten years if the minimum distribution rules applied only to assets over $100,000 in retirement accounts; this would enable almost 6 million households to avoid the computations associated with minimum distribution rules. (This is similar to the pension reform bill introduced by Representatives Portman and Cardin in the current Congress, but we abstract from the actual language of current bills (e.g., H.R. 1102) inasmuch as they set a cap of $100,000 on exclusions for IRAs and pension accounts separately.) However, older households would still have to determine which part of their retirement assets were subject to the minimum distribution rules, if any. Further, it is unclear whether households whose account balances were just below the exclusion amount when they turned age 70½, but whose account balances later rose above the exclusion due to superior investment returns, would later become subject to the minimum distribution requirements. Revenue losses would be only $8.5 billion over ten years if the minimum distribution requirements were delayed to households age 75, as proposed in a bill introduced in the current Congress by Senators Grassley and Gramm. The model assumes that the law change would apply to those currently receiving distributions between the ages of 70½ and 75; that is, these older individuals would not be forced to continue to take distributions until they turned age 75.

Table 7.A1
Assets in IRAs/KEOGHs and in pension accounts not being distributed, by age of older of spouse or respondent

	IRA/Keogh and pension accounts		
Age	Sum (Million $)	Mean ($)	Households (000)
60	45,489	75,146	605
61	40,706	92,447	440
62	49,276	90,442	545
63	64,118	99,256	646
64	40,573	69,001	588
65	66,502	123,450	539
66	51,835	99,508	521
67	63,934	125,729	509
68	51,317	81,356	631
69	32,136	81,006	397
70	34,112	77,640	439
71	18,021	67,291	268
72	16,048	40,322	398
73	25,809	80,641	320
74	10,859	36,633	296
75	44,447	111,403	399
76	3,270	39,650	82
77	6,472	45,185	143
78	11,903	39,381	302
79	7,246	77,474	94
80	4,844	36,136	134
81+	11,883	34,792	342
All ages	700,802	81,132	8,638

Source: Author's calculations based on data from the 1995 SCF, using the SCF survey weights.

Table 7.A2
Assets in IRAs/KEOGHs and in pension accounts not being distributed, by 1994 household AGI

1994 household AGI	IRA/Keoghs			Pension accounts			IRA/Keogh and pension accounts		
	Sum (million $)	Mean ($)	Households (000)	Sum (million $)	Mean ($)	Households (000)	Sum (million $)	Mean ($)	Households (000)
$42,350 or less	187,496	36,421	5,148	26,889	28,875	931	214,385	37,582	5,705
$42,351–102,300	151,458	76,824	1,971	83,627	132,151	633	235,085	107,769	2,181
$102,301–155,950	60,309	167,403	360	31,187	231,601	135	91,496	250,496	365
$155,951–278,450	54,232	217,572	249	33,751	315,819	107	87,983	350,994	251
Over $278,450	26,316	194,957	135	45,536	577,688	79	71,852	528,326	136
All incomes	479,811	61,014	7,864	220,990	117,274	1,884	700,802	81,132	8,638

Source: Author's calculations based on data from the 1995 SCF.
Notes: Calculations use the SCF survey weights. AGI is reported AGI amount on 1994 tax return. If household files separate returns, AGI is sum of AGIs on the separate returns. If household did not file, household is included in lowest income category.

Table 7.A3
Assets in IRAs/KEOGHs and in pension accounts not being distributed, by amount in accounts

Amount in account	IRA/Keoghs			Pension accounts			IRA/Keogh and pension accounts		
	Sum (million $)	Mean ($)	Households (000)	Sum (million $)	Mean ($)	Households (000)	Sum (million $)	Mean ($)	Households (000)
Under $25,000	40,368	10,609	3,805	8,033	10,398	773	41,522	10,741	3,866
$25,000–49,999	60,012	35,225	1,704	12,729	35,587	358	63,119	35,755	1,765
$50,000–99,999	95,853	68,311	1,403	19,865	68,600	290	106,449	68,158	1,562
$100,000–199,999	73,219	138,582	528	22,923	128,727	178	103,505	144,668	715
$200,000–299,999	43,548	236,203	184	21,670	224,776	96	64,526	228,864	282
$300,000+	166,811	697,417	239	135,770	714,450	190	321,681	718,758	448
All incomes	479,811	61,014	7,864	220,990	117,274	1,884	700,802	81,132	8,638

Source: Author's calculations based on data from the 1995 SCF.
Notes: Calculations use the SCF survey weights. Amount categories are specific to each column.

Table 7.A4
Assets in IRAs/KEOGHs and in pension accounts not being distributed, by amount in accounts and 1994 household AGI

Amount in account	1994 household AGI					
	$42,350 or less	$42,351–$102,300	$102,301–$155,950	$155,951–$278,450	Over $278,450	All incomes
Under $25,000	31,478	8,132	1,512	317	83	41,522
$25,000–49,999	45,132	15,507	1,607	358	515	63,119
$50,000–99,999	67,723	31,897	1,452	3,698	1,679	106,449
$100,000–199,999	35,303	44,580	8,203	8,747	6,671	103,505
$200,000–299,999	16,652	38,067	3,102	5,667	1,038	64,526
$300,000+	18,098	96,901	75,621	69,195	61,866	321,681
All incomes	214,385	235,085	91,496	87,983	71,852	700,802

Notes: Author's calculations based on data from the 1995 SCF, using the SCF survey weights. AGI is reported AGI amount on 1994 tax return. If household files separate returns, AGI is sum of AGIs on the separate returns. If household did not file, household is included in lowest income category.

Index